Margot

ADVANCE PRAISE FOR THE BOOK

'Reba Som unravels the journey of Margaret "Margot" Noble, better known to the world as Sister Nivedita, giving the reader an appreciation of how this truly remarkable and erudite individual, from a foreign land, went on to become a force in times of tumultuous change in India. This passionate chronicle of her life succeeds in giving us a rare glimpse of the individual behind the persona. Reba Som effectively brings Nivedita out of the shadow of her spiritual mentor, confidant and friend, Swami Vivekananda. A compelling read'—Shashi Tharoor

'A profound and searching biography that brings to life Sister Nivedita's journey through the spiritual landscape of her times. A remarkable record of an era and the extraordinary figures that inhabited it'—Namita Gokhale

'In Reba Som's timely, well-researched and engrossing portrait, Sister Nivedita, the iconic Irish–Hindu nun who consecrated her life to India, re-emerges as a sensitive, idealistic and daring young woman, who crossed boundaries and continents for her passion and belief'—Makarand Paranjape

REBA SOM

Margot

SISTER NIVEDITA
OF VIVEKANANDA

PENGUIN
VIKING

VIKING

USA | Canada | UK | Ireland | Australia
New Zealand | India | South Africa | China

Viking is part of the Penguin Random House group of companies
whose addresses can be found at global.penguinrandomhouse.com

Published by Penguin Random House India Pvt. Ltd
7th Floor, Infinity Tower C, DLF Cyber City,
Gurgaon 122 002, Haryana, India

First published in Viking by Penguin Random House India 2017

ISBN 9780670088799

Typeset in Adobe Caslon Pro by Manipal Digital Systems, Manipal
Printed at Replika Press Pvt. Ltd, India

www.penguin.co.in

*To the 'mother's heart and hero's will' in so many women that
I have been privileged to know*

Contents

The mother's heart, the hero's will
the sweetness of the southern breeze,
the sacred charm and strength that dwell
On Aryan altars, flaming, free;
all these be yours, and many more,
No ancient soul could dream before —
Be thou to India's future son
The mistress, servant, friend, in one

With the blessings of

Vivekananda

Written to Sister Nivedita on 22 September 1900

Preface

It was during the 150th birth anniversary celebrations of Swami Vivekananda in 2013 that I became curious to learn more about Sister Nivedita. The Ramakrishna Mission had booked all four galleries of the Tagore Centre at the Indian Council for Cultural Relations, Kolkata, of which I was then director, to host an art exhibition. It was well known that Swamiji and particularly Sister Nivedita were great advocates of Indian art. From what I knew, neither of them were artists as such, and I told myself the art connection needed to be researched further. Back in Delhi, I was amazed to find most people unaware of Sister Nivedita, who was often confused for a nun of the Missionaries of Charity. Yet on her cenotaph is written that Sister Nivedita had given her all to India. It convinced me then that her story must be told.

This then is a biography of Margaret Noble (1867–1911) of Ireland, called Margot by her family and friends, who came to India in 1898 inspired by Swami Vivekananda and made it her home. Named Nivedita (which means 'dedicated') by Swamiji, who initiated her into the vows of a *brahmachari* nun, she lived up to her given name and devoted herself fully to the cause of India.

On the eve of her 150th birth anniversary, this book captures the thoughts, emotions, concerns and doubts of a sincere and committed woman, voiced in over 800 letters, making this biography almost autobiographical. The letters that Nivedita regularly wrote to her close friends, in particular to Josephine MacLeod, whom she called Yum, Sara Bull, whom she often addressed as Saint Sara, and the journalist Ratcliffe, were practically in the nature of diaries. In her last years, aware that the novel of her life had unfolded in her letters, Nivedita, with a premonition that her end was near, sent her personal papers to her dear Yum and asked for her letters to be kept in safe custody. After her death, Josephine MacLeod decided to share Nivedita's personal papers and letters with Lizelle Reymond for a definitive biography of Sister Nivedita in French, which was translated into English as *The Dedicated: A Biography of Nivedita* (1953). In time, Narayani Devi serialized it in Bengali in the monthly journal *Basumati* in 1962, attracting a wide readership. The letters of Nivedita were sent by Reymond to India to remain in the possession of a Vedic philosopher named Anirvan who could utilize them for further research. Fortuitously, Anirvan selected Sankari Prasad Basu to receive and keep the precious collection. Basu, a well-known author whose painstaking seven-volume work *Vivekananda O Samakaleen Bharatvarsha* earned him the Sahitya Akademi Award in 1978, was considered the ideal recipient of this priceless legacy. Taken aback by the unexpected windfall, Basu went on to fulfil his promise to Anirvan, spending several years deciphering the handwriting, doing research on the letters, and translating many into Bengali for his five-volume work, *Nibedita Lokmata* (Ananda Publishers, Calcutta, 1968–94).

   Letters of Sister Nivedita was published in two volumes in 1982 by Nababharat Publishers and, as its editor, Sankari Prasad Basu in his introduction recounted the amazing circumstances in which he came to receive the letters. The third volume with a comprehensive introduction that he had in mind never appeared. Basu passed away in 2014 and the volumes of *Letters* are out of print. It was by chance that I secured from a bookseller on College Street in Kolkata two silverfish-eaten copies—the brittle pages and their musty smell adding to my excitement as I leafed through them. What I discovered was not necessarily Nivedita's 'world-moving power' that Basu had described but fascinating windows that opened through her eyes and keen observations into the social, cultural and political labyrinth of early twentieth-century India.

The letters revealed a flesh-and-blood Nivedita, who had embarked on a unique adventure in the quest of a larger dream. Leaving her country behind, she wished to learn the culture of faraway India so she could contribute towards the education of women in the light of their own civilizational values, rather than through the judgemental notions of an outsider. This was part of her training in the methods of education imparted by the nineteenth-century thinker Johann Heinrich Pestalozzi and adopted by his disciple Friedrich Froebel, which had inspired her in her teaching career in England. When she had first met Swami Vivekananda in England in 1895, it was not so much his spiritual thoughts of Advaita Vedanta, which in any case she concurred with, but his call to women with a Celtic dedication and determination who could address the crying need to educate women in India that appealed to her.

In India, she found herself in the midst of multiple and contradictory dynamics. She had to understand the multi-dimensional thought process of her guru's spiritual ideas, which often took her by surprise. Moreover, she found herself caught in the great contemporary debate between Reform and Revival. The Brahmo Samaj, which advocated comprehensive social and religious reforms, had been patronized by stalwarts like Raja Ram Mohan Roy and later by Rabindranath Tagore's father, Debendranath Tagore, encouraging women to step out of the inner quarters of their residences, the *andarmahal*, to educational institutions outside. Traditional worship of idols was replaced by Brahmo congregational prayers to the Universal Creator. The Hindus, threatened by this challenge to their ritual-based religious worship, socially ostracized the Brahmos. Nivedita found herself poised between reformers like

the Brahmo Tagore family, with whom she socialized well, and
the revival that was voiced by the Hindus, who viewed reform with
wariness, and with whom she now belonged.

Having come to India as an idealist, hoping to build bridges
between England and India, she soon became disillusioned to see
the racist and discriminatory policies of the British government. A
supporter of the Irish Home Rule movement, Nivedita was drawn
into the politics of the day and found herself sympathizing with
a burgeoning freedom movement in India. The British politics
of divide and rule, which culminated in the Partition of Bengal
in 1905, saw Nivedita turning to fully support the swadeshi and
boycott movements. Swamiji had passed away in 1902, and she now
came into close contact with the leading nationalists of the day,
from Aurobindo Ghosh to Congress leaders like Gopal Krishna
Gokhale. Nivedita was gripped by her theory of 'nationalism',
which drew on the underlying civilizational unity of India. India's
epics, folk legends, art, architecture and music revealed the path
to creating a civic bond among its people, which had the potential
to defeat British imperialism. This was very different from the
Western concept of 'nation', a mechanical homogenous unit bound
by a body of laws and a single shared language, which brilliant
minds like Rabindranath Tagore had critiqued widely since it could
never apply to India—a microcosm of the world. Nivedita felt that
the spirit of nationalism had to be aroused in a people who had
been led to believe that prior to the arrival of the Britishers, India
was not a unified entity.

As part of her nationalism project, Nivedita encouraged young
artists to draw inspiration from their indigenous art traditions
instead of turning to Hellenic and European sources, thereby giving
impetus to the Bengal Art Movement. As part of her mission to
spotlight the innate genius of India's finest minds, she promoted
the scientific work of Jagadish Chandra Bose. She took him under
her wing, reassured him in moments of despair, invited financial

assistance for his work and constantly edited and helped in the writing of his manuscripts.

In the short lifespan of forty-four years, Nivedita immersed herself in multiple activities with an unswerving dedication to causes she held dearly. Impulsive and excitable by nature, aggressive and confrontational when contradicted, Nivedita held her own in a world dominated by men, earning their grudging recognition and eventual respect. But she had her moments of doubt and weakness when her personal feelings clashed with the impersonal demeanour expected of her. Depression set in when she realized that her dreams could not be sustained. Such thoughts could only be shared through confidential exchanges in letters, which reveal her vulnerabilities and very human foibles.

At a personal level, my study of Nivedita occurred at a time when I was coming to terms with bereavement. After losing my husband, Himachal, I found myself in the secluded villa he had lovingly built amidst acres of an exclusive garden estate, with peacocks occasionally knocking on glass panes to see what lay within. In this ideal writers' retreat, it was total immersion in the world of Nivedita that enabled me to find answers to the riddles of life and death, which Vivekananda had expounded and Nivedita had so lucidly penned. The book is the result of rigorous historical research in the libraries of Kolkata and Delhi, a detailed study of primary material in the five-volume *Complete Works of Sister Nivedita*, two-volume *Letters of Sister Nivedita*, secondary work, including the five volumes of Sankari Prasad Basu's *Nibedita Lokmata* in Bengali, the two-volume *Life of Swami Vivekananda by His Eastern and Western Disciples* (Advaita Ashrama, first edition in 1912), major biographies such as Lizelle Reymond's *The Dedicated: A Biography of Nivedita*

(1953), Pravrajika Atmaprana's *Sister Nivedita* (first edition, 1961), Barbara Foxe's *Long Journey Home: A Biography of Margaret Noble (Nivedita)* (1975), and several other secondary books on the subject and the period of study.

My visit to the pristine and verdant Himalayan ashram Mayavati in the Kumaon region of Uttarakhand in October 2016 afforded me an insight into its deep spiritual energy, which had drawn Swami Vivekananda, Sister Nivedita and many personalities mentioned in this book to it despite the then arduous travel conditions. I was fortunate to be alerted by Swami Narasimhananda to twelve unpublished letters from Sister Nivedita to Patrick Geddes and Anna Geddes, which the Ramakrishna Mission had received from the archives of the University of Strathclyde and the National Library of Scotland, and which appear in the *Prabuddha Bharata* journal (July and August issues of 2015).

I have been supported in this project with an award of senior fellowship by the Indian Council for Social Science Research (ICSSR) and an affiliation to the Council for Social Development, Lodhi Road, Delhi.

While my sons, Vishnu and Abhishek, were glad to see me engrossed in this academic exercise, it was with my daughter-in-law Arundhati that I interacted regularly, sharing chapters and debating ideas.

I would like to thank Shri Rathin Mitra for sharing his exquisite line drawings of the buildings associated with Sister Nivedita. Finally, I express my deep appreciation for the painstaking editing of the manuscript by Richa Burman and Indrani Dasgupta of Penguin Random House.

Introduction

Colonial Bengal in the late nineteenth and early twentieth centuries was in the throes of a churning of social and religious ideas. In his seminal essay *Kalantar*,[1] Rabindranath Tagore mentioned the dawn of a new age, or the *nabayuga*, also called the Bengal Renaissance, when India stood at the crossroads. On the one hand, there was faith in British values and institutions, but on the other, serious opposition to foreign rule. There has been much historical debate on whether the term 'renaissance', borrowed from an Italian context, could apply to colonial Bengal and whether this age was indeed one of rebirth or a break with the past. It can be said, however, that it was an age when contact with the West became a catalyst in transforming modern Indian sensibilities, while reformist religious movements changed the whole aspect of Bengali life and thought. Western education brought with it the options of a better livelihood, family organization and even the construction of a social ideology based on Western egalitarian values, while the rise of a civil society in Bengal came with the introduction of a consolidated rule of law and the spread of print culture.

This turmoil of evolving ideas and attitudes that occurred among the Indians was often in response to the changing perceptions and policies of the colonial rulers. From the time of Edmund Burke to John Stuart Mill, roughly from 1784 when the British Parliament first regulated the East India Company's government in India until 1858 when Company rule was abolished and replaced by the rule of the British Crown, a host of Britons came into contact with India from all ranks and levels—soldiers, officials, political leaders, merchants, missionaries, historians, poets and philosophers.

The record of British corruption and plunder that had followed the Battle of Plassey (1757) made Edmund Burke and his contemporaries proclaim that India had to be governed according to Indian experience and tradition lest the fabric of Indian society be destroyed. There was a firm belief that a trained civil service for India had to be created, which would keep out graft and corruption, and that Britain had to recognize the peculiar characteristics and needs of India.

The College of Fort William established by Governor General Richard Wellesley in 1800 as a training centre for British civil servants enlisted the support of qualified Orientalists, a group of acculturated civil, military, judicial officials (and some missionaries) who were representatives of the British nation in India. While drawing on positive aspects of Western culture, the Orientalists had appreciation for Indian heritage and culture, which they wanted to explore and understand. Many Orientalists like William Jones, Henry Thomas Colebrooke, William Carey, H.H. Wilson and James Prinsep made significant contributions to the fields of Indian philology, archaeology and history. Apart from the large-scale English translations of Oriental classics that they undertook, there was also publishing and printing work in the Indian classical and vernacular languages. Through these activities, they came to form enduring relations with members of the Bengali intelligentsia, working with them to promote sociocultural change in Calcutta. Thus, in many ways, 'the Bengal Renaissance was a child of Orientalism'.[2]

With the Industrial Revolution in Britain, however, the intellectual outlook of the nation changed. There was now a focus on India's utility to Britain in terms of free trade and capital enterprise.

The laissez faire principles of trade had little understanding of the people, culture and institutions of India. James Mill, with his textbook knowledge of India, never having visited it, wrote his *History of British India* in 1817, which became a significant doctrine to transform India according to Utilitarian notions. Mill, as a Rationalist, attacked India's serious problems of poverty and ignorance and the treatment meted out to women. According to him, India's future lay in Westernization, the free spread of liberal knowledge and Christian truth brought in by the missionaries. The Orientalist position that the civilized achievements of India had to be preserved came under attack as being reactionary. Lord William Bentinck arrived in 1828 with openly anti-Orientalist views, dismantling the structure of the College of Fort William, which was formally dissolved by Lord Dalhousie in 1854. Bentinck's friend Thomas Babington Macaulay, president of the General Committee of Public Instruction, brought out his famous Minute in 1835, spelling out the Anglicist position advocating English education. Dismissing the lifelong work of Orientalists, he declared famously that 'a single shelf of a good European library was worth the whole native literature of India and Arabia'.[3]

With all these changes in British attitudes, Bengali intellectuals went through an identity crisis. It seemed an irony that although the Calcutta elite ultimately accepted Orientalism, the British civil servants for whom it was originally designed, challenged it. Severance from their own cultural and traditional past turned many to Christianity and the Brahmo Samaj. Even measures like Bentinck's anti-sati law in 1828[4] caused unanimous disapproval among the thinking elite in Calcutta, including Raja Ram Mohan Roy, who thought sati ought to die 'quietly and unobservedly'.[5]

An increasing frustration grew among the educated middle class with petty clerical jobs, who now had the stereotype of effeminacy stamped on them. The well-known diatribe by Thomas Babington Macaulay, law member for India in the 1830s, against Bengali men as being physically and mentally feeble, had been reproduced in many forms within official discourses. While the colonial masters had hoped, through English education, to bring up a whole generation of collaborators, Indian in features and English in thinking, the Indian Revolt of 1857 had brought home the realization that such an effort might have explosive consequences. There was, as a result, a hype in colonial projections, of natives who were babus or clerical pen pushers, servile in attitude, weak in constitution while dominating and subduing their womenfolk. This description was particularly directed at the Bengalis whose perceived lack of physical stamina excluded them from the British categorization of the so-called martial races developed after the Revolt for a reorganization of the Indian army. This classification differentiated between the manly Marathas, Rajputs and Sikhs and the supposedly effete, non-military and cowardly Bengalis.

The nationalist reaction to this projection was twofold. On the one hand, there was a self-appraisal, which grudgingly noted the verdict of physical effeminacy and ascribed it to the lack of adequate exercise and bodybuilding, excessive rice intake, early parenthood and so on. In the indigenous literature of this period, there was a prominent tendency to self-ridicule. The *Kalighata Patachitras* captured in cartoons ironic images of feeble men being castigated by strong spouses. On the other hand, almost as a foil to the image of a frail hero, the nationalists projected India as a strong and rich cultural tradition, with the Indian woman representing an impressive spiritual force. This nationalist effort received a fillip from the writings of a second generation of Orientalist writers like Max Müller (1823–1900) who focused on the achievements of the Aryans and explored the richness of the Vedic texts.

Many among the Bengali middle class found the message of Ramakrishna, expressed in rustic simplicity and promising validity to all forms and paths of religions, very comforting. Equally bracing was the message of Vivekananda that through physical fitness, Indian men could counter the stereotype of being emasculate and Indian women of being *abala* or helpless. Vivekananda inspired Indian youth to a robust life of dedication to the cause of nation-building, embracing celibacy until freedom was achieved and regarding women as mothers and sisters to be respected and protected. While urban Indian men had to contend with the colonial masters in the 'outer' public sphere and adapt to new ideas and social mores, they increasingly encouraged their women to remain rooted in the 'inner' realm of spirituality. At the same time, these women were acculturated in certain modern Western sensibilities of refinement and education, such as playing the piano, using cutlery, sporting Western clothes, and later the sartorial changes brought into sari-wear by the Tagore women. As the liberal values of the emerging Brahmo Samaj began to lead the women of established Calcutta families away from religious and social orthodoxy, late nineteenth-century Bengal witnessed an ideological turmoil.

It was into this Bengal, where ideas were confused, evolving and ambivalent, that Margaret Noble arrived in January 1898. Margaret Noble was not just a curious visitor to India. She was a woman of versatile interests with a committed dedication that had convinced Swami Vivekananda when he had met her in England that she would be ideal to do constructive work for the education of women. Her background equipped her for the mission she chose. Her father had been a priest who gave her the valuable lesson that service to mankind is true service to God. Her education, first in a church boarding school in London and later at Halifax College run by the Congregational Church, moulded her spiritual curiosity. Margaret lost her father at the age of ten and was brought up by her maternal grandfather, Hamilton, one of the front runners of the freedom movement of Ireland. His revolutionary idealism moulded young Margaret's mind.

What was the Calcutta society to make of this white woman crusader? Her immediate social acceptability was assured when, shortly after her arrival, Vivekananda at a public meeting at Star

Theatre in Calcutta introduced her as a 'gift' from England.
He followed this up by formally initiating her in the vow of
brahmacharya (lifelong celibacy), giving her the name 'Nivedita'—
the dedicated one. Initially, she stayed for a few days in a hotel
located in the anglicized quarter of Chowringhee but soon decided
to move out. She made her home in Bosepara, in the orthodox
environs of Baghbazar in north Calcutta, where at first no domestic
servant could be persuaded to work for her. Undeterred, she took
it as a challenge, thriving on fruits and wielding her own broom.
Later the same year, she opened her school in makeshift premises
in the presence of Sarada Devi, the revered widow of Ramakrishna.
But, by and large, across all sections of Calcutta society, Nivedita
appeared an enigma.

At a time when Western education was being welcomed,
Nivedita's stern admonishment of those who sought it was surprising
and antithetical. To the British population in Calcutta she appeared
as a 'gifted crank'.[6] Among the educated Brahmo families, where
Nivedita's erudition and congeniality found a favourable audience,
her seemingly uncritical acceptance of Hindu orthodoxy was not
appreciated and appeared inexplicable.

After Vivekananda's death, Nivedita reinvented herself and,
from 1902 till her death in 1911, her engagement with colonial
Bengal took on a totally different complexion. The political build-
up leading to the Bengal Partition in 1905 saw the coalescing of
a protest movement. This heralded the great national awakening
into which the nabayuga of the Bengal renaissance merged.
Nivedita's anti-imperialist political sensitivity now came to the
fore. Her sympathy and open support for the swadeshi movement
and to revolutionary groups discomfited many among the Bengali
bhadralok class and was viewed with deep suspicion by the British
government. In danger of deportation, she spent two years (1907–
08) in exile in England and USA only to return as a smartly dressed
Western woman, thus averting police recognition.

At the age of forty-four, in 1911, Nivedita passed away. Vivekananda had written in a poem dedicated to her, Nivedita combined in herself a 'mother's heart and a hero's will'. Yet Nivedita has remained an unsolved riddle to many.

It is the purpose of this book to try and understand what lay behind many of Nivedita's assumptions, to discover how she evolved in her thinking, to imagine what it might have been for a young, attractive woman in the late nineteenth century to renounce her culture and home for an alien country and adopt it with sympathy and compassion. Was there something in Vivekananda's message that resonated with her own values or was it because of her dedication to Vivekananda, whom she loved dearly and yet could never aspire to as a woman?

Soon after her arrival in India, Vivekananda had prescribed for Nivedita the role of a celibate nun, so that a watchful, conservative society would not be unkind to her. He sensed the depth of her love for him and resolved to keep it circumscribed, to prevent human weakness from getting the better of either of them. He openly spoke of 'the awful self-discipline' needed to love without attachment and warned of the 'danger that at any moment the most flower-like soul might have its petals soiled with the grosser stains of life'. He explained that 'the fight against passion was long and fierce, and at any moment the conqueror might become the conquered'.[7]

The restraint shown by both Vivekananda and Nivedita often told on their relationship, but they admirably sought to rise above any possible romantic compulsion. Following an intense emotional encounter with Nivedita in the Amarnath caves, Vivekananda moved Nivedita and himself definitively towards the worship of Goddess Kali, the divine mother, perhaps as a way of coping. By placing the woman on a pedestal as the Mother, he precluded any possibility of sexual interaction. Nivedita, in turn, realized with time that Vivekananda, who had attracted her initially as 'King', had to be viewed instead as the 'Master' who guided her and, finally, in the last stage as the 'Father' for whom her devotion was complete as a daughter. In her letters one can see the transformative change in the way she addresses him.

Nivedita's love for Vivekananda extended to an all-encompassing love for India, which could often be uncritically accommodating. The obvious disparities or social shortcomings did not deter her from embracing Indian society with a generous spirit. While her understanding of a complex environment grew over time, her observations tended to be spontaneous and were not always consistent. To see her evolving ideas as a well-defined body of thought and fault her for her biases, contradictions and oversights would be a mistake. Admittedly, she was idealistic, often utopian, and on occasion simplistic, but most important was the consistency in her concern for India and its future.

This unusual story may be studied as an intellectual history along with Nivedita's copious writings and letters. Her writings are replete with anecdotes, capturing the conflicting emotions she had experienced during her over-a-decade-long close association with India. Often through flashbacks and reminiscences, as in the first chapter of this book, I have taken the liberty to recreate the thoughts of Nivedita and Vivekananda, culled from their letters and writings. This is to provide an important background to the story that unfolds over the course of their lives as well as enable readers to experience the inner doubts and conflicts of the two principal protagonists.

Nivedita's chance encounter in London with Vivekananda in 1895 transformed her life completely. Although her time with her guru was limited to only four years before his untimely death in 1902, her relationship with him evolved sharply so that she saw him in rapidly changing roles. The Swamiji she had met in England with a magnificent, commanding presence, a baritone voice that broke into chants and an inspiring countenance, gave her confidence and assurance when she was emotionally vulnerable. Chapter 1, 'Inspired by the "King"', reflects the initial years of her association with her guru (January 1898–May 1899) when she was able to travel with him extensively and observe first-hand the incredible diversity in the life and terrain of India. Vivekananda's running commentaries on Indian history, culture and philosophy, as they travelled over wide expanses, gave her a rare insight and education, which later found expression in her literary works. After her emotionally powerful experiences with Swamiji in the Amarnath caves, she realized that her personal feelings for her guru had to change into an impersonal reverence towards a Master.

Chapter 2, 'Guided by the "Master"', describes her accompanying Swamiji on a sea voyage to England and then America (June 1899–November 1900), a period of intense interaction when she learnt about his philosophy and worldview. She also saw herself heading in a direction that was independent of her guru's path, although she was consistent in her defence of his message to the Brahmos and the Christian West alike. The next year, 1901, was spent away from India in introspection in England, pondering over the purpose of life as well as worrying about her guru's declining health.

In February 1902, Nivedita returned to India, and Chapter 3, 'Blessed by the "Father"', describes the last months she spent with Swamiji. By now, their relationship had evolved and was devoid of the earlier tensions. He blessed her as a father would. After his death in July 1902, Nivedita found a fresh focus in her work—not only running her school with Sister Christine but also finding herself drawn to the pulsating politics of the day. Her meeting with the Japanese savant Okakura, who had come to India to meet Vivekananda in 1900, had filled her with dreams of discovering an Indian cultural identity amidst its disparity. Gregarious and compassionate by nature, she soon realized that her friendship with the bohemian Okakura had to be reined in with an impersonal focus.

Chapter 4, 'Nationalism', describes the ideal that gripped Nivedita totally, namely to make India aware of its incipient civilizational unity developed over the centuries. She wished to challenge the received notion that before British rule India had no cohesive unity. She believed this would awaken among Indians a strength of character and purpose that would take the country forward in the anti-imperialist struggle. Nivedita's ideas need to be considered seriously in the context of a contemporary debate that has recently arisen on the concept of nationalism. Does nationalism mean an inclusiveness, a space for a multi-layered diversity or is it a prescribed voice of chauvinistic patriotism that rules out dissent or difference of opinion? Even during Nivedita's time, the concept of nationalism was interpreted differently.

Rabindranath Tagore and later Mahatma Gandhi were suspicious of the Western definition of nation as an artificial hegemonic entity bound by uniform laws and institutions into which a diverse people would be forcibly grouped. This kind of nation, they felt, would never work in India due to its multiple cultural and religious identities. The common perception that nationalism and patriotism are synonymous often made it problematic to understand the stand taken by Tagore in his famous 'Nationalism' lectures delivered in Japan and the United States, when he unequivocally attacked the aggressive nationalism of imperialist countries.

Nivedita's advocacy of nationalism and aggressive Hinduism initially worried Tagore until he realized that her definition of nation was a unique homegrown formula that was meant to arouse pride in the shared past of an enslaved nation, in their artistic heritage, in the scientific achievements of its men of genius and in the diversity of its religious traditions and cultures. Nivedita's aggressive Hinduism did not imply militancy but was an exhortation to Indians to shake off their apathy and the label of effeminacy given to them by their colonial masters. She encouraged them to work concertedly towards building a strong national character in light of the rich civilizational traditions they had inherited.

Chapter 5, 'Legacy', describes the substantial corpus of Nivedita's writings whether in her letters, articles, speeches, interviews or in her many published books. The five-volume *Complete Works of Sister Nivedita*, containing her major books as well as her lectures, articles and commentaries, is a testimony to her authorial competence. The two volumes of her *Correspondence* offer a useful thread to enter the labyrinth of Indian history, to discover its wonders and also its tensions and conflicts.

Her support of the scientific achievements of Jagadish Chandra Bose and her unstinted help in editing many of his manuscripts, which she wanted to promote abroad, won her his and his wife's lifelong friendship. Her exposition on Goddess Kali the Mother, highlighting the terrible, the ominous and yet unavoidable aspects of divinity—largely inspired by Vivekananda and tellingly enumerated in her writings and in her speeches to the orthodoxy—was exceptional. Her *The Cradle Tales of Hinduism*, easily comparable to classics like Charles Lamb's *Legends of Greece*, makes for delightful reading.

The encouragement she provided to artists to look for indigenous sources of inspiration for their art was significant. She also introduced them to the important exercise of art appreciation through her critical analysis of their paintings. Her meticulous notes on her travels in the Himalayas served as an important source of information. Aware that such details of itineraries in these remote areas were difficult to find, she felt it almost obligatory of those who undertook such journeys to publish their experiences.

Chapter 6, 'The Last Years', describes the final years of Nivedita's life, spent abroad and in India, when she had a sense of foreboding that her end was near and the work at hand should be completed. She found satisfaction that her most important work, *The Master as I Saw Him*, was completed during her visit to America and several other books were near completion or in print. It also gave her great satisfaction to help Jagadish Chandra Bose as he wrote some of his epoch-making chapters. This sense of personal fulfilment helped Nivedita come to terms with the general dejection she felt at the political impasse in the country. The swadeshi movement had been snuffed out with wholesale arrests. She had also witnessed the deaths of many of her loved ones, such as her mother in England, the death in India of Swami Sadananda, R.C. Dutt, the mother and grandmother of Swami Vivekananda, which gave her a sense of closure, and finally the death of Sara Bull in America in 1910. Nivedita had long pondered the inevitability of death and learnt to accept it philosophically. But she was totally unprepared for the vicious attack of Sara Bull's daughter Olea challenging in court her mother's will, which had generously provided for Nivedita and the scientific work of Bose. Dismayed and seriously ill with an infection caught in the hills during a visit with the Boses, Nivedita breathed her last on 13 October 1911 in Darjeeling.

How is history to judge Nivedita? She was not a kind of Jeanne d'Arc of the revolutionary movement that many hagiographic histories have tried to project,[8] but neither should she become a mere footnote of history. Nivedita has to be judged by other parameters. Her sincere and unalloyed dedication to India, which she made her home and which she sought to understand, can never be in question. What was unique was her entry into the largely male preserve of the Indian intelligentsia, on equal terms, owing to her erudition and assertiveness.

Questions have been raised about the apparently irreconcilable aspects in the personality of Nivedita as a spiritual or a political figure.[9] Although she was spiritually inclined, the Swami never envisaged Nivedita as a spiritual leader. After initiating her as a *brahmacharini*, he did not follow it up with the monastic vows of *sannyas*. He saw her role first as an educator and then as his spokesperson who could present his scattered thoughts on religion and society in a coherent and lucid manner through her speeches and writings, a responsibility she discharged to the full. After the death of Vivekananda, Nivedita found a new purpose in enunciating her theory of nationalism that she felt would have relevance in the charged environment of post-Partition Bengal. Aware that her political interests were not welcomed by the Ramakrishna Order, she formally severed connections with them. However, in her mind there was no contradiction between the path she had taken by supporting the Swadeshi Movement and her allegiance to the thoughts and philosophy of her Master. Until the end, she maintained this credibility by signing herself as 'Nivedita of Ramakrishna-Vivekananda'.

Perhaps one of the most balanced appraisals of Nivedita is by Tagore in his Bengali article 'Bhogini Nibedita'.[10] Tagore confessed that though on the one hand he had felt considerably provoked by Nivedita's outspoken combativeness, on the other hand she had perhaps done him a service as no other. Her defence of India had given him great confidence at a time when his self-esteem as an Indian was coming under attack. Her self-effacing dedication, her defiance of the government run by her countrymen made her unique. Tagore believed that the considerable sacrifice Nivedita made had not been fully appreciated. There was an indomitable will behind her resolve, which is often forgotten, while there is a tendency to gloat over the fact that Nivedita had embraced Hinduism.

It would be unfair to judge Nivedita from a Saidian framework and dismiss her as an obscurantist Orientalist.[11] If Hindu religion and society were to see themselves from a historical and scientific perspective, as Nivedita did, they would break the blind beliefs and unfair practices that go in the name of religion. Nivedita is to be admired and respected not as a Hindu but as an outstanding human being. Her uniqueness lies in the fact that she was both a thinking, analytical individual and a tireless worker—a rare combination. She gave a gift of selfless love as a mother to an adopted nation. Hence, she was given by Tagore the title 'Lok Mata' or People's Mother.[12]

1

Inspired by the 'King'

It was a cold January morning in 1898 at Tilsbury Dock, London, where a small group surrounded Margaret Noble to say goodbye, as she was about to set sail for India aboard the *S.S. Mombasa*. Her mother Mary was in tears and yet remembered how, from the time of her daughter's birth, she had always known that she would leave home for a larger mission.[1] Her sister May, on whom Margaret had left the responsibility of running her school in Wimbledon, seemed anxious. When would she be released from this responsibility, to live her own life and get married? Her brother, Richmond, feared for his sister as she was moving away from hearth and home to unknown surroundings so far away. Artist Ebenezer Cooke, Margaret's close associate in school and at the Sesame Literary Club where they both belonged, knew her calling had come.

Once on the high seas, Margaret's thoughts kept turning to that fateful day over two years back, which had proved to be the turning point in her life. Lady Isabel Margesson, a strong advocate of social and educational reform and secretary of the forward-looking Sesame Club, had invited an Indian monk to speak to a select gathering at her well-appointed West End home in London. Margaret recalled that cold Sunday November afternoon in 1895, when Swami Vivekananda had sat facing a small audience with the fireplace behind him, answering questions and breaking into Sanskrit chants from time to time. So intimate had been the image, she was to recall later, that it had seemed a close variant of an Indian scene, when at twilight a group of listeners sit by the side of a well under a tree listening to their sadhu.[2] The Sanskrit verses that he recited in a sonorous voice sounded like Gregorian chants while his look of 'mingled gentleness and loftiness'[3] seemed like the look on Raphael's *Sistine Child*.

Vivekananda's main assertion was that the truth in all religions was equal since they were expressions of a Universal Oneness. Although instantly appealing, it was not a very novel idea, thought Margaret with an initial scepticism. However, after attending several of his lectures she felt his message growing on her. The fact that he always preached in philosophical terms, quoting only from the Vedas, the Upanishads and the Gita, and did not bring in images or stories from Hindu mythology nor mention his own Master, made him gradually acceptable. 'As great music wakes in us, grows and deepens with its repetition',[4] Vivekananda's discourses heard by her over the next few weeks gained a new plausibility.

Nivedita was living in a time of tremendous religious uncertainty and realized that 'belief in the dogmas of Christianity has become impossible to us, and we had no tool, as we now hold, by which to cut away the doctrinal shell from the kernel of Reality, in our faith'.[5] Vivekananda's call, that 'I am God', that divinity lay within each one of us, was startling in its direct simplicity and seemed as 'living water to men perishing of thirst'.[6] Margaret was quick to realize how difficult it must have been for him to explain many of these concepts in a borrowed tongue the way she struggled to understand the concept of maya. It was neither 'delusion' nor 'magic' but 'that shimmering, elusive, half-real, half-unreal complexity, in which there is no rest, no satisfaction, no ultimate certainty, of which we become aware through the senses and through the mind, as dependent on the senses'.[7] It is by going beyond this bondage of maya that one could find freedom—mukti or nirvana—and the religious quest was therefore always to go from the direction of being to becoming.

Coming from a family of pastors, Margaret found much peace in Swami's words. While her grandfather John Noble, of Scottish descent, had been a Protestant minister in a Wesleyan church, her father Samuel, who began his career as an apprentice to his uncle, a cloth merchant, gave up his business and went to England to enrol as a student of theology in a Wesleyan church in Manchester.

One-year-old Margaret, who was born on 28 October 1867 in the town of Dungannon in County Tyrone in Ireland, was left under the care of her maternal grandmother. She was able to join her father only three years later on his return to a church in Oldham, England, and met her younger sister May for the first time. Oldham, however, never suited the family, and Samuel's health deteriorated. They moved to the more healthy environs of Devonshire in Great Torrington, where they spent a few happy years, with young Richard joining the family as the youngest sibling. Margaret was very close to her father and discussed theological matters from an early age. However, tragedy struck when Samuel died of consumption at the age of thirty-four. Margaret's maternal grandfather Hamilton, a retired cork merchant and one of the pioneers of the freedom movement of Ireland, now took over the charge of the girls' education. He sent them to study at Halifax College, run by the Congregational Church. Margaret's participation in church-sponsored activities gave her a Catholic zeal, while her spiritual curiosity made her delve into various books on religion, including Buddhism.

Perhaps what fascinated Margaret most was teaching, which she began in 1884 at the young age of seventeen, after leaving school. She taught children at an excellent private boarding school in Keswick in the Lake District. After a few years, she found it more challenging to try a new experiment of working in an orphanage in

Rugby, where charity girls were trained to be domestic servants. At twenty-one, she applied as mistress of a school in Wrexham, a large mining centre in north Wales, where she became familiar with the lives of miners by visiting their shabby, dreary homes. However, misfortune hit hard when the twenty-three-year-old Welsh engineer she had planned on marrying died prematurely. Margaret now sought a transfer to Chester so that she could relocate her mother and siblings to Liverpool nearby. In her fifth year of teaching, Margaret got interested in the Pestalozzi–Froebel method of new education, which not only altered her perspective on education but also significantly changed her approach to life in general.

Johann Heinrich Pestalozzi (1746–1827), a product of the French Revolution, was an educator who believed that the science of education could only be built up on a keen and continuous observation of the laws of the mind. His student Friedrich Froebel (1782–1852), helped carry his ideas out and laid the foundation of modern education based on the recognition that children have unique needs and capabilities. The process of 'psychologizing of education'[8] involved training the child to learn from concrete experience and in a manner that was true to his innate nature and racial background. In other words, foreign norms or examples could not yield desired results when imported into his environment. The ideal kindergarten or garden of children was best at home with the mother as the gardener. Local folklore, mythology, handicrafts could all be employed for the efflorescence of culture which was typical to its civilizational ethos. Margaret decided to help try out this new education in a school in Wimbledon, which was opened by Mrs de Leeuw, a Dutch woman who had been Froebel's pupil. After two fruitful years, in the autumn of 1895, Margaret was encouraged to open her own school, Ruskin School, in another part of Wimbledon, not only for children but also for adults who wished to study modern educational methods.

This was a milestone in Margaret's life since she now attracted the cooperation of several celebrated teachers such as Cooke, who was at that time a fashionable painter of children's portraits. Her work was discussed in the salon of Lady Ripon, Ebenezer's friend, which developed into the Sesame Club frequented by George Bernard Shaw, T.H. Huxley and other men of letters and science and patronized by educators like Lady Isabel Margesson. Margaret became an active member of the Sesame Club.

Soon after arriving in London, Margaret also joined the 'Free Ireland' group working for home rule and wrote pro-Boer articles in papers such as *Daily News*, *Research* and *Review of Reviews*, whose editor William Stead became a personal friend. Prince Pyotr Alexeyevich Kropotkin, formerly of the Russian royal family now living in exile in London, often spoke at the 'Free Ireland' circle. He and his wife not only befriended Margaret but also became ideologues of sorts to her. His anti-establishment anarchist views fired the rebel in Margaret, while his theory of mutual aid based on collaboration, rather than the Darwinian theory of competitive struggle for survival of the fittest, appealed to her.

What attracted Margaret to Vivekananda at this point in her life was not only his doctrine of Vedanta, of preaching to men their innate divinity, conducted in weekly classes in London, but also the larger 'man-making' mission of educating people to become aware of their inner strength and improve themselves and their nation. When he spoke of the acute need to start an institution in India for the education of girls on nationalist lines, producing not only ideal wives and mothers but brahmacharinis, celibate women, working for the betterment of the womanhood of the country, Margaret felt the moment had come to carry her educational ideas to another country. The belief gradually grew in her that she had to go to India, never to be critical but to sympathetically understand Indian society under the lessons, guidance and direction of Vivekananda. It took several months for Margaret to ponder over this important decision and when Vivekananda returned to London again from America, in April 1896, she began discussions with him. On his return to India, he wrote to her on 29 July 1897,

> Let me tell you frankly that I am now convinced that you have a great future in the work for India. What was wanted was not a man, but a woman; a real lioness, to work for the Indians, women specially. India cannot yet produce great women, she must borrow them from other nations. Your education, sincerity, purity, immense love, determination and above all, the Celtic blood make you just the woman wanted.[9]

But he was candid too in cautioning her that—

> . . . The difficulties are many. You cannot form any idea of the misery, the superstition, and the slavery that are here. You will be in the midst of a mass of half-naked men and women with quaint ideas of caste and isolation, shunning the white skin through fear or hatred and hated by them intensely. On the other hand, you will be looked upon by the white as a crank and every one of your movements will be watched with suspicion.
>
> Then the climate is fearfully hot; our winter in most places being like your summer and in the south it is always blazing. Not one European comfort is to be had in places out of the cities. If in spite of all this you dare venture into the work, you are welcome, a hundred times welcome.[10]

Margaret stood by her decision and was much reassured when Vivekananda wrote back to her, 'I will stand by you unto death, whether you work for India or not, whether you give up Vedanta, or remain in it. The tusks of the elephant come out, but they never go back. Even so are the words of a man.'[11] She was undeterred by reports of India's poverty for had she not observed at close quarters in Wrexham, 'networks of slums and alleys, wherein dwells a race whose habits and surroundings are a blot on our civilization, a foul canker eating into the very heart of our Municipal life . . . where life is a perfect epitome of degradation and uncleanliness'.[12]

At a time when she was facing personal crisis with the untimely death of her fiancé and another failed relationship,[13] Margaret felt grateful that such an opportunity had arisen for her. Recalling this moment, she was to write to her friend many years later, 'Supposing he had not come to London that time! Life would have been like a headless torso—for I always knew that I was waiting for something. I always said that a call would come. And it did.'[14]

While the ship was on the rolling seas, the compassionate Margaret found much to keep her engaged. She found a passenger who was leaving his country with a heavy heart having proved to be a burden to his family owing to his intemperate nature. She befriended the dejected man and presented him her gold watch gifted by her mother. She extracted from him a promise never to pawn it but keep it as memento from one who gave him courage. The news of his death a year later in South Africa was conveyed to Margaret by his mother, who added that he had remembered the compassionate soul on the ship who had inspired him to turn over a new leaf.[15]

On 28 January 1898, after three weeks at sea, the ship neared the coast of India and the shoreline in the Calcutta harbour became increasingly distinct. Margot, as Vivekananda called her using her pet name, felt suddenly anxious. Would he be there—her 'King', for whom she had left her country to make a new home in his land?

Vivekananda stood at the Kidderpore Docks along with a fellow monk who carried a garland of flowers to welcome Margaret. Vivekananda was troubled. Was it the right decision to accede to

Margaret's wishes to come? Would she be able to make India her home? How would Indian society view her and would her presence not add to the aspersions already cast on Vivekananda for having Western women disciples? Deep in thought, he reflected on how unpredictable his life had been.

Born on 12 January 1863, in his ancestral home in Simulia, in north Calcutta, Narendranath Datta came from a well-established family of distinguished lawyers. In his youth, he showed great promise in athletics and had a mellifluous voice. Beginning his studies in the arts in Presidency College, he was, however, unable to continue due to ill health and completed his bachelor's degree in philosophy from Scottish Church College. Following discussions about the presence of God during a class with Professor Hastie, he, along with a few friends, made a trip to the Kali temple at Dakshineswar on the banks of the Ganga. The unlettered priest of the temple, Ramakrishna, had reportedly announced on many occasions that he had been blessed with a vision of god. An intense association followed between the two, during which Narendranath slowly came under Ramakrishna's inspired spell.

Meanwhile, family fortunes fell dramatically with the premature death of his father and property disputes, which left his immediate family in a state of penury. It was Ramakrishna's inspiration and support that helped Narendranath cope with his difficult circumstances. Having been a member of the reformist Brahmo Samaj, Narendranath questioned icon worship and engaged Ramakrishna in endless debates until one day, when persuaded to enter the Kali temple to pray for his family's well-being, he felt he was in the presence of a living, divine mother.

After graduation, Narendranath gave up his legal studies and became the chief devotee among the band of disciples that Ramakrishna had gathered around him. Ramakrishna, then ailing from cancer, declared Narendranath as his chosen successor. After Ramakrishna's death in 1886, Narendranath, along with the principal disciples, set up a monastery in Baranagore where the Ramakrishna brotherhood could assemble. This was moved to Belur in 1898.

The years immediately following the death of Ramakrishna filled Narendranath with great restlessness. In 1889, he renounced his family, took up the vows of a celibate monk and began an arduous journey throughout the length and breadth of India in an attempt to get to know his country well. He embraced total austerity and frugality in his travel, often travelling on foot, begging for food, accepting alms and food from people of all castes and religions, meditating in open spaces and periodically facing ill health.

The diversity of the Indian people, the multiplicity of its religions and an architectural heritage of contrasting civilizations impressed him greatly. But behind all contrasts, Narendranath found an underlying commonality. He visited places of worship of all religions—Hindu, Buddhist, Jain, Christian—and concluded that they all endeavoured to assist believers to discover the divinity that lay within them. But the poverty of the Indian masses, their superstition-laden beliefs and lack of education overwhelmed him. For Narendranath, the need of the hour was to raise the masses from the depths of ignorance and penury, and for this, he sought to engage the princely heads of states through which he passed, for leadership and direction. He accepted the hospitality of many of these princes and addressed large gatherings of intellectuals and politicians while staying with them, surprising all with his erudition, vast knowledge of various subjects and excellent command over the English language. It is from the princes that he heard about the forthcoming Parliament of Religions being held in Chicago in 1893 and was persuaded to attend it to disseminate the fundamentals of the Hindu religion. It was also his fervent wish to garner support for a Ramakrishna Order that could devote itself to philanthropic causes for India's destitute and needy. At the request of the Raja of Khetri, he decided to adopt the name Vivekananda for his America visit. He also accepted with gratitude the financial and infrastructural support that had been initiated by the Raja and several others to facilitate his visit to the Chicago Conference.

In the great enthusiasm to attend the Chicago Conference it had been overlooked that he was travelling several months before the event and was not carrying the mandatory letter of invitation to the Parliament of Religions! How such a hopeless situation turned into a resounding success is quite another story.

As his finances dwindled due to mounting hotel costs in Chicago, Vivekananda suddenly remembered a pleasant acquaintance he had made on the train journey from Vancouver to Chicago a few weeks back. Kate Sanborn, a lecturer and author who lived in Massachusetts, had been very impressed by the handsome Indian monk who 'spoke better English than I did, was conversant with ancient and modern literature, would quote easily and naturally from Shakespeare or Longfellow or Tennyson, Darwin, Muller, Tyndall; could repeat pages of our Bible, was familiar with and tolerant of all creeds. He was an education, an illumination, a revelation!'[16] She had naturally extended to him an invitation to visit her in Boston and he now took up this offer.

In her country home 'Breezy Meadows' near Boston, Vivekananda regaled intellectuals and academics, among whom was John Henry Wright, professor of Greek history at Harvard University, who now invited him to spend a weekend with him at Annisquam Massachusetts, a quiet village resort on the Atlantic seaboard. When Vivekananda shared his grave concern that he would have to forgo attending the Parliament of Religions since he had not carried the proper credentials, Prof. Wright exclaimed, 'To ask you, Swami, for credentials is like asking the sun to state its right to shine!' Introducing Vivekananda in a letter to the chairman of the Committee for the selection of delegates as 'a man who is more learned than all our learned professors put together',[17] Prof. Wright presented Vivekananda the fare to Chicago and handed him letters of introduction to the Committee. One would have thought the travails of the venerable monk were over! But by a strange quirk of fate, Vivekananda found when he reached Chicago that he had misplaced the address of the Chairman of the Parliament's General Committee where he was to report! Unable to get help and with night coming on, Vivekananda stretched himself into a huge empty box in the railway yard and fell asleep. When morning dawned, he emerged and walked past stately mansions on Lake Shore Drive. There he rang the bell at a few places to get some help but failed completely, as his strange appearance was viewed suspiciously. Resigning himself to fate, he sat by the lake completely exhausted. Suddenly a door opened in a mansion opposite and an elegant lady asked if he was a delegate to the Parliament of Religions. Inviting him into the house, she and her husband provided him warm hospitality and accompanied him to the offices of the Parliament of Religions. Among others, George and Mrs Hale and their three children became Swamiji's closest friends in America.

The Parliament of Religions, which was held in connection with the World's Columbian Exposition in Chicago from 11 to 27 September 1893, was an epoch-making event with delegates from around the world. Overawed by the large Congress and without having brought a prepared speech, Vivekananda missed several turns to speak. As he confessed to a disciple later, 'Of course my heart was fluttering and my tongue nearly dried up—I was so nervous!'[18] When eventually he spoke, addressing the gathering as 'Sisters and Brothers of America', he was taken aback at the spontaneous wave of enthusiasm that greeted him with a long standing ovation! The speech itself was short but its spirit of universality, its fundamental earnestness and broadmindedness completely captivated the audience. An eyewitness, Mrs S.K. Blodgett, later recalled that scores of women walked over the benches to get near him and she could not help saying to herself,

'Well, my lad, if you can resist that onslaught you are indeed a god!'[19]

Vivekananda had indeed created history. For the next four years, he stayed on in America, with short visits to England, preaching practical Vedanta through a series of courses, lectures and workshops across the country. He positioned himself as representative of an impoverished India in serious need of material aid from the West but with a wealth of spiritual wisdom to offer in exchange. The phenomenal success of Vivekananda, however, drew the wrath of detractors such as the Christian missionaries, who realized that there was a sharp fall in monetary contributions to their causes. Vivekananda was periodically heckled by questions such as, 'Do the people of India throw their children into the jaws of crocodiles?' or 'Do they kill themselves beneath the wheels of Juggernaut? or, 'Do they burn their widows alive?'[20] Vivekananda tried his best to respond to these with customary wit and humour, refusing to be dragged into discussions of India's superstitious rituals and practices since it made little sense to wash one's dirty linen in public.[21] He was aware that he was being watched by the close circle of friends of Ramabai, the erudite Hindu widow who had embraced Christianity and spoken extensively of the ills of Indian widowhood. Vivekananda went to great lengths to speak of the virtues of the Hindu woman as wife and mother and some of his devoted followers sent a card during Christmas to his mother, in grateful recognition of her life and work in and through her son![22] Perhaps the most scathing attacks on Vivekananda were by his erstwhile friend and fellow speaker at the Chicago Parliament— Pratap Chandra Mazoomdar of the Brahmo Samaj who now questioned his credentials as a non-Brahmin, cigar-smoking monk to represent Hinduism. Aspersions were also cast on his character and his close association with several Western women disciples.[23]

The delay in the Indian press to acknowledge his success added to Vivekananda's woes since he was keen to counter this negative publicity. Eventually, accolades poured in for him in the Indian press, but the mischief had been done. When Vivekananda returned to India in 1897 to a hero's welcome, he also sensed disapproval in some quarters that he had crossed the seas and not made ritual penance. At the Dakshineswar temple for instance, where he paid obeisance to the cherished Kali image along with the Raja of Khetri, he was not greeted by the proprietor of the temple who decided to remain absent. In the outcry over this incident that appeared in the newspapers, the proprietor explained that the temple precincts would have to be ritually purified after it had been defiled by the visit.[24] Such ironies were not lost on Vivekananda, who was to address the issue of caste purity in a novel way later.

Vivekananda's visit to the West had not yielded any substantial financial resources from his lectures or engagements. However, he did realize his desire to gain a select number of disciples with whose spiritual earnestness and sincerity he could form a core that would be instrumental in spreading his message. Among his staunchest supporters who stayed loyal to him till the end, with substantial financial pledges and emotional support, was Sara Bull, the rich, independent widow of Norwegian violin virtuoso Ole Bull, forty years her senior. Mrs Bull offered hospitality to Vivekananda in her home in Massachusetts and remained his close financial supporter; he saluted her composure by calling her 'Dhira Mata'. There was also Josephine MacLeod, eminent socialite of New York, who preferred to be seen as his friend rather than disciple, affectionately called Jo Jo. The monks in the Ramakrishna Order addressed her as their beloved Tantine, or 'aunt' in French. Captain James Henry Sevier, a retired British army officer, inspired by Vivekananda, sold off his property in England and acquired a beautiful hill house in Kumaon. This, he developed into the Mayavati Ashrama along with his wife, Charlotte, both of whom regarded Vivekananda as a son. There were two others who joined this foursome but were not destined to remain with them for long—Henrietta Muller, who became his disciple in England and offered him her generous hospitality, and Josiah John Goodwin, a professional stenographer, who had decided to dedicate his services to Swamiji. All of them were to converge in Calcutta soon. And to join this group would be Margaret Noble.

Vivekananda was shaken out of his reverie as he saw the first passengers alighting from the ship *Mombasa*, which had just docked into the harbour. It did not take long for him to spot the 'the distinctive woman with luminous grey blue eyes, with hair light golden brown, with a complexion radiant and with a smile ingratiating and alluring'.[25] Margot was delighted to find her 'King' waiting to welcome her to India.

It was arranged that Margaret would stay for a few days at 49 Park Street in the European quarter of the city of Calcutta until she was joined by Henrietta Muller. They had planned to jointly start an institution for the education of Indian women. Vivekananda lost no time in getting her started with Bengali tuitions. Margaret's first impressions after arriving in Calcutta are captured in her letter to her friends, the Hammonds, in England. 'It is so funny to get to a country in the time of roses and green peas, and to value a rose just as one would do at home. The weather is perfect—not a bit too hot.'[26] In March 1898, Vivekananda bought a piece of land, over seven acres in extent, together with an old decrepit building, in Belur, on the west bank of the Ganga. The purchase price of Rs 39,000 had been gifted by Henrietta Muller. Mrs Sara Bull, who along with Josephine MacLeod had arrived in Calcutta in February, now pledged to make a substantial financial contribution for the building of a shrine and the creation of an endowment for the monastery, which on completion came to be known as Belur Math.

After a few days in a hotel, both Sara Bull and Josephine MacLeod offered to repair and furnish the old riverside house and make it their home for a few months, where they were joined shortly by Margaret.

Thus began a close historic association between three dedicated and committed women, whose lives had changed remarkably following their encounter with Swamiji. Among his Western disciples, he was closest to the independent-minded Josephine, whom he regarded as an equal and whose judgement he could trust. He considered Jo Jo his 'good luck'.[27]

Josephine as Yum Yum[28] to Nivedita was a mother figure. Mrs Bull, who looked upon Vivekananda as a son, became Grannie to Nivedita. Vivekananda could hardly believe how the old rundown riverside cottage had been transformed by the efforts of these enthusiastic women. In a letter he wrote, 'My, these Yanks can do anything! It is wonderful how they accommodate themselves to our Indian life of privation and hardship. After the luxuries of Boston and New York to be quite content and happy in this wretched little house!!'[29]

The two months spent in the riverside cottage in close association with Vivekananda were described by Josephine MacLeod as 'perhaps the most beautiful time we ever had with Swamiji. He came every morning for early tea, which he used to take under the great mango tree'.[30] This was an important period of training for his Western disciples and Vivekananda revealed the Indian world to them—its history, its folklore, its caste system and its customs.

To Margaret, the Swamiji she had known in the West as a religious teacher with Buddha-like calm was very different from what she now saw of him in his 'home-aspect' with the relationships of his own life.[31] From the moment of her landing, Margaret sensed that the personality of her Master was caught in fruitless torture and struggle, like a lion trapped in a net. She tried hard to understand the root cause of this struggle. On the one hand, he warmly welcomed his Western guests with deep consideration of all their needs and requirements and on the other he struggled hard to keep his involvement impersonal and detached. His vow was 'to accept nothing, however pleasant, if it concealed a fetter; at a word to stand ready to sever any connection that gave a hint of bondage'.[32] Yet he realized his responsibility of training his guests in Indian ways, protecting them against the censure of an orthodox society and acculturating them to many Indian norms that seemed strange. Margaret recalled, 'We were even called upon to understand a thought immeasurably foreign to all our past conceptions of religion, in which sainthood finds expression in an unconsciousness of the body, so profound that the saint is unaware that he goes naked. For that delicate discrimination of a higher significance in certain cases of nudity, which, in Europe, finds its expression in art, in India finds it in religion. As we, in the presence of a Greek statue, experience only reverence for the ideal of beauty, so the Hindu sees in the naked saint only a glorified and childlike purity.'[33]

His Western disciples were called upon to accept Indian practices, including eating of food with fingers, sitting and sleeping on the floor, performing Hindu ceremonies and adhering to the feelings and observances of Hindu etiquette so that the orientation to a Hindu consciousness would come easily. At the same time, Vivekananda had to ensure that his monks of the Order could accept dining with the Westerners whom their leader had accepted. By calling his Western disciples true Brahmins and Kshatriyas, eating in public the food they cooked for him from time to time and even making his brother monks do the same, he gave them a social standing unacceptable to the orthodox Hindus. Margaret recalled being asked by Swamiji to cook some special food as a sick diet and being disappointed on learning that he had hardly partaken of the dish. It was only gradually that she realized the pains Swamiji went through to make a place for her as a foreigner in Hindu society.[34]

What took Margaret by complete surprise was the discovery of a significant element in the spiritual consciousness of Vivekananda. In England and America, the realization of the Brahman was his only imperative, Advaita philosophy his only system of doctrine, the Vedas and the Upanishads his sole scriptural authorities. Yet, alongside this, in India the words 'Shiva' and 'Mother' were always on his lips. This transition from non-dualism or monism to dualism perplexed Margaret. He now spoke of the divine mother as a living reality and over time explained to Margaret how in the incarnation of Kali, the mother goddess embodied not only sweetness and joy but also evil, terror, sorrow and annihilation. During conversations, he would often break into chants of 'Shiva, Shiva, Shiva'. It was Margaret's former training as an educationist that enabled her to accept the many-layered consciousness in Vivekananda's life and thought.[35]

Margaret's first public appearance in Calcutta was in the Star Theatre, where on 11 March she spoke at a meeting presided over by Vivekananda under the auspices of the Ramakrishna Mission, on 'The Influence of Indian Spiritual Thought in England'. Introducing her to the audience, the Swami called her 'another gift of England to India'—the others being Annie Besant and Henrietta Muller, all of whom he said had consecrated their lives to the good of India. In her talk, Margaret said, 'You have the ingenuity of 6000 years of conservatism. But yours is the conservatism of a people who have through that long period been able to preserve the greatest spiritual treasures for the world, and it is for this reason that I have come to India to serve her with our burning passion for service.'[36] Vivekananda was delighted with Margaret's lecture and wrote to her on 16 March that he felt convinced that it was from the public platform that she would be able to help him the most, apart from her plans for education of women. He confided in a brother monk, 'Miss Noble is really an acquisition. She will soon surpass Mrs Besant as a speaker, I am sure.'[37]

Vivekananda now sought the blessings of Sarada Devi, the widow of his guru Ramakrishna, for his Western disciples. The Holy Mother, as she was addressed, readily welcomed all the friends of her dear Naren as her children. Even the aged Gopaler-Ma, who had been regarded as a mother figure by Ramakrishna, warmly accepted the new friends of Naren. Breaking all orthodox norms, she even agreed to dine with them, and a week later, to live with them for a few days.

Margaret's first impressions of Sarada Devi, as recounted in her letter to her friend, make for delightful reading.

> I have often thought that I ought to tell you about the lady who was the Wife of Sri Ramakrishna, Sarada as her name is. To begin with, she is dressed in a white cotton cloth like any other Hindu widow under fifty. This cloth goes round the waist and forms a skirt, then it passes round the body and over the head like a nun's veil. When a man speaks to her, he stands behind her, and she pulls this white veil very far forward over her face. Nor does she answer him directly. She speaks to another older woman in almost a whisper, and this woman repeats her words to the man. In this way, it comes about that the Master [Vivekananda] has never seen the face of Sarada! Added to this you must try to imagine her always seated on the floor, on a small piece of bamboo matting. All this does not sound very sensible perhaps, yet this woman, when you know her well, is said to be the very soul of practicality and common-sense . . . Sri Ramakrishna always consulted her before undertaking anything and her advice is always acted upon by his disciples. She is the very soul of sweetness—so gentle and loving and as merry as a girl . . . And she is so tender—"my daughter" she calls me. She has always been terribly orthodox, but all this melted away the instant she saw the first two Westerners—Mrs Bull and Miss MacLeod, and she tasted food with them! . . . This gave us all a dignity and made my future work possible in a way nothing else could possibly have done.[38]

Eventually, Sarada Devi was persuaded by Mrs Bull to be photographed for the first time. Although Nivedita was inspired by Josephine to call Sarada Devi her 'dear Mother', while inwardly the claims of her own mother tugged at her heart,[39] she realized that apart from love and blessings there was little more she could expect from the Holy Mother. As she astutely observed, 'In thought, outside the range of practicality and experience, these ladies have no range; it is in *feeling* that they are so strong. You see they have never had the education that would enable to frame a thought that would appeal to a stranger.'[40]

Preparations were now made by Vivekananda for the formal initiation of Margaret Noble. On 25 March, the Christian Feast of Annunciation, the Swami took Margaret to the shrine room and taught her the worship of Shiva. With a simple ritual of initiation, she was made a brahmacharini, embracing the vows of celibacy, and given the name 'Nivedita', the dedicated one. After the ceremony, Vivekananda introduced to all his Western disciples the concept of Shiva by himself donning the matted locks of Shiva, smearing ash on his body, putting on bone earrings, singing devotional songs and directing all to culminate the worship by offering flowers at the feet of the statue of the Buddha, who had always held a special place of reverence for him.[41] Nivedita, who shared her guru's veneration for the Buddha, treasured this day of initiation as the day of her new birth with a new name.

In May 1898, plague struck Calcutta. Although it did not reach epidemic proportions, Vivekananda sought to create awareness about the event and forestall a panic reaction by asking Nivedita to write about it extensively in the English newspapers. 'Calcutta Notes—By An English Lady' found among the papers of Sister Nivedita, was obviously written for some English newspaper or journal. A first-hand report of Calcutta in the plague days of 1898, it recounted the panic of families fleeing in terror with household effects not from plague, which had not yet found a foothold, but from fear that the proposed Segregation Act might come into effect. The decision to stay on, of a few families like the Tagores, did little to allay such fears. Finally, a government announcement of optional inoculation making segregation unnecessary brought the crisis under control. A walk through the city by Nivedita and a Western friend gave her a hands-on feel of the extent of ignorance and mass hysteria. Mischievous rumours were being spread about innocent people being compelled to submit to pseudo-inoculation due to which the victims died within six hours of great pain. To dispel the fears of the mobs surrounding her, who were 'as ignorant as children and as sensitive as racehorses,' Margaret offered to take the inoculation herself. She and her friend were then amused to be led in a procession with a drummer leading all the way to the boat that would take them back to the safety of their home. Her reason for not fearing the mob is insightful, 'As they were all Hindus we took no notice—had they been Moslem we might have felt some alarm. The Hindu whatever he might say, loves the Englishman. The Mohammedan never can forget that we robbed him of empire.'[42]

Once the stringent plague regulations were withdrawn and the possibility of an epidemic was over, Vivekananda took his Western disciples on a long tour to understand the 'real' India. Apart from Mrs Bull, Josephine and Nivedita, the group included Mrs Patterson, wife of the American Consul in Calcutta, who had befriended Vivekananda earlier in America. This tour, which lasted over several months through the summer of 1898, caused 'hidden emotional relationships'[43] to surface and brought into sharp focus how the individual equation of Nivedita with Vivekananda had gradually evolved in character. As Nivedita had written elsewhere to her friend Nell Hammond, 'I love to connect and watch people's attitude. To you he is the Master, to me the King, to *her* [Mrs Bull] the *Sistine Child*. Isn't that a beautiful idea? And I think one can't help catching the resemblance too, the minute it is mentioned.'[44]

However, it was not as the gentle *Sistine Child* that Vivekananda appeared to Nivedita. This was a period that Nivedita herself described as one of 'clash and conflict . . . I had been little prepared for that constant rebuke and attack upon all my most cherished prepossessions which was now my lot. Suffering is often illogical and I cannot attempt to justify by reason the degree of unhappiness which I experienced at this time as I saw the dream of a friendly and beloved leader falling away from me, and the picture of one who would be at least indifferent, and possibly silently hostile, substituting itself instead'.[45] There is no doubt that Vivekananda suffered equally from deep emotional turmoil and a sense of helplessness when he saw the vulnerability of his spontaneous, ebullient, adoring disciple with her flashing Irish eyes. Perhaps the harshness with which he tried to impose a moral discipline on Nivedita was his way of defending himself and her from the passionate adoration she had for him. As Josephine was to later analyse, 'Although Nivedita's feelings for him were always absolutely pure, he perhaps saw their danger.'[46]

Vivekananda tried to do two things, harshly and precipitously. One, he urged her, 'You have to forget your own past and cause it to be forgotten. You have to lose even its memory.'[47] Nivedita, who still considered herself as 'the most loyal English woman that ever breathed in this country,'[48] felt 'I cannot yet throw any of my past experience of human life and human relationships overboard'.[49] In fact, she confessed, 'It is the dream of my life to make England and India love each other.'[50] It was only later, once she became aware of the extent of British racial arrogance and the unfair discriminatory policies they practised against Indians that she adopted India completely and spoke for its people as one of her own. But that took some time.

The second attempt of Vivekananda was to point out aspects of her behaviour, such as constant expressions of feeling, whether of pain, admiration or surprise, which to him seemed 'shocking' and 'ill-bred'. She needed, he felt, to learn reserve, reticence and be reflective in meditative silence. Perhaps he saw the sharp contrast between the shyness and withdrawn demeanour of Bengali women with Nivedita's outspoken, often argumentative personality. He advised her to 'Hinduize' her thoughts, needs, conceptions and habits since 'your life, internal and external, has to become all that an orthodox Hindu Brahmin brahmacharini's ought to be'.[51] The decision to embrace the life of a celibate, he pointed out, came with a strict lifestyle. Vivekananda confessed that 'shadows of home and marriage cross your mind sometimes. Even to me they come now and again!'[52] But he had steeled himself to accept brahmacharya, the vows of celibacy, which meant renunciation of private pleasure for public good. In his conception, true manhood could not be without the control of manhood.[53] Therefore, Nivedita realized, to him marriage would be the first of crimes. 'To rise beyond the very memory of its impulse was his ideal and to guard himself and his disciples against the remotest danger of it, his passion. The very fact of "un-marriedness" counted with him as a spiritual asset.'[54] But as Nivedita also understood, Vivekananda's dread was not of women but of temptation. Many of his disciples and co-workers the world over were women but he sought to give each of them the title of a family relationship—whether of sister, mother or daughter. What had particularly thrilled him in America was the ease with which women played men's sports, studied the same disciplines at university since knowledge has no sex and were free to choose their own marriage partners. In India, he realized that marriage by arrangement had inflicted much pain on many but hoped that examples from the West would indicate other possibilities. The ideal marriage in Vivekananda's view was one where there would be man's acceptance of his wife as the mother, as he had seen in the case of his master Ramakrishna.

It goes to Nivedita's credit that she withstood Vivekananda's harsh discipline, although she did have emotional breakdowns from time to time, when she was comforted by Mrs Bull and Josephine. At the end, she could admit, 'I understood, for the first time, that the greatest teachers may destroy in us a personal relation in order to bestow the Impersonal Vision in its place.'[55] Reflecting on this relationship, Romain Rolland was to write,

> The future will always unite her name of initiation Sister Nivedita to that of her beloved Master . . . as St Clara to that of St Francis, although of a truth the imperious Swami was far from possessing the meekness of the Poverello and submitted those who gave themselves to him, to heart-searching tests before he accepted them. But her love was so deep; Nivedita did not keep in her memory his harshness—only his sweetness.[56]

Many years later, Romain Rolland analysed that the harshness with which Vivekananda often treated Nivedita was his own way of defending himself against her 'worshipful passion'. Perhaps Nivedita had for Vivekananda a 'lover's adoration', similar to what Madeleine Slade was to have for Gandhi, but the age difference between Gandhi and Slade was thirty years as against the five years between Vivekananda and Nivedita. Rolland concluded that although 'the sentiment of Nivedita had always been one of absolute purity maybe Vivekananda understood the danger'.[57]

The summer tour of Swamiji began on 11 May 1898 when he boarded the train at Calcutta's Howrah station with a large group of disciples. They were headed to Kathgodam, at the foothills of the Himalayas, from where they would proceed by trekking and riding on horseback to Nainital and then further along the scenic mountain route towards Almora. On the train journey, which lasted for two nights and a day, Swamiji gave a running commentary on the diversity of Indian culture and history as the train went through various cities and changing terrain. The wealth of information and experience gathered by Nivedita was to find expression later in her many writings, from travelogues to mythological tales, descriptions of history and architecture to serious analysis of the Indian societal framework. She began to spin the 'web of Indian life' (as one of her most well-known books came to be named) from the word pictures that the Swamiji lovingly painted for them. Nivedita was to reflect, 'The summer of 1898 stands out in my memory as a series of pictures, painted like old altar-pieces against a golden background of religious ardour and simplicity, and all alike glorified by the presence of one who, to us in his immediate circle, formed their central point.'[58]

A highlight during the halt at Nainital was Swamiji's meeting with a Muslim, Mohammed Sarfaraz Hussain, who was an Advaita Vedantist at heart and considered himself one of his disciples under the name Mohammedananda. From Almora a month later, Swamiji was to write to him a letter, which significantly speaks not of mere toleration of religious difference but acceptance of oneness.

> Whether we call it Vedantism or any ism, the truth is that Advaitism is the last word of religion and thought, and the only position from which one can look upon all religions and sects with love . . . I am firmly persuaded that without the help of practical Islam, theories of Vedantism, however fine and wonderful they may be, are entirely valueless to the vast mass of mankind . . . For our own motherland a junction of the two great systems, Hinduism and Islam—Vedanta brain and Islam body—is the only hope.[59]

Another interesting experience in Nainital, recorded in Nivedita's writings, was how despite general outcry and disapproval, Swamiji allowed two nautch girls into his presence to receive his blessings. His compassion and understanding were perhaps the result of his experience years ago in the palace of the Raja of Khetri, where the nautch girl's plaintive song, begging not to be despised since the name of the Lord was Same-Sightedness, had made a profound impact on him.[60]

At Almora, Swami and his brother disciples were guests of James and Charlotte Sevier at Thompson House, while the Western disciples were lodged in the nearby Oakley House. Now began a period of rigorous training for Nivedita—'A going-to-school had commenced', she was to write. He took upon himself the task of attacking the age-old prejudices and preconceptions, harboured in the West about social and artistic practices in India, of which he became aware of during his visit to the West. Additionally, he sought to gauge Nivedita's full commitment to India without which he felt it would be futile to work in any meaningful way. Constantly he raised the topic of her loyalty, often resulting in fireworks. Recalling these exchanges, Nivedita mentioned how he had surprised her one day by asking her directly to which nation she now belonged. Her candid answer pledging her loyalty to the British flag disappointed him. He continued in his efforts to make her realize that Britain was acting in India from narrow self-serving reasons and was bitterly blunt in saying, 'Really patriotism like yours is sin! All that I want you to see is that most people's actions are the expression of self-interest and you constantly oppose to this the idea that that a certain race are all angels. Ignorance so determined is wickedness!'[61] Realizing that he was testing her, Nivedita did not fight shy of arguments and nor did Vivekananda take offence. As he explained to her, he himself had put up a five-year fight before accepting his own Master's ideas. In course of time, Nivedita became the severest critic of the British government and adopted India as her country.

However, during their stay in Almora, when the tussles went beyond control, making the suffering to Nivedita unbearable, the two older women, Mrs Bull and Josephine, often interceded with the Swami, bringing him to his senses. On one occasion, he left for a while to reflect and on returning admitted with the simplicity of a child that they were right. Observing the new moon that was feted by Muslims, he promised to make a new beginning. Although Nivedita knelt to receive his blessing in acceptance of 'a moment of wonderful sweetness of reconciliation' she was to admit that 'such a moment may heal a wound. It cannot restore an illusion that has been broken into fragments'.[62] Already the 'King' she worshipped was becoming the 'Master' she had to obey.

In Almora, Vivekananda met Annie Besant twice. Vivekananda had been having a running battle with the Theosophists. He had been peeved when Colonel Henry Steel Olcott had not given him any reference when he was on his way to America. The Theosophists in America had also joined the chorus of opposition raised by the Christian missionaries against him. Although he spoke well of Mrs Besant, whom he had met earlier in England, he was consistently critical of the occult practices of the Theosophists. Mrs Besant now appealed to Swami for friendship between their organizations. At Almora, the police kept watch over the Swami's movements, particularly his association with Nivedita, whose fiery writings on Irish home rule in British papers were well known.

The Swami also received the sad news of the untimely death of his trusted secretary Goodwin, who had been sent to Madras to spread the message of Vedanta. He prevailed upon Mr Sevier to take a place near Almora where the journal *Prabuddha Bharata* (Awakened India), the notable instrument for the dissemination of Vedantic knowledge, could continue publication. The Seviers bought a new property in Mayavati for the purpose and developed it into Advaita Ashrama in March 1899. The uniqueness of the ashram lay in its total commitment to the Advaita philosophy of non-dualism, and hence no idols were kept there, nor was worship of Ramakrishna allowed.

On 11 June, exactly a month since they had left Calcutta, Vivekananda decided to proceed with his disciples to the valley of Kashmir where began a period of intense interaction between him and his Western disciples, particularly Nivedita. Leaving the deodar and pine forests behind, the group retraced their steps to

Kathgodam from where they now took a train to Punjab. Passing through Ludhiana, Lahore and racing across the Doab, they arrived in Rawalpindi, from where, by tonga, they reached the hill station of Murree where they spent a few glorious days. Then began their long journey, partly by tonga and boat, through the valley of the river Jhelum, first to Baramulla and then after a few days they reached Srinagar, the capital of Kashmir. The period from 22 June to 25 July was spent on houseboats on the Jhelum, in and around Srinagar. In subsequent letters, Josephine MacLeod and Nivedita were to repeatedly remember these weeks with great nostalgia. The overpowering beauty of the surroundings has been lyrically described in Nivedita's books:

> For as one returns upon that time . . . its record is found in a constant succession of scenes of loveliness . . . I might linger over the harvest merriment of the villagers playing in reaped fields on moonlit evening; or talk of the red bronze of amaranth crops, or the green of young rice under tall poplars at Islamabad. Forget-me-nots of a brilliant blue form the commonest wild flower of the Kashmiri fields in summer; but in autumn and spring, fields and river banks are violet-tinged with small purple irises and one walks amongst their spear-like leaves as if they were grass.[63]

An avid botanist, Nivedita collected specimens of various species of flowers from edelweiss to anemones, columbines to Michaelmas daisies and wild roses.

But the days passed in the Jhelum valley were not merely idyllic. There were daily informal discussions with Vivekananda on history, culture and religion. Often he took pains to point out the commonality of religions and share his own views about them. Buddhism for instance, in his opinion, was born from and remained within Hinduism. Commonalities in the ritual observances of Roman Catholicism and Vedic practices, as for example in observation of Mass, offering of food to God which was like the prasad in Hinduism, and the use of incense, lights and music fascinated him. Islam, he felt, was the only religion where the idea of the priest had completely broken down, with the leader of the prayers standing with his back to the people and only the reading of the Koran was from the pulpit. Vivekananda had his doubts about the historicity of Jesus Christ and believed that 'Indian and Egyptian ideas met at Alexandria, and went forth to the world tinctured with Judaism and Hellenism as Christianity'. Of the early figures of Christianity only St Paul, he felt, was historical and could be credited with galvanizing into life an obscure Nazarene sect of great antiquity, around a mythic personality as a focus of worship.[64] Views such as these were constantly debated by his disciples in a healthy atmosphere of intellectual and philosophical discussion.

Vivekananda also took his disciples to the Mughal Gardens, explaining their significance, and to several monuments of historical antiquity such as the temples of Avantipur, the ruins of Martand and the architectural marvel that was the temple of Pandrethan. He dwelt on the different civilizational influences that had left their imprints on such sites. These talks proved to be a vital source of information for Nivedita, which she elaborated with customary eloquence in her books. Teaching his disciples the techniques of meditation too formed a part of the Swami's training process, which he imparted often by leading them to forest expanses and setting up camps. The Swami was not the serious teacher all the time. Often enough he regaled his guests with humorous lighthearted banter, or cooked special dishes for them, which he enjoyed preparing. But the focus on celibate brahmacharya never wavered and it upset him considerably to see Nivedita playing with others a fun game with cherry stones to see when she would get married.[65] Deciding that the education of Nivedita as a future worker remained incomplete without a direct knowledge of the ritual practices of Hinduism, he selected her to accompany him, along with the thousands of pilgrims who had assembled, on the annual pilgrimage to Amarnath, the mountain cave perched at a height of 18,000 feet, where there was a natural formation in ice of an emblem of Shiva.

To Nivedita, the experience was to assume great significance not only for its novelty and for what she learnt, but principally because it was during this pilgrimage that she came face to face with her King in a shared spiritual experience of great emotional and transformative intensity.

Leaving the rest of the group behind in Pahalgam, a quaint village by the gushing waters of the river Lidder, Nivedita set off with Vivekananda on 29 July for the glacial gorge, trekking, halting for the night and setting off again at dawn. They traversed some of the most picturesque terrain in the country, which appeared to Nivedita like 'the scenery of Switzerland or Norway at their gentlest and loveliest'.[66]

She observed with wonder how at nightfall a whole canvas town would spring up with incredible rapidity, to vanish in no time the next morning, before the trek began afresh. She also noticed how Swami undertook to perform minutely all the ritual observances required. While acceding to orthodox opinion to have the tent of his foreign disciple moved to a distance, he also made sure to take Nivedita round the camp to be blessed and to distribute alms. A steep climb, after crossing an ice bridge on foot just after Chandanwari, saw them above the tree line on slopes carpeted with edelweiss and other flowers, with the road winding past the lake Sheshnag, fed by two small glaciers. The next day saw them crossing a high mountain pass to reach Panchtarani, where five streams ran through a dry gravel riverbed. Nivedita observed how Swami performed the mandatory bathing in each of the streams, going from one to the other in wet clothes, unmindful of his sheer exhaustion. On 2 August, there was the steep ascent to a glacier by a flowing stream, where pilgrims bathed before entering the Amarnath cave.

Nothing could have prepared Nivedita for the sight of the voluminous cave large enough to hold a cathedral, with a huge iced

Shivalingam enthroned as it were on its own base. Vivekananda entered the shrine, naked except for his loincloth, body smeared in ashes, prostrating himself in adoration and almost swooning with emotion. As he narrated later, he felt that he was in the presence of Shiva who granted him the grace of Amarnath (Lord of Immortality) to be able to choose the moment of his own death.[67]

Nivedita was the stupefied observer of this scene. Caught in this moment of intense spiritual wonder, she felt certain that Swami had also dedicated her to Shiva. But conflicting emotions gripped her. Mentioning none of these in her book *The Master as I Saw Him*, she laid bare her soul in her letter to Mrs Eric Hammond on her return. Swearing her to secrecy and confidentiality, Nivedita confessed how left out she had felt at that moment of spiritual intensity and how, although 'deeply and intensely glad' of the revelation that her guru had experienced, she felt 'terrible pain to come face to face with something which is all *inwardness* to someone you worship, and for yourself to be able to get little further than externals. Swami could have made it live—but he was lost'. She had longed for that moment to be supremely meaningful, when he would impart to her, through a touch perhaps, a spiritual knowledge such as his Master had given him. That moment would then have glowed in her memory. Instead, she felt excluded from his defining moment of spiritual realization.

In vain did she plead with him to climb down from the position of Master and realize that 'we were nothing more to each other than an ordinary man and woman'. Holding on to his uncompromising reserve, Vivekananda tried valiantly to reason with her, but as she confessed later, she was inconsolable and 'angry with him and would not listen to him when he was going to talk'. In retrospect, she realized with bitterness how wrong she had been and how she had lost a chance that would never come again. What she had perhaps sought was an initiation by Vivekananda at that auspicious moment into the divine knowledge and transcendental experience that he seemed to have received. Sensing the anguish and disappointment of his disciple, Vivekananda explained gently to her the next morning on their return journey, 'Margot, I haven't the power to do these things for you—*I* am not Ramakrishna Paramhamsa.'[68] He had already explained his position to her clearly a year before she came to India. He had written,

> The great difficulty is this: I see persons giving me almost the whole of their love. But I must not give any one the whole of mine in return, for that day the work would be ruined. It is absolutely necessary to the work, that I should have the enthusiastic love of as many as possible, while I myself remain entirely impersonal.[69]

What Vivekananda did from this point onwards was to overtly turn the focus of his adoration from Shiva to the mother goddess. By exalting a woman to the raised status of the divine mother or by adoration of a pre-pubescent girl child as divinity, he could sidestep the sexuality of the feminine principle while lauding its compassion and strength. This was to become an example emulated by young men dedicated to the cause of India's freedom, who took up their war cry in the name of the divine mother, postponing familial compulsions, including marriage, until their motherland achieved freedom.

On his return from Amarnath, Swami went into a phase of silence, austerity and withdrawal. Retreating to a solitary place for meditation, his internal turmoil found release in the worship of the 'terrible' manifest in the image of Kali. Penning his thoughts in his poem 'Kali the Mother' in a fit of ecstasy, he dropped to the floor unconscious just as the last word had been written.[70] Returning to his disciples, he now gave constant explanations of the worship of Mother, who was the harbinger not only of joy but also of disaster. The refrain in his celebrated poem was 'Come, Mother, come/ For Terror is Thy name/Death is in Thy breath/And every shaking step/Destroys a world forever.' He now repaired to the temple of

Kshir Bhavani, where he spent several days alone performing the severest austerities, making ritual offerings, and as a special prayer, worshipping every morning the Brahmin pandit's little daughter as Uma Kumari, the Divine Virgin. When he returned to Srinagar to his disciples, his was a transformed presence. Placing floral offerings on each disciple, he proclaimed 'No more "Hari Om"—it is all Mother now!'

He had reinvented himself and seemingly moved away from his customary role as teacher or patriot. On his changed attitude, Nivedita reported, 'It is too great for words. My pen would have to learn to whisper.' Enveloped in an overwhelming tide of love, he questioned his role as a teacher, adding, 'Swami is dead and gone'. As an onlooker, Nivedita wrote: 'The mingled solemnity and exhilaration of his presence have made me retire to the farthest corner, and just worship in silence all the time.'[71]

Having left all his 'careless combativeness' behind, it now became a mission for Vivekananda to explain to Nivedita the philosophy behind Kali worship by going through every word of his poem 'Kali the Mother' and making her repeat the lines.[72] Explaining how he had fought against the acceptance of the Kali figure at Dakshineswar for several years before being enslaved by the goddess under the directions of Ramakrishna, Vivekananda pointed out to Nivedita the importance of symbols, which were particular to each civilizational context. For instance, to the Arab of the desert, with their patriarchal practices, god was visualized as the Father who protects, defends and nurtures. However, central to the Christian conception of God was a Child in his Mother's arms. Jesus himself had the essence of the eternal feminine when he promised to draw into his loving arms all who needed to be comforted. But it was in India that the thought of the Mother had been realized in its completeness but under the strangest of guises. Whereas in the West, art and poetry had exhausted all means of expression to describe the tender nurturing Mother and the Holy Child, in the Indian Kali was portrayed 'a terrible extraordinary figure'[73] of a blue–black

woman, nude with flowing hair, with four arms, two in the act of
blessing and two holding a knife and bleeding heads respectively,
garlanded with skulls and dancing with a protruding tongue on
the prostrate figure of a man, all white in ashes! The depiction was
loaded with symbolism, which Vivekananda proceeded to explain.

Nature always expressed itself through a duality—whether of
light and shade, attraction and repulsion, microcosm and macrocosm,
cause and effect and in humanity as man and woman, of soul and
body. On the plane of symbolism, the soul of things somehow became
associated with the manly form and the manifested energy or nature
with that of woman. The complementarity of the two as purush and
prakriti, soul and energy, went to form one existence. Vivekananda
repeated to Nivedita what Ramakrishna had explained to him—
'Brahman and Shakti are one, even as fire and its heat, even as milk
and its whiteness.' Using the metaphor of a flame, Vivekananda
described its blue neck as Shiva and its fiery body as Kali.[74] In the
Kali image was captured a dramatic moment when shakti (energy)
looked upon a supine Shiva and in a spark of touch and sight there
was the manifestation and realization of divinity. Shiva, the great
god of Indian imagination as the benevolent destroyer of ignorance,
was depicted as the embodiment of renunciation, as a wanderer,
covered in ashes, hair untended and with nothing but a tiger skin for
meditation. As the purush or soul, he was the consort and spouse of
maya or nature, the fleeting diversity of sense. It was in this relation
that he lay at the feet of Kali, who after a wild dance of carnage
steps unwittingly on his body, and in their gaze lies the ecstasy of
recognition when he calls her 'Mother'. But how did he behold her?
Not as a picture of green fields and smiling skies and flowers steeped
in sunshine. Elaborating on Vivekananda's thoughts later in her
book *Kali the Mother*, Nivedita wrote:

> Under the apparent loveliness, Shiva saw life preying on life, the
> rivers breaking down the mountains, the comet poised in mid

space to strike. Around him rises up the wail of all the creatures, the moan of pain, and the sob of greed, and the pitiful cry of little things in fear. Irresponsible without mercy seems the spirit of time—deaf to the woes of man or answering them only with a peal of laughter. Such is the world as the Hindu mind is predisposed to see it. 'Verily,' says the heart wearily, 'Death is greater than Life and better'.[75]

The ease with which Nivedita, with a critical mind of her own, accepted Vivekananda's interpretations was the result of her basic philosophy, garnered from a study of Pestalozzi, that the belief system of a people had to be judged in the context of their own historical, religious and social consciousness. She elaborated: Everything in my past life as an educationist had contributed to impress on me now the necessity of taking on the Indian consciousness' and with 'the personal perplexity associated with the memory of the pilgrimage to Amarnath . . . I set myself therefore to enter into Kali worship, as one would set oneself to learn a new language, or take birth deliberately perhaps in a new race.[76]

On her return, Nivedita stayed for some time at Sarada Devi's residence at 10/2, Bosepara Lane in north Calcutta before shifting to number 16, Bosepara Lane, which became her home for the next several months. After her initiation she tried hard to live up to the ideals of purity, simplicity and austerity required of a brahmacharini. For days, she lived on milk and fruit, sleeping on bare boards, denying herself the luxury of a fan during the hot months. Her immediate commitment was to open her school and on Kali puja on 12 November 1898, the Girls' School was inaugurated by Sarada Devi in the presence of Vivekananda and some of his disciples at Nivedita's residence. Golap-Ma and Jogin-Ma, two elderly disciples of Ramakrishna, were also present. Jogin-Ma even taught in the women's section of the school. But perhaps the most unique bond of love was formed by Nivedita with Gopaler-Ma, the octogenarian, who was at first horrified to see a foreigner in the household of Sarada Devi but later showered affection on her as the 'daughter of Noren'. It was Nivedita's home that she moved into in 1903 when she needed to be looked after. Nivedita took on the responsibility of looking after her 'dear little grandmother' and 'dearest treasure' till she passed away in 1906.

The school began with a few girls of the neighbourhood, who were brought in under supervision. Classes in botany, physical education, drawing, clay work and sewing were drawn up and a beginning was made. Delighted that the children exhibited great artistic power with their impressive brushwork and colour selection, Nivedita slowly gained the confidence of the mothers, who were welcomed by her at all times. The reticent and orthodox women reached out with acts of kindness such as sending her fruits or milk when she needed them. However, Nivedita felt handicapped when Henrietta Muller, who had promised to help her and had been a generous benefactress to Swamiji, decided to return to the Christian faith. She left Vivekananda with personal attacks and outbursts against Hinduism, which pained him considerably. Nivedita had been clear in her own mind that the school was to be 'at first only tentative and experimental', her role being to assist the learner to development in her own way; she in turn hoped to gain valuable experience and education from the process.[77] In a short while, however, it became evident that the idea was not proving viable and funds were insufficient. Vivekananda too felt despondent after Henrietta Muller's defection. He was afraid for the future of the prospective students, many of whom were widows, who would be thrown back to their families if Nivedita could not somehow deliver. He was brutally frank with Nivedita, wondering if she should not perhaps return to England since there was no money, nor was there any hope of raising any.[78] Eventually in 1903, with the good services of Sister Christine, one of Vivekananda's American disciples, the school was to rally around and Nivedita became actively associated with its activities.

Adding to Nivedita's mood of despondency at this time was the arrival in March 1899 of Vivekananda's American disciple Marie Louise, whom he had renamed Swami Abhayananda as a *sannyasini*. Actively associated with his Vedanta programme in America, she received on arrival in India a rousing welcome in Madras and Bombay before proceeding to Calcutta, where she gave a few lectures before accompanying Vivekananda to Dacca for more public addresses. However, her interaction with Nivedita proved to be unpleasant, as she slighted her for not being of the Order yet as a sannyasini and dismissed her adoration of her guru as 'very foolish and emotional'.[79] This emboldened Nivedita to ask her guru for a greater recognition and be made 'a member for life' on 25 March, which would be the first anniversary of her initiation. In her letter to Josephine, Nivedita gushed about how her 'King' had taught her to do puja, led her like Gabriel into the chapel asking her to also make floral offerings to Buddha and regaled her with *jataka* stories. Given a *rudraksha*, a rosary of sacred seeds, she was to wear a white robe from then onwards.[80] But she was deeply disappointed that she was not made sannyasini as expected, but a *naishtik* brahmacharini (eternal celibate), which was the revival of an old celibate order of south India. Realizing that she could not continue to feel aggrieved, she asked Swamiji at the earliest opportunity, 'What perfection could I strive for in order to be worthy of being a sannyasini?' Refusing to get drawn further into the discussion, Swamiji's comment was, 'You just keep as you are.'[81] Since Nivedita was not initiated into sannyas, she never wore the *gerua* (saffron) habit of a sannyasini. She usually wore a white dress, and Abanindranath Tagore, who met her in 1902, described her as *Mahasveta*.[82]

Perhaps Vivekananda now envisioned a different future for
Nivedita. With her sincerity and commitment never in question,
her ability to grasp his ideas, her eloquent prose, her gift of public
speaking, the ease with which she could mingle with the Europeans
and act as a bridge with the Brahmo elite in Calcutta society were
well appreciated by Swamiji. As early as 17 February 1896, in a letter
to his benefactor and supporter Alasinga Perumal, Vivekananda
had expressed his dream 'to put the Hindu ideas into English and
then make out of dry philosophy and intricate mythology and
queer startling psychology a religion, which shall be easy, simple,
popular, and at the same time meet the requirements of the highest
minds'.[83] He now found Nivedita to be the right person to carry out
his dream. Already, a month back, she had created waves with her
speech on Kali to packed audiences at Calcutta's Albert Hall.

The invitation to Nivedita to speak on Kali on 13 February 1899
had not only taken her by surprise but also 'shocked' the educated
elite of Calcutta to whom Kali worship remained associated with the
temple practices of daily goat slaughter. Indeed no one was prepared
to chair the meeting after the Principal of Vidyasagar College,
N. Ghosh, who had previously agreed, backed out at the last
instance. Nivedita, however, was not to be deterred and decided
to go ahead nonetheless.[84] Vivekananda, who had welcomed the
opportunity so that he could get even with his detractors, who
had criticized his Kali worship despite his belief in monotheism or
Advaita, was convinced that a talk on Kali by his foreign disciple, and
a woman at that, would be a befitting reply. He could never forget
how his beloved Dakshineswar Kali temple continued to remain
out of bounds for him on the specific instructions of the temple
authorities. Vivekananda took on the challenge by thoroughly
briefing Nivedita on the subject and reading through her prepared
speech. Curiosity about her and what she would present resulted in
large numbers turning up. Dr Mahendranath Sarkar, well-known
physician, agreed to chair the meeting but being avidly opposed

to idol worship, he raised provocative questions about why such regressive moves to worship the Kali were needed, leading to a fracas with a member of the audience calling him 'an old devil'.[85] It required the grace of Nivedita to restore decorum and proceed with a well thought-out lecture, in which she not only voiced her guru's ideas but also couched them in her own world view.

Beginning with a disclaimer that without a knowledge of Sanskrit or Indian history she was hardly suited to lecture on Kali, Nivedita declared her right as an English woman to publicly regret the vilification carried on by her countrymen of this religious idea. She said that instead it could be approached as a subject with a certain freshness of view, and by drawing comparisons with another faith. She went on to speak of the three aspects of the mother goddess—Durga, Jagadhatri and Kali—as embodiments of power and energy evolving to the final incarnation as Kali or Death bringing the ultimate freedom. Bluntly, she went on to say, 'Religion is not something made for gentlehood . . . to refine is to emasculate it . . . God gave life, true. But he also kills. Let us face also and just as willingly, the terrible, the ugly, the hard.'[86] The depiction of the naked and violent Kali went against the accepted notion of womanliness associated with the Hindu woman. But as Nivedita explained,[87] since Kali depicted maya, which was unreal, she had to be painted as the ideal non-woman. Her real existence lay in Brahman and by going beyond her present form, she had to be realized as *Brahmamayi* (pervaded, interpenetrated, overlapped and full of Brahman), so eloquently sung by the devotee Ramprasad.

The resounding success of the lecture was evident in favourable press reviews. A correspondent in the *Indian Mirror* was to write, 'It was a novel thing to hear an English lady speaking in support of Kali-worship . . . and her explanation was a most rational and philosophical one . . . free from orthodoxy and bigotry.'[88] Nivedita was relieved since she knew how ignorant even the educated English were about the symbolism in the Hindu religion. Indeed, she was to write that many thought that Kali was a real woman who had killed her husband.[89] Her King 'was greatly pleased about the lecture', and the invitation that followed soon after, for her to speak on Kali at the Kalighat temple itself, seemed 'the greatest blow that could be struck against exclusiveness'.[90]

At the second Kali lecture, which Nivedita delivered at the famous Kali temple of Calcutta in Kalighat on 29 May 1899, Vivekananda was asked to preside but declined. Prompted by Sarada Devi, he came to Nivedita the previous morning at six and stayed for a couple of hours, briefing her over cups of tea and a smoke. He had already given strict orders about the lecture, where the audience would not be given chairs but would be seated instead on the floor around Nivedita, who would be on the steps with a few guests. He reminded her that she would also have to ensure that the European and the Brahmo guests removed their shoes and hats. While discussing the coming event with Nivedita, Vivekananda confessed, 'How I used to hate Kali and all her ways.' It was a six-year-old fight with his guru Ramakrishna, whom he often thought was 'simply a brain-sick baby, always seeing visions and things—I hated it—but I had to accept her too!' When Nivedita pressed him to reveal what had led to a change in mind, he merely said that family misfortunes had made him turn to Kali and he had been enslaved. But the actual details 'will die with me'. But in the end, he was convinced that universal oneness was manifest in Brahman as well as in the gods. And there was no contradiction there. He cautioned Nivedita, 'But these things must never be told to anyone—never.'[91]

The second Kali lecture was the same in the substance as the previous one at Albert Hall but it was followed by some explanations she offered to questions that were raised. Drawing a comparison between the fearful image of Kali and the sombre, nearly sinister, visage of Mother Mary in Byzantine icon paintings, Nivedita spoke of the need to recognize that divinity lay beyond form.[92] Faced with critics who spoke against animal sacrifices offered during Kali puja, Nivedita asked if the same critics had also raised their voices against the many abattoirs in the city. Nivedita had consciously decided not to criticize Indian tradition but rather try to understand it. Relieved at the success of her lecture, she wrote to Mrs Bull that Kalighat was prepared to reprint the speech in thousands.[93] But she admitted that she had roused a controversy and feared lest her views on Kali travel abroad to orthodox Wimbledon and embarrass her poor sister.[94]

In the months of March and April, between her first and second Kali lectures, Nivedita was horrified to see the return of plague to the city of Calcutta, this time as an epidemic. Under Vivekananda's supervision, the Ramakrishna Mission plague service swung into action, forming a committee, which included Nivedita and others, to organize volunteers to clean infected city slums and distribute pamphlets with instructions on preventive sanitation and hygiene. Abanindranath Tagore recalled how Nivedita accompanied his uncle Rabindranath on daily inspections of the various localities where plague had struck, which sadly had claimed his little daughter as victim.[95]

Nivedita began lobbying in right earnest with key European individuals, so that her letters of awareness and appeals for help could be brought out in the English papers. With stinging irony, she hoped to rouse from apathy 'those who can daily feast their sense of sight and smell on the fresh air and beautiful flowers of private gardens and the maidan, those to whom cleanliness of roads and surroundings is no luxury but a first need, will they do what they can towards such ends for those who cannot hope to enjoy even the least of them otherwise?'[96] In response to this letter, Nivedita was to write, funds started to come in.[97] In another letter she listed out simple measures to be adopted, such as the distribution of the inexpensive perchloride of mercury, which could be kept in solution in all places for frequent flushing.[98]

At a lecture on 'Plague and the Duty of Students' on 22 April 1899, Vivekananda, who presided, exhorted students to throw off lethargy, prove themselves to be men for practical action and not remain puppets shut in a glass case for show. In her lecture that followed, Nivedita gave a graphic description of the unimaginable filth of the affected areas, observing that the contrast between the cleanliness of the inside of the Hindu huts with the filth outside was perhaps due to the women being subject to seclusion in the zenana system, and being totally unaware of their outside surroundings. Anticipating Gandhi in later times, she appealed, 'Let us with our own hands perform the necessary service. Let us glory in the shame of such service before the people. And in that way and that alone they be made strong to grapple with those facts of life in which they see its degradation.'⁹⁹ At the end of the lecture, many students responded to her call and enlisted as workers. With the help of Sadananda, the Swami assigned to her by Vivekananda from the outset to help her settle down, Nivedita began her vigil of the roads, nursing the sick, tending to the dying and supervising the cleansing of the area. A twelve-year-old boy died in her arms mistaking her, in his last moments, for his mother. Praising the efforts of Sadananda, who worked like a 'hero' along with her, Nivedita wrote, 'The gang loves him, the women welcome him, the children carry his opinion, and the men trust him. I just dread the day when he tires.'¹⁰⁰ Sanitation and cleanliness were restored in their area and the Government Plague Committee, which inspected the work, proclaimed the area they had overseen to be 'model bustees'¹⁰¹ but plague had travelled to other areas. Vivekananda objected to Nivedita hazarding her own health. As she confessed to her beloved Yum,

He says my great fault is attempting too much—in which he is emphatically right. I am to give up all thought of Plague nursing and throw my whole heart and soul still deeper into the Sanitation that we have now on hand. Won't I just? This is an infinitely higher proof of self-sacrifice and obedience on my part as you know well dear Yum than the delightful excitement of risking Plague would be.[102]

Nivedita loved to live dangerously. 'Plague nursing', having children die in her hands, gave her a sense of total involvement, which she sardonically put as 'delightful excitement' and which the Swami forbade, as it would expose her to the danger of infection. His advice that she keep busy with managing sanitation seemed tame to her and yet one she had to obey.

Nivedita was irrepressible. She was now well known in the Calcutta society and her gregarious and spontaneous nature helped open many windows in orthodox families. Her entry into many of the celebrity homes offered her a key insight and enabled acquaintance with some eminent personalities. Vivekananda, as her King, felt protective about her and wanted to have a control over whom she met or socialized with. However, Nivedita's rebellious heart cried: 'Love for Swamiji does not prevent one's loving others, and loving them does not seem untruth to him.'[103] Although she realized that perhaps she had 'deeply grieved' him by going into society, Nivedita justified it to herself saying, 'It was right enough I feel sure—for I had to learn my India.'[104]

2

Guided by the 'Master'

Nivedita's efficient management during the plague crisis and the surprising success of her Kali lectures had created a curiosity about her in elite Calcutta circles. Already, she had been encouraged by Vivekananda to 'carry on a Crusade' and enthuse Calcutta with lectures in theatres. 'Make inroads into the Brahmos,' he exhorted.[1] Accordingly, on 27 January 1899, Nivedita organized a tea party where she invited eminent Brahmo families. Among the guests were the poet Rabindranath Tagore, his sister Swarnakumari Devi and her daughter Sarola Ghoshal, Mr and Mrs P.K. Roy, Mohini Chatterjee and many others. She could hardly contain her excitement knowing that Swamiji would address the gathering and that she would become hostess 'with such a very big lion on the show'.[2] She made arrangements for the tea party in the yard outside her home, and added in her comments that she looked magnificent in the gown and white sun hat that Josephine had left behind for her. Apprehensive that she would be closely observed, Nivedita felt nervous. She was well aware of 'the suspicious eyes that watch and the sharp tongues that wag in India—over a society where men and women of the country mix—but all said and done I fear, I fear, I fear'.[3] Although she admitted it had been 'a brilliant gathering' after all, where Tagore regaled those present with three of his own compositions in a lovely tenor, and the Swami was 'lovely', she sensed that 'only there was some cloud—I could not tell what'.[4]

Perhaps she sensed an underlying tension between her two illustrious guests, born only two years apart, in close proximity in north Calcutta—Rabindranath Tagore and Vivekananda. Interestingly, there is no evidence of much contact between these two personalities, nor is Tagore on record for any comments made after Vivekananda's remarkable performance in Chicago. Perhaps music was a common link. It is known that Vivekananda sang several of Tagore's spiritual songs to his guru Ramakrishna, but he certainly did not approve of Tagore's love poetry. He was focused on India's man-making mission, which would make a subservient, enslaved people strong and able to resist bonds such as marriage. With his view on strengthening their moral character, Vivekananda attacked any cultural influence he perceived as effeminate or emotional, that could emasculate or weaken a people. While in Almora in the summer of 1898, he had expressed his views with brutal frankness to Ashwini Kumar Dutta, the patriot who had visited him. In an interview, he had said,

> And wherever you hear the Radha-Krishna songs going on, use the whip right and left. The whole nation is going to rack and ruin! People with no self-control indulging in such songs! We have long sung and danced: no harm if there is a lull for a while. In the meanwhile, let the country wax strong.[5]

In a similar vein, he went on to tell Nivedita, 'As long as you go on mixing with that Tagore family, Margot I must go on sounding this gong. Remember that, that family has poured a flood of erotic venom over Bengal.' Describing some of this 'decadent' poetry, he concluded that his mission was not Ramakrishna's or Vedanta's but simply to bring Manhood to this people.[6] Perhaps to make a distinction from the refined, elitist and aesthetic quality of Tagore's prose, Vivekananda chose for himself a popular, colloquial style, which Nivedita suspected was 'a deliberate maltreatment of the

Bengali language, which makes him about as difficult to read as Thomas Carlyle when he first appeared and which is purposed to serve certain tremendous ends!⁷ Certainly Sarola and many members of the Tagore family considered Swami's language of a 'loose set, and vulgar'.⁸

Secretly, Nivedita admired Tagore and admitted, 'I prefer, when I do take a holiday, to go to the Tagores'. The Poet has asked me—and in that house there will always be common interests in poetry and music and the chance of carrying an idea.'⁹ The sudden decision to accompany Vivekananda on his subsequent trip abroad made her decline the 'fascinating invitation' of the Poet to his river house. She wrote how disappointed she was that she would miss 'long talks with him on all sorts of delightful things'. She had hoped that as they both had a mutual friend in the scientist, Jagadish Chandra Bose, she could be friends with the Poet too.¹⁰ A few years later, in 1904, Nivedita visited Bodh Gaya in a large group that included, among others, Jagadish Chandra Bose, his wife, Rabindranath Tagore and his son. Analysing the qualities she discovered in Tagore, she wrote,

> The Poet, Mr Tagore, was a *perfect* guest. He is almost the only Indian man I have ever seen who has nothing of the spoiled child socially about him. He has a *naif* sort of vanity in speech, which is so childlike as to be rather touching. But he thinks of others all the time—as no one but a Western hostess could. He sang and chatted day and night—was always ready—either to entertain or be entertained—served Dr Bose as if he were his mother—struggles all the time between work for the country and the national longing to seek *mukti*.

This experience made Nivedita wonder why her Master had been so harsh about him. She exclaimed that 'never was any man so *ridiculously* maligned when suspected of things vulgar and immoral'. But in conclusion, she felt, 'But for all this, Mr Tagore is not the type of manhood that appeals to me.'¹¹

This feeling was quite mutual. Although Tagore had great admiration for Nivedita's total devotion to India and was struck by how a 'delicately nurtured lady' could live 'uncomplaining and cheerful in conditions of sheer squalor', he found her uncompromising attack on Western civilization ironical since the ideal he held for his own university, Visva-Bharati, was cultural cooperation between the East and West. Several years later in a private conversation with Edward Thompson, Tagore confessed when asked about Sister Nivedita, 'I didn't like her. She was so violent. She had a great hatred for me and my work, especially here (Santiniketan) and did all she could against me. She was so confident that I was unpatriotic and truckling to modern thought.' Asked to explain what he meant by her violence, Tagore explained that 'she could be *ferocious* at any wrong or injustice to my people'.[12] This was particularly evident soon after the Bodh Gaya trip, when the group was returning to their respective destinations. At the railway station, Jagadish and Abala Bose faced discrimination from white passengers in the first class compartment of the train, who protested against their entry. Nivedita's angry and forceful intercession on their behalf brought the dispute to a halt, allowing their entry into the train. When her train came, Nivedita refused to get into the first class compartment reserved for whites. She chose to enter the next compartment where an Indian gentleman courteously made way for her to settle in, drawing from her the remark that such generous hospitality can only be expected from Indians.

Rabindranath's first encounter with Nivedita had puzzled him. He had assumed that Nivedita was a missionary who could be requested to teach his daughter English. He was totally taken aback when Nivedita declined, arguing sternly that education should stem from inherited cultures and not imported language traditions. At a time when Western education was being welcomed, Nivedita's admonishment of those who sought it was anathema.[13] Over time, Tagore came to appreciate that unlike most foreigners, Nivedita did not stop to generalize but proceeded to 'discover our soul that has living connection with its past and is marching towards its fulfilment'. She was unique in totally identifying with India, adopting its concerns and problems. As Tagore put it, 'She lived our life and came to know us by becoming one of ourselves.'[14] Rabindranath's association with Nivedita grew with visits to her home and renditions of his songs that she deeply appreciated. She was to write to Josephine, 'I cannot forget the lovely poem Come O Peace [*Esho Shanti*]—with its plaintive minor air that Mr Tagore composed and sang for us the other day'.[15] When Nivedita faced a problem about where to house her school, it was Tagore who offered his own. But he could never fathom how Nivedita, with a rational, discerning mind, was totally subservient to the call of her guru. He recalled a certain morning, while they were discussing a difficult philosophical text in Bengali, when a messenger from Belur announced that Vivekananda wanted to see her. Nivedita broke off in the midst of what she was saying and immediately decided to leave since the blessing of her Swami was on her. Her abrupt leave-taking and total subservience to her guru both peeved and fascinated Tagore, who realized how completely she had found the object of her devotion.[16] He wondered if Vivekananda could have been Vivekananda without obtaining the complete submission of Nivedita, whose devotion or *tapasya* to him was like that of Sati.[17]

Tagore's association with Nivedita continued well into the years after Vivekananda's death in 1902. It is quite possible that the forthright views of Sister Nivedita, an erudite, sincere and committed friend of India, might have triggered off conflicting thoughts in the Poet and in many ways her bold stances could have appeared as a sounding board for another point of view. Tagore decided to vent these thoughts in the medium he knew best. His novel *Gora* took shape over these years and was situated in the debate about the cultural identity of India and the place of religion, caste and class in it.

The Brahmo-Hindu tension expressed in *Gora* is through the opposing stands taken by the main protagonists. In the novel, we are told that Gourmohan, or Gora, like other English-educated young men of his generation, had first been drawn towards the reformist Brahmo faith, which sought to purge Hinduism of elaborate rituals, caste hierarchy and idol worship. Incidentally, Narendranath Datta, before he became Vivekananda, too had been drawn briefly to the Brahmo Samaj. The novel begins at the point when, after his brief infatuation with the Brahmo way of thinking, Gora turns to a loud and flamboyant brand of Hindu orthodoxy. 'Bharatvarsha' is a key concept in Gora, denoting more than a geographical area or an administrative unit. The emotive and abstract form of Bharatvarsha crystallizes in Gora's mind after his visits to rural areas in an attempt to connect with the masses. In many ways Gora's efforts to discover his India are reminiscent of Vivekananda's travels as a wandering monk to different parts of the country or Nivedita's later travels with her guru. For Gora, the final delinking of Hinduism from the concept of Bharatvarsha is achieved when he is told that he is no Brahmin but was born to Irish parents and given to a Brahmin couple for adoption to save him from the violence following the Revolt of 1857. This knowledge liberates Gora from an intolerant orthodoxy. He is able to realize that he is a true 'Bharatiya' for whom there is no conflict between communities—whether Hindu, Muslim or Christian. He claims all castes of Bharat as his caste and declares himself free from all inhibitions of food. The thawing of Gora's rigidity in the later part of the novel also includes a sweeping change in his attitude to women. Under the influence of Sucharita, a Hindu woman raised by an enlightened Brahmo mentor Poreshbabu, Gora can see clearly the major flaw in his earlier concept of Bharatvarsha in excluding women altogether. He slowly comes round to accepting that women are individuals rather than static icons of culture. The novel ends with Gora extending his hand to Sucharita, inviting her on a journey of self-discovery so that she can avoid being cast with any particular group.

Several models have been suggested for Tagore's fictional hero Gora.[18] Vivekananda (born in 1863), six years younger than Gora, (alleged birth in 1857) might have been the real life character. Ashis Nandy[19] makes a strong case for Brahmabandhab Upadhyay being the inspiration for Tagore while Bimanbihari Majumdar has suggested Sister Nivedita.[20] Nivedita had visited Tagore in his riverine estate at Shelidah in 1904 where the poet had discussed the plot of *Gora* with her. But when he recounted the ending he had in mind for *Gora*, namely that Sucharita, on discovering Gora's Irish parentage, rejects him, Nivedita was very disturbed. According to Tagore, in 1904, he wanted to convey to his Western guest the strength of orthodox prejudice. Nivedita, on her part, was in disagreement with this interpretation, declaring that Tagore was doing a disservice to Hindu women. This persuaded Tagore to change the ending of *Gora* (1909)[21] as he admitted in a letter to William Pearson, who translated *Gora*. Tagore wrote,

> You ask me what connection had the writing of *Gora* with Sister Nivedita. She was our guest at Shilada and in trying to improvise a story according to her request, I gave her something which came very near to the plot of *Gora*. She was quite angry at the idea of Gora being rejected even by his disciple Sucharita owing to his foreign origin. You won't find it in *Gora* as it stands now.[22]

Nivedita's interaction with the Tagores spanned three generations. Her interest in Maharshi Devendranath Tagore, the grand patriarch and founder of the Brahmo Samaj and Rabindranath's father, was aroused when Vivekananda recounted his experience as a youngster, of having posed to the Maharshi the question, 'Have you seen God?', as he was resting in a houseboat on the Ganga. Devendranath apparently responded in the negative, adding that with the eyes of a yogi, Naren must be patient and will find the answer. With Vivekananda's permission, Nivedita went to meet

Devendranath Tagore in his ancestral home in Jorasanko, where he lived in the privacy of his sunlit room on the terrace. As she offered her respects with pranam, she added that she was paying the respects of Vivekananda as well. This made the old man respond that he remembered well their early encounter and would look forward to meeting with him again. Vivekananda was 'wonderfully moved'[23] to hear that and decided on their visit, which took place a few days later.

Realizing how thrilled Mrs Bull would be to be told of this historic encounter, Nivedita sent her a detailed letter describing how in the presence of Devendranath, Swami *said* pranam while she *made* it, offering a couple of roses.[24] Obviously, Swamiji had folded his hands in pranam while Nivedita bent low as if to take the dust of his feet, a more authentic Bengali gesture of pranam, and sought to point out the difference. To the surprise of many members of the Tagore family present, and much to Vivekananda's 'shyness', Devendranath recounted to Vivekananda how he had followed with intense pride and pleasure the many successes in his career, including the doctrines he had preached.[25] After receiving his blessings, Vivekananda hoped to leave quietly but was persuaded by the Tagore family to join them for tea, which he declined though he agreed to have a smoke. As the conversation came to veer round the subject of Kali symbolism, Nivedita 'thought for a moment he was going to fight' but Vivekananda deftly turned the conversation around by mentioning that he considered Raja Ram Mohan Roy to be 'the greatest man modern India had produced'. He also agreed in a tone that was 'exceedingly conciliatory' that the Brahmos had adopted the true Hindu doctrine but could also acknowledge the relationship of symbolism to it. Nivedita felt delighted 'that there is plenty of consciousness on both sides of the real position' and that she found herself as 'a real living link between Swami and his own people'.[26]

Among the third generation of the Tagores with whom Nivedita established a close relationship, were Surendranath Tagore, the son of the Poet's elder brother Satyendranath Tagore, with a strong commitment to social development, and Sarola Devi, the independent-minded daughter of the Poet's sister, Swarnakumari Devi, who had postponed marriage to devote herself to programmes that would instil in the youth, martial vigour and commitment to the cause of the motherland. By closely associating with them, Nivedita hoped that 'a new period may prove to have opened in the matter of our relations with the Brahmo Samaj'.[27]

Considerable interest was expressed in her school, and Nivedita had several visits by Brahmo ladies and also a visit, organized by Surendranath, of the Maharaja of Natore, who was curious about Nivedita's educational ideas. Constant hospitality by the Tagores saw Nivedita visiting their grand homes often, of which she wrote extensively to her beloved Yum. 'For the first time in India, I saw a drawing room that might have been the royal nest of European taste and intellect of the first water. Magnificent carved bookcases surrounded the room three-fourths of the way up. An irregular line of shelf held pictures, busts, statues and objects of art. So were precious things scattered about the room. The decorations were severe Japanese—magnificent.'[28]

Often, however, Nivedita felt as awkward as 'a fish out of water. I go in simple white amongst their gorgeous silks and finery—and it is absurd'.[29] Elsewhere she was to write that she had vowed not to go out anymore for dinner. The frugal and unostentatious Nivedita wailed, 'I wish food did not exist'.[30] Although Nivedita felt self-conscious in her plain outfit in the presence of the glamorously clad ladies of the Brahmo Samaj, to the artist Abanindranath Tagore she presented a refreshing contrast. Writing about a party held by the Oriental Art Society, attended by the social elite of Calcutta, consisting of British officials and well-placed Indians amidst high fashion and music, he mentioned that Nivedita made a dramatic entrance in her white outfit, strings of rudraksha beads round her neck and her hazel brown hair swept into a top knot. With his colourful artistic temperament, Abanindranath noted that the majestic moon had descended suddenly amidst a galaxy of stars! The beautiful ladies present suddenly seemed to lose their lustre while the British men vied with each other to meet her. Abanindranath went on to say that he had glimpsed the 'ideal beauty' that day. From the pages of *Kadambari*, Banabhatta's seventh-century classic romantic novel, *Mahesveta*, the heavenly damsel dressed as an ascetic, seemed to have emerged![31] Reminiscing that he had on occasion also met Vivekananda, Abanindranath concluded that his beauty was no patch on that of Nivedita, who had a rare purity in her unadorned demeanour. Like a snow peak emerging in moonlight, Nivedita radiated an unparalleled luminance.[32]

Vivekananda had encouraged the line of communication that Nivedita had opened with the Brahmos. At a lecture on the 'Young India Movement' that Nivedita gave at the Minerva Theatre on 26 February, he was happy to note the presence of the Tagores, who had appeared in their Bengali dress. Nivedita confessed to Yum that she had first tried on her little muslin gown but abandoned it for the brahmachari Kashmiri gown that she had gotten used to. In her speech, she referred to both Ram Mohan Roy and Devendranath Tagore, of course 'with the King's own sanction'.[33] When the lecture was over, Swamiji, standing at the porch with Sarola, congratulated her saying, 'You have done splendidly Margot!' On the way back, Nivedita narrated to Yum 'all the criticisms and hints were reserved for the carriage—*there* I had done splendidly'.[34]

Shortly after, at the invitation of Vivekananda, Sarola and Suren visited Belur Math and Dakshineswar. After visiting the shrine of Ramakrishna at the Math, where Swamiji prostrated himself and Sarola 'held aloof',[35] at dusk they were invited to accompany Swamiji across the river to Dakshineswar. While Vivekananda did not alight from the boat, Nivedita and other monks accompanied the guests to the room of Ramakrishna and the precincts of the temple, since the temple itself was closed. With her customary eloquence, Nivedita wrote to Yum, 'How beautiful Dakshineswar was! We sat under the tree—Sarola, Suren and I—and as we rose to go, Sarola pointed out the spaces of moonlight on the steps of the seat, all outlined by the leaves and branches it had fallen through. On the other side of the river were the lights of lamps and two great blazing corpse fires and the great boats were going up the stream with sails full set.'[36] Increasingly Vivekananda felt that the liberated Sarola, 'a jewel of a girl', was set to 'do great things'.[37] He considered her to have received a 'perfect education' where she was securely grounded in an Indian consciousness while having received the best of Western education.[38] Recounting a Sunday lunch prepared by Vivekananda himself, which was also attended by Sarola, Nivedita described with delight the menu of the 'geographical meal' he had planned. The first item on the list was titled 'Yankee' and included fish chowder; the second had fish balls under 'Norwegian'. Vivekananda had warned that the third item, boarding house hash under 'English', would contain nails, which turned out to be cloves! The fourth dish was mince pie a la Kashmir (meat with almonds and raisins) and the fifth one was Bengali rasgulla and fruit.[39]

Though the Brahmos were coming round to accepting Vivekananda, they were not willing to accept the avatar worship of his guru Ramakrishna. Nor was there a proper understanding of the call for detachment and renunciation. Sarala Ray, a distinguished Brahmo social worker and educationist, was to write to Nivedita that renunciation, self-annihilation seemed cowardice at a time when the need of the hour was engagement.[40] Clearly, Vivekananda's message of dedicated action with full participation and involvement of others in various programmes of nation-building, rather than ascetic withdrawal in isolation from the world, for which he faulted even Buddha, was not fully understood. Often Nivedita found herself fending off these attacks. Confessing to Yum, she mentioned one occasion, while dining with the P.K. Roys, how she had been 'disgracefully short tempered under criticism of Shri R.K. (Ramakrishna) and his movement. I am so sorry—for as Swami says fighting does no good'.[41]

Sarola wrote to Vivekananda soon after their visit, that out of a common love for their country, she and all others would be happy to join in his efforts, if only 'he would sweep away the worship of Ramakrishna'.[42] She was also certain that she would not be prevailed upon to believe in *Kalitatva* as easily as he had inculcated in his Western disciple, Nivedita, who had been persuaded to speak publicly on it.[43]

Swamiji's response was measured. While he was willing to hear the objections of Sarola and her friends, he felt the issue of Ramakrishna worship was too small a matter to inhibit burning patriotism. Indeed if he was convinced that it would be beneficial to humanity, he himself would sweep away that worship.[44] Although disappointed with Sarola's letter, Nivedita was very appreciative of the thoughtful gift made to her by Sarola, Suren and others, of a McIntosh bicycle, which would grant her added mobility.[45] But she felt aggrieved when Sarola told her that their association as it was would diminish her family's reputation and all that it stood for. 'So we are to give up a custom deep in the hearts of all who knew Him, in order to save the honour of the Tagores. After all, who are the Tagores?' she asked angrily.[46]

Among the other acquaintances that Nivedita made at this time was the famous theatre personality Girish Chandra Ghosh, with whom she shared her literary interests. She often exchanged books and discussed ideas with him. 'Mr Ghose is so delighted with Ibsen. He loved Brand and then brought me the *Master Builder*[47] from somewhere,' she was to write to Mrs Bull.[48] Nivedita offered to translate Girish Chandra Ghosh's *Bilwamangal*, an old morality play of a sinner's emergence into sainthood, which met the approval of

Vivekananda. This, from the same Vivekananda who had criticized Tagore as effeminate and felt that his romantic poetry would be a dangerous example for a nation already lacking in manly qualities.[49]

Perhaps the most endearing and enduring relationship that Nivedita made was with the celebrated scientist Jagadish Chandra Bose and his wife Abala. Professor of physics at Presidency College, Bose had been at the receiving end of considerable discrimination and racial insults, being denied his title, given limited laboratory access, and paid a considerably lower salary than his English colleagues. After several years of struggle, when the Royal Society of London offered him a scholarship, the government was forced to give him his title retroactively. It was only after learning about his travails that Nivedita came to realize the full implications of imperial racialism. The profound despair and loneliness of the scientist deeply touched her. After the great ecstasy of scientific success abroad, he seemed to have come back home to 'slow crucifixion'. The indignant Nivedita expostulated, 'I hate my own people.' She reminded Mrs Bull, 'Do you remember how I told Swami that I could never fire on the English flag? But I LONG with all my heart for the day, when I may be reincarnated to cry "Young India" when the time comes to snatch the country's freedom from us.'[50]

Not only did she decide to take Bose under her wing, but she impressed upon Mrs Bull the need to nurture his scientific talent with support and encouragement. She urged, 'Become a second mother for him as you are for Swamiji. He [Bose] is sick of life, yet honestly anxious to hold on, to prove to his countrymen that their chances of success in experimental science are as great as those of any European!'[51] Although nine years younger than Jagadish, Nivedita adopted him as her 'bairn'[52] exclaiming to Yum that 'at last the friend I loved and craved is mine—and how great! how simple! and through what suffering!'[53]

Jagadish Chandra, a staunch Brahmo, though grateful for her friendship was, however, unable to accept Vivekananda's worship of Kali and of his guru Ramakrishna. He admitted how thrilled he had been to hear Swamiji's mission to bring manliness to the people and how disappointed he was when Swamiji on return, proceeded with Kali and avatar worship.

'The man who had been a hero had become the leader of a new sect.'[54] In vain did Nivedita argue that Ramakrishna the avatar had not created another sect but had spoken of an all-embracing religion, which would unify all sects.[55] She despaired when she saw a great thinker and scholar take a position of seeming ignorance and superstition compared to reason and science.[56]

Various factors combined at this time to make Nivedita increasingly troubled. She realized her Swami was very unwell with asthma and persisting diabetes. In addition, his peace of mind was shattered by property disputes initiated by his 'wicked aunt, villain of the piece'.[57] In despair, she consulted astrologers to recalculate his horoscope and was relieved to be told that the influence of Jupiter would protect him till 6 December 1899 and if he could fight off the negative influence, he had nine more years to live.[58] Of course, when she shared this with Vivekananda, he laughed it off saying, 'Not another word on superstition. We are going to sweep it all away and make places for Advaitism pure and simple—one in the Himalayas and one here if you like.'[59]

The financial crunch at the Math had also made it clear to Nivedita that her prolonged stay would be difficult. Vivekananda had made it known that he had lost hopes of any improvement in the financial situation and that she should perhaps leave. Additionally, Nivedita was facing pressures from her family in England. Already she had a sense of guilt at not corresponding with them enough since her world had moved so drastically away from theirs. But her sister May's appeal that she should be given respite from the school's responsibilities so that she could marry increased Nivedita's sense of guilt. It had been decided that Vivekananda would be proceeding on a tour abroad to England and America but it was uncertain as to who would accompany him. At a time, it was thought that perhaps Sarola would go along with him.[60] Sarola recognised well that despite her misgivings about aspects of his belief, Vivekananda deeply appreciated her. In many ways, she vied with Nivedita for Swamiji's approbation. Her family was, however, reluctant to agree to her journey West with Swamiji. In the meantime, Nivedita grew increasingly anxious and wrote to her confidante Josephine, 'I just keep the ghost (my family) at arm's length and try to forget that they exist. My worst crime, in these moods, is that I love my life here. So if you can minister to a mind diseased—for once Dearest Joy let that mind be mine.'[61] Agonizing over the thought of being separated from her Master, she poured out her heart to Yum, 'While he is alive and here, I will not stir out of reach of him—I could not bear it—I worship, idolize, love him—I dare not risk his wanting me and not being there.'[62] Nivedita realized that her almost daily exchanges with Josephine were more like diaries than letters and requested her to save them since they were her only record of her meetings with the King.[63]

Nivedita's prayers were answered when she received financial support to travel with Vivekananda and Swami Turiyananda by the *S.S. Golconda*, which was to set sail on 30 June. It would call at Aden, Port Said and Naples before reaching England. Suspecting that Sara Bull, along with Josephine, had contributed to her succour, she wrote about her sense of relief—'It's like the great stone rolled away from the mouth of the sepulchre.'[64] With tears, she thanked Josephine, 'You have made me free for India—free with a light heart too—and the rest of my life shall be an attempt to prove not utterly unworthy'.[65] Repeating a favourite phrase of the King, she concurred that after all, 'Mother knows best.'[66]

The sea voyage of six weeks was the longest uninterrupted period that Nivedita was to spend with Vivekananda. Looking back, she felt that this had been indeed the 'greatest occasion' of her life, when she had been enriched by 'one long continuous impression of his mind and personality'.[67] As Master, Vivekananda's continuous explanations on assorted subjects such as challenges in life, Hinduism, the importance of Buddha, glimpses of saints, mythological stories, medieval history, juxtaposed with comments on the history, culture and location of the places they went through, provided a rich reservoir of information for Nivedita, who took copious notes, much of which found place in her writings. She felt that she had a responsibility to transmit Swamiji's ideas to others, and the books she went on to write were in a sense all Vivekananda's, since he gave her the power and inspiration.

There were also private moments when Vivekananda confided in Nivedita his guilt for having caused anguish to his mother. He said, 'I would undo the past if I could—I would marry, were I ten years younger, just to make my mother happy—not for any other reason,' to which Nivedita exclaimed, 'But I'm awfully glad you're not ten years younger,' which made them both laugh.[68]

Nivedita was filled with an overwhelming sense of devotion and love for her King, while he felt protective of her when he cautioned that she must not travel with him to America, so as to avoid objectionable attacks from missionaries.[69] He described himself to be a man of extremes. 'I eat hugely; I can go without food altogether; I smoke quantities; I don't smoke at all; as much power as I have in the control of the senses I have also in the senses themselves. Else what would the control be worth?'[70] For Nivedita, however, the toughest test was to exercise this control over the irresistible love that she felt for her King. To Josephine, whom she chose to address as Dear Lady Lakshmi in this letter, she wrote how love for Vivekananda had totally absorbed her, adding, 'Blessed be God for making it possible to love like this.'[71] But the transparency of her love often invited derisive comments from many, such as Mary Hale, daughter of one of Vivekananda's earliest benefactors during his first visit to Chicago. During the America tour, Mary said Nivedita was being silly with her 'hero worship', which she found irritating.[72] Vivekananda admitted that as a sannyasi he had found the strength to accept the sense of loss when, on many occasions, some of his disciples had left him, but he confessed that personal love would hurt him.[73] Nivedita, on the other hand, confessed that even after 'that awful time at Almora, when I thought he had put me out of his life contemptuously . . . I have grown infinitely *more* personal in my love.'[74] Vivekananda analysed that her spontaneous outbursts of affection came from an impulsive nature and worried about possible consequences. For instance on the ship, when the Captain had an attack of serious neuralgia, Nivedita volunteered to treat him and foment his face, which resulted in rapid recovery. When she laughingly told the King how grateful the Captain was, plying her with gifts, Vivekananda retorted that she had been 'imprudent', which, to make matters worse, she heard as 'impudent' and was reduced to tears. Later, assuaged by consoling words from Swamiji, she was told how he feared that people like Henrietta Muller might malign her for travelling on the ship with Vivekananda. He went on to analyse the three kinds of charity mentioned in the Gita: the *Tamasic*, which was impulsive, when one acted on one's desire to help, without a thought about consequences; the *Rajasic*, when one offered charity for one's own glory; and the *Sattvic*, when charity was offered at the right time, in the right way and quietly. He concluded that Mrs Bull seemed to be of the Sattvic kind, adding, 'But you see, Margot, I think yours was like Tamasic charity.'[75]

Even in England, Nivedita was known to voice her decided opinion on several compelling issues of the day at the Sesame Club. But when she had decided to come to India, she had taken a conscious decision to rein in her subjective feelings and try to understand a new culture with an open mind. While Nivedita was a good student in grasping the nuances of India's historical and cultural diversity, she could not help being impulsive and found it hard to hold back in her personal relations. Swamiji saw in this a vulnerability that he feared others could take advantage of. Throughout her short life, even as Nivedita tried to strike out on a path of her own on a number of occasions, she realized repeatedly the wisdom of restraint as had been advised by her dear guru.

The *S.S. Golconda* sailed into Tilsbury Dock in London on 31 July 1899. Nivedita's mother and sister were at the Dock, overjoyed to welcome her back. Accompanying them were a couple of American disciples of Vivekananda, including Christine Greenstidel, who was later to go to India and take over the reins of the school in Calcutta that Nivedita had started. Conspicuous by his absence to receive Vivekananda was Sturdy, Swamiji's disciple who was in charge of the Vedanta mission in London and who was to look after his stay. Like Henrietta Muller earlier, Sturdy too had decided to abruptly leave Vivekananda, much to his sadness and disappointment. Nivedita made alternative arrangements for Swamiji's stay in a lodging house in Wimbledon, very close to the house where her family lived. This gave him an opportunity to get to know the Noble household, which was preparing for May's forthcoming wedding. Vivekananda was fascinated to see the reverence with which Nivedita's family received him. While they knelt around him with deep interest in his talks, her mother Mary Noble cared for him like a son. Vivekananda warmed up to Richmond, Nivedita's younger brother, who jokingly informed Swamiji, much to his alarm, how the whole household had been put on alert not to have roast beef, so as to comply with Indian practices. Vivekananda promptly took Richmond to a restaurant and ordered for him a well-done steak.[76]

Swamiji, accompanied by Turiyananda, travelled to Glasgow by train on 16 August, in time to board the *S.S. Numidian* for America the next day. When she had travelled from India on the long sea voyage, Nivedita had discussed with Vivekananda her plans to travel to America in the hope of earning through lectures and articles, so that she could start a school in Calcutta for girls and widows. Swami had encouraged her and suggested she create a cottage industry with girls making green mango chutney and jams, which would contribute to earnings for the proposed school. She had also spoken of her intention to travel to towns where Ramabai had lectured attacking Vivekananda, where the plight of widows had already been raised, so that she could carry forward sympathy for this cause through donations and support for her project. Vivekananda had been tentative about this. On a more serious note, he asked her, 'Do you think, Margot, that you can collect the money in the West?' to which she answered with confidence, 'I don't think Swami—I *know*.'[77]

Now that Swamiji had left, Nivedita decided to join him immediately after the wedding celebrations of her sister May were over. Josephine had thoughtfully sent her frocks and gowns that she could wear during the festivities. A delighted Nivedita thanked her for the 'divine' dresses, adding that she had proved to be a wonderful Mother.[78] But she wondered if it would be appropriate after all to wear these dresses when she joined Josephine's household in America. While the feminine in Nivedita delighted in how 'awfully nice' she had looked and went into details with diagrams to explain how she had skilfully improvised a hat which was to go with her dress,[79] the brahmacharini in her made her declare that after this wedding she would be free to decline a new gown for the rest of her life.[80] Already she felt like a stranger in her own country. Disillusioned with Catholic orthodoxy, a visit to the Anglican Church made her declare in anguish, 'How unutterably and awfully mean and low it seemed!'[81] Declaring that she was hungry to get to work, she was reassured by the financial support from Mrs Bull to travel. Her Master's last words before leaving—'Come on as fast as possible'[82]—echoed in her ears as she wrote about her travel plans to her 'dear King', signing off as 'your daughter Nivedita'.[83] She arrived in New York on 20 September on the *Mongolian* of the Allan Line.

At the stately Ridgely Manor, overlooking the scenic Hudson River on the outskirts of New York, Nivedita found herself enjoying the gracious welcome of the Leggetts, friends of Vivekananda from his previous stay in America. Betty Leggett, the older sister of Josephine MacLeod, was well known in the elite social circles of Paris and New York and, with her husband Francis, had come to admire and revere Vivekananda. She now offered the hospitality of her lovely home to Vivekananda and his disciples Turiyananda and Nivedita. Joining them in their stay were Josephine Macleod, Nivedita's favourite Yum Yum, as well as 'grannie' Mrs Bull, with her highly strung daughter Olea. It was a rare moment for the three women to catch up and remember with nostalgia their days together on the Jhelum with Swamiji. Reflecting on this friendship, Nivedita was to write that they had grown into each other and how difficult it was to think of them as divisible. Nivedita felt comforted in the knowledge that both regarded her as their spiritual child.[84]

For the next two months Nivedita found herself under the Master's gaze, with his attempts to rein in her impulsiveness, offering advice and instructions for her to toughen up for her work ahead. Reporting to her beloved Yum how he had been pacing up and down for an hour and a half like a caged lion, Nivedita wrote how he warned her against external exclamations of politeness, of this 'lovely' or that 'beautiful' instead of internalizing these emotions silently. 'Therefore, Margot you fool,' he had continued candidly, 'get rid of all these petty relations of society and home—hold the soul firm against the perpetual appeals of the sense—realize that the rapture of autumn trees is as truly sense-enjoyment as a comfortable bed or a table dainty.' The ideal he held up was: 'Hate the silly praise and blame of people.'[85]

Nivedita sought to distance herself from the socializing and parties of Ridgely Manor, and went to a retreat for a fortnight (18 October to 1 November), in which she could concentrate on her writings. Vivekananda encouraged Nivedita to write—to produce literature. On the evening before she went into retreat, he wrote a poem titled 'Peace' and gave it to her.[86]

Behold it comes in might,
The power that is not power,
The light that is in darkness,
The shade in dazzling light.

It is a joy that never spoke,
And grief unfelt, profound,
Immortal life unlived,
Eternal death unmourned.

It is not joy nor sorrow
But that which is between
It is not night nor morrow,
But that which joins them in.

It is sweet rest in music;
And pause in sacred art;
The silence between speaking;
Between two fits of passion—
It is the calm of heart.

It is beauty never seen,
And love that stands alone,

It is song that lives unsung,
And knowledge never known.

It is death between two lives,
And lull between two storms,
The void whence rose creation
And that where it returns.

To it the tear-drop goes,
To spread the smiling form
It is the Goal of Life,
And Peace—its only home!

One of the projects Nivedita took up immediately was to complete the manuscript *Kali the Mother*, with further inputs from Swamiji. She dedicated it to Vireshwar—a name for Shiva given to Vivekananda by his mother, who had prayed at Shiva's temple in Benares before being blessed by his birth. Published in 1900 from London by Swan Sonnenschein, the book's review in the *Brahmavadin* (1901) spoke of 'the mystic glow of loveliness' in the 'poetic prose of Nivedita's booklet, which in several places mirrors forth the sentiments of Swami Vivekananda in all the glory of an English woman's language and imagery'.[87]

After a few months of hard work, Nivedita was able to form 'The Ramakrishna Guild of Help in America' with Mrs Betty Leggett as president and Mrs Sara Bull as the honorary secretary. A booklet describing the project of setting up the Ramakrishna School for Girls was sent to donors. Mr Leggett contributed 1000 dollars to Nivedita to start her work. The school course was to be founded on the kindergarten system and include English and Bengali languages and literature, elementary mathematics, some basic science and handicrafts with a special bearing on the revival of old Indian industries so that pupils would be equipped to earn their own livelihoods.

Perhaps the greatest worry of Vivekananda related to how finances could be garnered to sustain Nivedita's lecture programme. On 5 November at Ridgely Manor, soon after breakfast, his pent-up anxieties burst like a 'volcano'. Nivedita was to write to her 'sweet Yum Yum . . . he turned on me before everyone and asked how much longer I intended to hang on. He was quite abusive and then he uttered a relenting word—you know how.' With her flashing Irish eyes, Nivedita replied that there was no need for harshness since she had been only too anxious to be at work and had been kept where she was by his express instructions. At this point, Olea's offer to take Nivedita to Chicago immediately assuaged his fears and he insisted that Nivedita take up the invitation. Nivedita commented that 'waxing glorious' Vivekananda ended with a blessing in which 'the Guru was lost and it became all Father'. He told her to go out into the world and fight for him.[88] Nivedita recalled how Vivekananda had subjected Josephine to similar outbursts, reducing her to tears. Although smarting from his admonishment, she took solace from the realization that 'where he loved most he scolded most'.[89]

Perhaps to atone for the stern chiding of the morning, Swamiji called both Nivedita and Mrs Bull in the afternoon of the 5th, in what proved to be for Nivedita 'the event of my life—the great turning point'. Giving them both pieces of cotton cloth of gerua colour, he draped one round Mrs Bull like a skirt, putting the other piece like a *chudder* (stole) over her shoulder, calling her a sannyasini. Placing a hand over their heads, he pronounced that he had given all that Ramakrishna Paramhansa had given to him. He went on to exult that women's hands would be best to hold what came from a woman—the Mother, who might be, for all he knew, a disembodied spirit but certainly felt like a real presence.[90] His last word to her as she took his leave was that she should always say 'Durga, Durga, Durga' before beginning anything or going anywhere, as a protective utterance.[91]

Soon after this, both Vivekananda and Nivedita went along their own travel paths through America—one in his quest to disseminate practical Vedanta by setting up more missions and the other in her endeavour to create more awareness of India, of Hinduism, of the need for the education of women in India and to try to raise money for her cause.

After visiting the Vedanta Society in New York and spending weeks in lectures and classes, Vivekananda headed for California, stopping over in Chicago for a week and catching up with his old friends the Hales and Emma Calve, the famous opera singer, whom he had met before. By early December, he reached Los Angeles, to be met by Josephine, who had come earlier to nurse her terminally ill brother, after whose death she now felt free to accompany Vivekananda. The series of lectures and talks he gave were profound yet carried simple truths. Josephine noted the ease with which Swamiji could pass from a sombre note to a mundane one. She wrote that after an outstanding lecture on Christmas day at the Home of Truth on Jesus of Nazareth, when she imagined him covered in a halo of distinction, he mentioned on their way back that he had finally realized how it is done. After a tantalizing wait, he explained that it was how they put a bay leaf in the mulligatawny soup that made the difference![92] January 1900 saw Vivekananda in South Pasadena, where he gave wide-ranging talks on subjects such as women of India, yoga, Universal Religion, Buddhist India, Indian epics, mythological legends and Persian Art. But he soon realized that he was losing the zest for such work, which was no longer raising funds. During this period, his ardent followers had formed Vedanta Societies in Los Angeles and Pasadena. In general, finding the Pacific coast more conducive to his Vedanta ideals, he headed to San Francisco, where the focus of his talks was on the Advaita truth, that man had to realize and utilize the divine power latent in him. After the inauguration of the Vedanta Society of San Francisco, Vivekananda felt a deep sense of peace and release from work. In a letter to Josephine dated 18 April 1900, he admitted,

> Behind my work was ambition, behind my love was personality, behind my purity was fear, behind my guidance the thirst for power! Now they are vanishing and I drift. I come, Mother, I come, in Thy warm bosom—floating wheresoever Thou takest me—in the voiceless, in the strange, in the wonderland. I come, a spectator, no more an actor![93]

While in California, Vivekananda received an invitation from Mr and Mrs Leggett, then in London, to join them in Paris in July to attend and speak at the Congress of the History of Religions, which was to be held in September in conjunction with the Paris Exposition of 1900. Accepting the invitation, Vivekananda now headed back to New York, where he decided to spend a few months before sailing to Europe. In June, he met up with Nivedita, who had also returned to New York after her long tour around the country. In the Vedanta Society rooms in New York where he held Gita classes, they both lectured on aspects of Hinduism. Nivedita's talk on the 'Ideals of Hindu women' was a lucid and sympathetic account of their simple life and thoughts, which created keen interest among the audience, who, to Vivekananda's satisfaction, raised many questions.[94]

Nivedita's travels around the country in the past several months, however, had not been up to her expectations. She had pinned her hopes on meeting the circle of Vivekananda's friends who could help make her lecture tour a success. But she was soon to discover that not all had the same commitment as her Yum or 'Grannie'. Although Olea, Mrs Bull's daughter, temperamentally lacked balance, she had been very helpful in introducing her to Chicago. Nivedita felt encouraged by the warm hospitality extended by Mary Hale, despite her initial impatience with Nivedita. But both Olea and Mary felt that Nivedita should discard her nun's outfit and wear modern clothes, and speak on general issues more as a journalist than as representative of a religious leader. She was reminded how Vivekananda after all had invited a lot of criticism with his forthright speeches. Nivedita herself experienced at times how association with her guru adversely affected the success of her talks. While in India, her audiences had felt encouraged by her strong support of Indian cultural and religious traditions, in America audiences questioned how a foreigner had the authority to speak on such matters. She put it down to sheer jealousy and venting her frustration to Yum exclaimed, 'I felt as if I could crumple the whole audience up in my hand.'[95] Nevertheless, Nivedita remained adamant, saying she was following her Master's instructions. When Mary Hale tried to reason with her that Swami was often not right and on occasion she had disagreed with him, Nivedita replied that as a friend, Mary could be counted an equal, but as disciple, she had to respect her subservience. Later of course, Nivedita regretted her own obstinacy, because as it turned out, her lectures did not ensure a big draw.[96] Even the lectures before the Hull House Arts and Crafts Association, on the ancient arts of India, Kashmiri shawl-making, etc. resulted in a payment of 15 dollars only, with many orders for brass utensils and embroideries, which she would find difficult to organize. Also, her idea of raising funds by charging only one dollar per year for ten years from several hundreds of people for her proposed school for girls did not take off. Although Mrs Bull had seen some sense in the concept, Vivekananda had been doubtful. While she raised some paltry amounts from the public, the elite families remained unenthused by her. Often she was grilled about the depressed status of women in India and the system of polygamy that existed. Her spirited defence made some people think she sounded as a Mormon.[97] Feeling suffocated as if she were in 'a lunatic asylum' Nivedita now, more than ever, realized how trying it had been for her Master to get his message across.[98] Exhausted and without any financial support, Nivedita felt dejected. But her spirits revived when Mrs Bull assured her that financial concerns should not stand in the way of her plans and she should be released from the burden of asking for money.[99] Accordingly, Nivedita travelled from Chicago over large expanses, visiting and lecturing in Kansas, Cleveland, Minneapolis, Ann Arbor, Detroit, Boston and Cambridge in Massachusetts. Her lectures were on various topics covering aspects of the condition of Indian women, the concept of Mother Worship, the ancient arts of India, etc. Her presentations of mythological tales interested audiences since she linked themes from across cultures to express an underlying commonality. Thus, starting with the Christ Child, she would go on to the Indian 'Christ Child', Krishna, and then add stories of Dhruva, Prahlad and Gopala, often giving a geography lesson that carried her audiences on a journey down the Ganga or visiting the Taj and the Fort in Agra.[100] She was encouraged when a person associated with a public school felt that the stories had the makings of a book. When Nivedita clarified that all her stories were learnt from her Master, she was assured that surely her Swami could not provide the actual feel of conversing with little children as she had. She also felt her academic scholarship might not be scrutinized as minutely as that of her Master if he were to write the book.[101] Later this was to take the form of her well-known book *The Cradle Tales of Hinduism*.

Although Nivedita briefly met Swamiji in Chicago, she did not mention to him her problems. She looked for every sign that could herald a better future for her. Thus on 6 December, when the astrologers had predicted that Swamiji would be freed from the negative influence of the stars, Nivedita finally earned public attention and press coverage when she forcefully spoke as a respondent at a public lecture on America spreading Anglo-Saxon civilization over the world. She seemed to believe that as daughter of the Master, she was receiving Kali's blessings.[102] Despite her elation, Vivekananda by now had realized that her lecture tour was not going as well as she had hoped. He wrote, 'Your work in Chicago will not do much I fear save give you education in methods here.'[103]

Nivedita's staunch loyalty to her guru and open criticism of the Brahmos irked many such as Bipin Chandra Pal, the Indian nationalist leader who was visiting America at that time and who was a guest of Mrs Bull in Boston along with Nivedita. Pal noted in his journal how Nivedita's uncompromising defence of Hindu tradition and aggressive rejection of all criticism resulted in stormy arguments between them, embarrassing his hostess and compelling him to leave. Nivedita was not prepared to hear that the Christian missionaries, who had insulted Vivekananda on many occasions, were helpful, as Pal claimed based on his experiences. Nor did she want to hear that her Guru was only a social reformer and not a Hindu guru since orthodox society would never accept a non-Brahmin to be eligible as such. Pal and Nivedita were to meet again shortly after, at a conference of the Free Religious Association, which Sara Bull had arranged, where both were speakers. When she heard Pal speak eloquently on 'India's Contribution to Free Religion' Nivedita was charmed and all memories of past differences were forgotten. In her speech on 'Our Obligations to the Orient' that followed, Nivedita spoke convincingly of how in India there were a series of possibilities of worship—from fetish[104] worship to the idea that the whole universe is God. Bipin Pal observed in his journal, 'At this Congress of Religions session, both of us putting India on a pedestal bound us in a friendship that a hundred differences of opinion would leave unbroken.'[105]

By May 1900, Nivedita confessed to Yum, 'I feel weary to death of my own incapacity and remorseness in a hundred directions.'[106] She longed for her Master and yet knew that he expected her to deal with her own disappointments. He had told her clearly, 'If you are really ready to take the world's burden, take it by all means. But do not let us hear your groans and curses. Do not frighten us with your sufferings, so that we come to feel we were better off with our own burdens.'[107] When she was to meet him in New York in June, she realized how he held her life 'in the hollow of his hand'.[108] But there also grew in her the realization that she had to think afresh about where she should be heading.

This opportunity was provided by the chance encounter she had with Patrick Geddes (1832–1954), a Scottish biologist and sociologist and one of the foremost twentieth century thinkers on civics, planning and urban development. Nivedita had been seeking him since the time she had been facing personal problems in England. Referred to Geddes as the person who could change her attitude to life forever, Nivedita had instead ended up meeting Vivekananda at that time, who came to loom large in her life. But her interest in Geddes had remained, as he was seen as the first sociologist since Herbert Spencer to produce a new and living theory of society with a future in it. With an interdisciplinary approach, Geddes sought to address questions of urban planning and social improvement by taking into account the interlinked characteristics of geographical location, workplace and family patterns. Nivedita wanted to learn the methods of social science to apply them to Indian life so that she could write a book about the cultural life of Indians. Describing the 'kind, wise, horned owl' appearance of Geddes to her 'dearest Father' Vivekananda, Nivedita wrote excitedly about the genius of this biologist, who could inspire people from across disciplines. Calling his analysis more psychological than sociological, Nivedita described how Geddes had persuasively argued how the occupation patterns of humans had always been moulded by habitat or in response to family needs.[109]

Finding much encouragement in the advice of her dear Yum Yum, 'Live your own life, speak your own message,'[110] Nivedita decided to offer her services in response to the need expressed by Geddes, for help during the Paris exhibition. Taking heart in Vivekananda's message 'Death for the cause, not success is your goal',[111] Nivedita set sail for Paris on 28 June 1900. Although Swamiji had always feared that her impulsive decisions might dissipate her energies and rob her of her focus, he accepted the inevitable.

A month later, Vivekananda headed for France. He stayed for a while as a guest of the Leggetts in their prestigious residence in the Place des Etats-Unis in Paris and then chose to move to the quieter home of M. Jules Bois, a well-known occult philosopher and writer, where he hoped to hone his skills in the French language. At the various social occasions to which he was invited, he met many luminaries that included the philosopher Prince Kropotkin; Hiram Maxim of the machine gun fame; opera singer Emma Calve, whom he now met again and who taught Swami the song 'Marseilles', the tune of which had captivated him; the Duke of Richelieu; the sculptor Auguste Rodin; Jagadish Chandra Bose, who had come on a scholarship, and whom he described to acquaintances as the 'pride and glory of Bengal'; and Prof. Patrick Geddes, who had been invited to participate in the Paris Exposition as an organizer and presenter, and who gladly took Swamiji around to visit it and explain the exhibits. In connection with the Paris Exposition, Sorbonne University hosted the Congress of the History of Religions in the first week of September, where Swamiji was invited to make his presentation. He was soon to discover that the Congress, with its focus on scholarly and academic presentations, had no room for debates on doctrines and beliefs, which had distinguished the Chicago Parliament of Religions. Despite his ill health, reports in the *Indian Mirror* indicate how he had impressed all with his presentation in French.[112] Swamiji also had the opportunity to participate in talks as a respondent, refuting charges of the Shivalingam being a phallic symbol, suggesting the influence of the Buddhist stupa instead on such structures. He also challenged the theory of Greek influence lying behind all aspects of Indian culture.[113]

While in Paris, Vivekananda had the occasion to meet Nivedita on social occasions in the company of Josephine and her friends. But a distance had now crept up between them. He admitted that they were both headstrong and obstinate but he felt that she should create fresh energies instead of scattering them by constantly giving. Nivedita disagreed. Dejectedly, she wrote to Mrs Bull, 'The most futile will-o'-the-wisps in the whole wilderness are those dreams of helping others, that lead us farther into the morass of hope . . . One does not desire to receive, but the dream of giving dies hard.'[114] Vivekananda resigned himself into accepting that Nivedita was now on her own. He had been hurt by the defection of close disciples in the past and now chose to be detached. He felt that his journey on earth was coming to an end and sought to break free of all emotional bondage. He formally relinquished charge of the Ramakrishna Mission and declared that he had freed himself of all responsibilities and obligations.

Nivedita, however, was distraught. She had been staying with the Geddes couple ever since she arrived in Paris but her work with the famous sociologist from Edinburgh University had not proved successful. With her Guru not accessible to hear her woes, she poured out her heart to Yum, her confidante. While Geddes had wanted her to collate his documents, draw up reports and abstracts of his lectures and establish in three months a specialized library, Nivedita found the work mechanical and soulless, with no scope for her individual input. 'He wants a voice that will utter his thought as he would have done. I try, then to make a mosaic in which the bright bits are his words, and I provide only grey cement of mere grammatical context. You can imagine how feeble this is!' she wrote.[115] It increasingly dawned on her how different Swami had been when he had asked her to pen his thoughts, giving her the freedom to do so in her own way. To Mrs Bull, she wrote how

Geddes had clearly expressed his displeasure by announcing that her work was 'quite unfit for his purpose' apart from criticizing her for her 'flamboyance'.[116] Nivedita nevertheless acknowledged her debt to Geddes when she wrote,

> No words can tell you how much I have learnt from doing this and I do hope you may feel yourself able to use it in some form or other soon . . . and if you say it is quite useless, I shall of course be sadly disappointed but I shall quite understand.[117]

Nivedita yearned again to be led by her Master to divine knowledge, as he himself had been by Ramakrishna. She was certain that she could never reach it on her own 'unless Swami will give it by a miracle'. But the question remained with her: 'Will he give it?' Convinced that 'he has it—and the power to give it' she feared that alas, he 'could not'.[118]

In the meantime, she observed how much Vivekananda admired Madame Emma Calve, who had risen from dire poverty to become one of the highest paid opera icons. She was famous for her leading role in *Carmen*, the sensational opera classic that had created a stir at that time, for the open passion with which a gypsy seduces a soldier, lures him away from his wife, only to give her affections to another, bringing on her violent murder. Vivekananda's decision to view *Carmen* resulted in a disagreement with Nivedita, who feared that he would come in for criticism. Not only did Swami attend the performance but he also congratulated Calve in the dressing room.[119]

Nivedita was aware that her abrupt departure for Paris to help Geddes had deeply pained Swamiji, who commanded her single-minded devotion to the cause she was committed to. But as she admitted to Yum, while being steadfast in her love to him, it was hard to love no one else.[120] Trying to soothe a distraught Nivedita, Mrs Bull invited her to spend some time in August at the house she had rented in Perros-Guirec, a small village on the English Channel in Brittany, where she hoped that the sea air would restore her. Introspecting over their misunderstanding, Nivedita now decided to write to Vivekananda. But her blunt charge to Swami of being jealous of her making new friends she regretted as soon as she had sent it, with the realization that she could have put across her views to him very differently.[121] The damage was done. Vivekananda replied forthwith, declaring, 'You must know once and for all I am born without jealousy, without avarice, without the desire to rule— whatever other vices I am born with.' The reason he cited for his displeasure was that he feared that Nivedita, with an impulsive and persuasive nature, might foist her ideas on others who did not see their merit or were not ready for them. Detaching himself fully, he declared to Nivedita, 'You are free, have your own choice, your own work . . .'[122] Admitting that, 'Swami has cut me off by a well-deserved stroke',[123] Nivedita steeled herself to a decision that she would remain in Europe and work there. Sara Bull, to whom Swami had given the responsibility of Nivedita, now invited her to spend the winter in London, where she would be cheered by the presence of her favourite 'bairn', Jagadish Chandra Bose, and his wife.

Before her departure for England in late September, she had an unexpected surprise when suddenly Josephine, accompanied by Swami, visited them in Mrs Bull's house in Brittany. He asked Nivedita no questions. Days passed in discussions on the life and thoughts of Buddha. On the last evening before Nivedita was to leave, Vivekananda asked her for a walk in the garden. He explained that a guru, after preparing his disciples, had to leave, for they could never come into their own in his presence. Now he was just a wandering monk. Giving her his blessings, he said:

There is a peculiar sect of Mohammedans who are reported to be so fanatical that they take each newborn babe and expose it saying, 'If God made thee, perish. If Ali made thee, live!' Now what they say to the child I say, but in the opposite sense, to you tonight: Go forth into the world, and there, if I made you, be destroyed. If the Divine Mother made you, live.[124]

Vivekananda's parting gift to her was a poem he wrote in English titled 'A Benediction', which conveyed his aspirations and good wishes.

The mother's heart, the hero's will,
The sweetness of the southern breeze,
The sacred charm and strength that dwell
On Aryan Altars, flaming, free;
All these be yours, and many more
No ancient soul could dream before—
Be thou to India's future son
The mistress, servant, friend in one

On the day she left, Nivedita found that Swami had come soon after dawn to wish her farewell. One of the lingering memories that she cherished was of her leaving in a peasant market-cart and looking back to see his silhouette against the dawn sky with his hands uplifted in blessing.

Vivekananda left Paris on 24 October on the famous transcontinental train, the Orient Express, in a group that included Josephine MacLeod, Madame Calve, M. Bois and others. After some historical sightseeing in Vienna, they reached Constantinople. After a few days, they took a steamer to visit Athens and the old port of Piraeus and then on another ship they travelled to Egypt. After visiting the museum and historical sites, Vivekananda grew restless to return to India, predicting to Madame Calve that he would die on the 4 July.[125] His return was promptly arranged with the generous support of Madame Calve. On 9 December 1900, Vivekananda surprised his brother monks at Belur Math, Calcutta, by making an unannounced appearance.

While the Swami's first visit to the West had impressed him with its organization and democratic processes, this last visit exposed some of its exploitative practices for privilege and power. But the Swami took all in his stride, being at complete ease among imperialist aristocrats and American millionaires as well as those not so fortunate. 'Monk and King,' he said, 'were obverse and reverse of a single medal. From the use of the best, to the renunciation of all, was but one step.'[126]

Nivedita, now in England, felt the happiness of a child when she received the 'blessings of the howling dervishes' that Swami sent from his travels. She was at peace that in their relationship, Vivekananda had evolved from being a King to a Master and now was the Father. This was 'the sweetest of all relationships,' she was to write to Yum, since 'the world is before one—every soul is free to be served by one—nothing is shut off, even no degree of love is forbidden to one'.[127]

Just as Swamiji had placed women on a pedestal, addressing them as mother or sister, thereby distancing himself from implicit gender tensions, Nivedita too found her liberation by placing her adored King on a pedestal as Father. She had found freedom from her own internal struggle and from his control and discipline.

3

Blessed by the 'Father'

In England, away from the 'Father' for nearly sixteen months before her return to India, Nivedita had ample time for introspecting, exploring her own ideas and thoughts, pursuing whatever programmes she felt were best for the cause of India and getting back to writing, which the Swami had consistently encouraged.

The opportunity of interacting closely with Jagadish Chandra and Abala Bose, whom she had already adopted as her family, proved enriching on many counts. She came to realize under what pressures of discrimination the great scientist worked, which added to her growing disillusionment with the colonial rule. It led her to explore alternative theories of governance put forward by social scientists and theorists such as Geddes and Kropotkin. Besides, she found in Jagadish not only a formidable scientific mind but also a friend with whom she could share ideas. For one, she was curious to know the Brahmo point of view and gently persuaded a reluctant Jagadish to explain his reservations about icon worship. As she wrote to Yum, 'I am trying to get the whole of the Brahmo feeling and tradition honestly . . . You will remember that we (or at least I) did not love Shiva and Kali at first . . . Even S.R.K [Sri Ramakrishna] cannot have loved all religions equally. So I can say without any disloyalty to the effort

I am making, that at present it is dreadfully like the Puritanism of my childhood.'[1]

After much soul searching, Nivedita had a sudden realization while giving a lecture at a Sunday religious service at Thenbridge Wells. It appeared to her that probably she had been groping in the dark by 'using images to thwart and blind my vision of the One. That until I have achieved that vision, I may not go back to the Image. I cannot tell you the peace of this discovery,' she was to write to Yum. For after all that was the core of Advaita belief, which her Swami had inculcated over her. Although initially she had shuddered to think of Swami's disapproval over her delving into Brahmo beliefs, she now realized that 'every path means faithfulness to him'.[2] Distance had given her objectivity and as she wrote, 'I do see some value in the soul of R.N. Tagore for instance, even while I also see more clearly than I ever thought possible, the probable truth in all that the King had said.'[3]

She hastened to assure Yum that despite this, she did not cherish any idea of going out to tea with the Brahmos regularly when she got back. She was also slowly getting convinced that her future work lay not only with girls and women but also men, for the larger cause of India's regeneration. Voicing for the first time what her future preoccupation would be, she said, 'I belong to *Hinduism* more than I ever did. But I see the *political* need so clearly too!'[4]

Nivedita was fascinated by the scientific ideas and experiments of Jagadish. Only recently had the Institute of Electrical and Electronics Engineers acknowledged that Bose's demonstration of the remote wireless signalling preceded that of the Italian inventor Guglielmo Marconi. Bose being relatively unknown and his work unpatented, Marconi went on to receive the Nobel Prize. Bose also demonstrated that metals respond to stimulus, show fatigue, could be stimulated by certain drugs and killed by poisons. Dissolving the boundary lines between living and non-living matter, he in effect vindicated the Vedantic principle of a fundamental unity that existed in the apparent diversity of nature. Nivedita was keen to assist Bose to articulate his thoughts, which she could then capture in lucid prose. As she described to Yum, 'Dr Bose is like one who walks on air. Discovery succeeds discovery, one instrument follows another and the brilliant intention becomes the measured fact. It is breathless awe with which one watches.'[5] From the serious academic interaction that followed between the two and extended until the end of her life, there emerged several volumes of Bose's works of which Nivedita was often the willing scribe and editor. Describing her busy time in London, she wrote to Yum, 'I cannot write letters . . . Whole days pass in Science and in translating and talking India.'[6]

Nivedita could sense Bose's anxiety about the approaching presentation of his experiments that he would have to make at the Royal Society. Conscious that the crude homely apparatus that he had used would not perhaps receive the same attention as a proper apparatus might have, he felt some diffidence, which told on his health. However, the presentation went well and soon after he had completed arduous laboratory work, he surrendered to doctors on the operating table for an overdue surgery, announcing dramatically, 'Now gentlemen, you may cut away!'[7]

Nivedita brought him and his wife over to her mother's home in Wimbledon for post-surgery recovery. Through the many discussions they had, Nivedita discovered that Jagadish's scientific temper had room for belief in the Advaita concept of Universal Oneness. Moreover, with his interest in Indian mythology he encouraged Nivedita to pen the tales that she often narrated so dramatically in her lectures.

Knowing the academic jealousy and racial discrimination that Bose faced, Nivedita was constantly planning ways of securing his future. In response to her appeal, Rabindranath Tagore managed to persuade the Maharaja of Tripura to undertake some of the cost of supporting Bose and his scientific work.[8] Nivedita also appealed

to Dr Bose's friend Romesh Chunder Dutt, who after twenty-five
years of distinguished service in the Indian Civil Service had come to
England, where he was in the faculty of history at the University of
London. Mr Dutt's considerable literary talent had found expression
in historical novels, poems and the abridged translation into English
verse of the Indian epics and the Rig Veda. Now absorbed in
writing the economic history of India, he found Nivedita, whom he
called his god-daughter, receptive to many of his ideas on India's
economic crisis and the problems of industrialization. He responded
enthusiastically to her invitations to give lectures on India at various
literary meetings.[9] To Dutt too, Nivedita broached the question of
finding a financial solution for Bose's scientific career. Dutt agreed
that Bose had to be 'released from his chains' and calculated that he
needed an annual sum of a thousand pounds a year for life. But, as
Nivedita wrote to Mrs Bull, in the light of the academic jealousy that
Bose faced, 'It has to be begged secretly in India.' Dutt guessed that
Tagore, to whom he too had written, would be helpless to assist.[10]

Mrs Bull, who had also adopted Jagadish and in the end was the
one to provide him the necessary financial support, was then in
London and was also exploring career options for her favourite 'son'.
Jamshetji Tata, distinguished Parsi industrialist and philanthropist,
was also in London to find means to establish an independent
university for Indians to encourage scholarship and scientific
research. On hearing this, Mrs Bull arranged a small lunch where
she invited Sir George Birdwood of the India Office, in charge of
educational affairs, and asked Nivedita to join them. Although she
had hoped to steer the conversation in a fruitful direction, Nivedita
returned disappointed and angry. In a detailed letter to Jagadish
recording her experience, she spoke about the superciliousness of
the British attitude. Apparently, Sir George had turned down the
proposition that appointments to the proposed university be reserved
for meritorious Indians alone. Claiming that the Indian universities
were in a state of deterioration, without having produced a single

person of pre-eminence in the sciences or arts in fifty years, he felt
that the entire project of Tata be unreservedly turned over to the
British government. He added that 'the people of India will never
rise against us. They are all vegetarians.'[11] An irate Nivedita sent
a press circular stating that the British government sought to fill
the advisory committee formed to discuss Tata's scheme with its
own nominees, rather than invite educated members of the native
community and impartial English people with an experience of
India to it. Her plea received many signatories, including William
James, who also commented that 'the infatuated pretensions of
the Anglo-Saxon' had to be resisted in favour of the best-educated
native opinion.[12]

During this time, Nivedita engaged in sundry writings in
newspapers and enjoyed translating a few of Tagore's short stories.
It was at Jagadish Chandra's persuasion that Tagore had agreed to
allow some of his short stories to be translated. Jagadish had written
to his Poet friend that although he occupied the foremost literary
position in India, he was unknown in Europe, where Rudyard
Kipling remained the favourite. Exhorting his friend to emerge
from the rural villages where he had been hiding, Bose asked for
some of the short stories from the just-released first volume of
the famous collection *Galpo Guchho* to be translated. Somewhat
apprehensive about the project, Tagore replied with customary
humour that his creative Lakshmi, while being presented to the
outside world should not like Draupadi, be stripped of the Bangla
language which clothed her.[13] Three short stories were given to
Nivedita for translation. She reported to Mrs Bull, 'Cabuliwallah
and Leave of Absence [*Chhuti*] are both Englished now and I have
Giving and Giving in Return [*Dena Paona*] ready for the last finish'.
She added that in memory of Cabuliwallah she had made an ink
impression of her right hand![14]

It was after Nivedita's death that the manuscript of Cabuliwallah
was recovered from her papers. In November 1911, at Tagore's

request, it was published in the *Modern Review*, making Nivedita the first translator of Tagore's short stories. Unfortunately, although Cabuliwallah had found much appreciation among her friends like Kropotkin and was submitted by Bose to *Harper's Magazine*, it was declined because the West was not sufficiently interested in Oriental life![15]

Nivedita increasingly veered to the anarchist position of the 'utter needlessness of governments', claiming that 'it matters little therefore who is on India's throne—Edward VII of England or the Tsar of all the Russias—her real hope lies in the education of her people'. This education, as propounded by Kropotkin, was to be obtained through long years of writing, printing, lecturing and propaganda, which would only bear fruit at unexpected moments. Nivedita dreamt of a day when, without bloodshed, the Viceroy could be informed that his services were no longer required.[16] Against the raging intellectual debate of the nineteenth century sparked off by the survival of the fittest doctrine of Herbert Spencer (1820–1903) and Charles Darwin 's origin of species (1809–82), Prince Kropotkin's theory of mutual aid struck a note of hope. Not all mankind could be perceived as caught in a struggle against one another unto death. Struggle, bloodshed and mutual conflict were not the only determinants of the history of the races, and the role of co-operation, fraternity and solidarity finding expression in institutions of mutual aid was, if anything, of greater consequence. This was proclaimed by religion even as it was attested by science. In a favourable review of Kropotkin's book, *Mutual Aid*,[17] Nivedita concluded, 'The history of Humanity may, after all, prove to have been less of a battlefield than of a garden, of a family, of a home.'[18] Had Vivekananda not come to the same conclusion in discussions with his disciples, including Sister Nivedita, following a visit to the Calcutta zoo in 1898? He had explained that Darwin's theory might be applicable to the animal and vegetable kingdom but never to the human, where reason and knowledge were highly developed.[19]

From early 1901, Nivedita began extensive lectures in England on Indian topics thrice a week, in the hope that her earnings would contribute towards the school for girls and widows, a dream she had not yet abandoned. In February, she went on a fortnight's lecture tour to Scotland, where she visited Patrick Geddes. She was pleased to discover that he had put behind him the failure of their Paris collaboration, which he explained was more in the nature of a misunderstanding. He now offered her the position of lecturer in the India section of the Glasgow Exhibition and invited her to spend some time with them in Dundee. Nivedita never failed to acknowledge to Geddes that 'the intellectual impulse' he had given her was 'so real and true'.[20] Geddes' argument was that the family was the central biological unit of human society from which all else developed. Physical geography, market economics and anthropology were all related in a single chord of social life, much as the petals of a flower. In Nivedita's perception this seemed to echo the Eastern philosophy that saw life as an interrelated whole. With enthusiasm, she wrote, 'I am very sure that your own philosophy would grow immensely if you had the chance of study which the East presents.' Her own view had always been that 'soil and race' gave 'the real basis for work, family, etc.' and Geddes' theory further 'illumined' her understanding of India, which he had not yet seen.[21]

Once back in India, Nivedita implored Geddes to visit and write a book on his theory of synthesis, which lay at the root of the Indian ethos. 'The world needs this idea,' she wrote, 'it is not this thing or that thing that is not good—it is the all-together. I have seen this so clearly for India. Not one creed or another—not one race, or idea, or state but all of them.'[22] She even offered to write for him on those lines, suggesting to Mrs Geddes, 'I still feel that if I could only have sat down and written from his dictation for hours and days, I could afterwards have served him well by arranging and altering and preparing a book for the press, and could have at the same time assimilated perhaps his whole idea, myself.'[23]

Nivedita's Edinburgh lectures were marred by the fierce opposition she faced from the Christian missionaries and their damning attacks on India. Her rejoinder was in the form of her publication *Lambs among the Wolves*. Quoting the guidelines given to early Christian missionaries to enter their mission as lambs among wolves, with humility, modesty, austerity and thrift, Nivedita pointed out how missionaries had now lost their compassion in their zeal to condemn and criticize Indian societal practices. Highlighting Shakespeare's unique gift of bringing out the compulsions of the 'other', whether the Jew, the Moor or the hapless prince of Denmark, Nivedita went on to explain how this ability to discern different cultural responses was lost on the missionaries. They sought only to castigate and generalize, using their own cultural norms as the standard for judging what was correct or incorrect. She lamented how the missionaries lost their best energies 'forcing round pegs into square holes, destroying in the process, poetry and mythology and folk custom, as well as rare and beautiful virtues that they are too ignorant to appreciate'.[24]

Emotionally drained by the tense exchanges during her Scottish tour, Nivedita spent a week in the 'Home of Retreat of the Sisters of Bethany' in London on her return from Scotland. Here she enjoyed the routine of devotion and meditation, which reminded her of the Holy Mother's home in Calcutta. Beset by anxiety over the uncertainties of her life, her thoughts often took her back to India, which she missed and her concern for Vivekananda's declining health lingered. Although she repeated in her letters to Yum how she was 'dying to get back' and 'just longing to get there', she could not get herself to write to Vivekananda on his birthday in January, confessing that she had torn up the sheet she wrote.[25] Once more, it was Mrs Bull who came to her rescue. Nivedita had often addressed Mrs Bull in her letters as her 'darling Mother-in-law', privileging her own relationship with Vivekananda, Sara's adopted son.[26] At this time, Sara Bull was planning to go to Norway for the unveiling of a bronze statue of her late husband, violin virtuoso Ole Bull, on 17 May, the day of Norway's freedom. Nivedita decided to accompany her, and stayed for weeks in Lysoen, Bergen—'A green gem set in blue sea'—recovering slowly from what she later described to friends as a nervous breakdown. She was gripped by a desire 'to do, and do and never dream anymore'.[27] Convinced that she could not return to India unless she was strong again, she took pains over her diet, breaking all rules and eating mutton, fish and eggs, sleeping out of doors, bicycling and recuperating fast.[28] She knew that she was on the verge of deviating from the exclusive mission of educating women, which Vivekananda had spelt out for her. 'At times I think of Swami and shudder—for I do not think *he* could understand or approve,' Nivedita wrote.[29]

She was now increasingly attracted by a broader mission—that of helping shape a national opinion in India that would rely on its own strength in asserting against colonial domination. She wished to spread the message of freedom and awareness not only among women but among the entire nation. Thoroughly incensed by the manipulative practices of imperialist control over a helpless people with whom she totally identified, Nivedita felt an urgency to return to India to take stock of the political developments. She was willing to support the early initiatives of the Indian National Congress while engaging in Vivekananda's man-making mission to prepare the youth across the country for any eventuality if intervention with the British government failed. Nivedita, with little faith in the British royalty, was slowly coming to believe that the destiny of the Indian people lay in their seizing the momentum with their own hands once the occasion presented itself. But there were preparations to be made for that, by forming networks across the country, providing physical and ideological training to the youth, making stirring speeches and writing enthusing articles so that public opinion was galvanized. Nivedita was also aware that just as she had successfully been a bridge between the Brahmos and the Hindus, she could also act as a bridge for the growing patriotic opinion by virtue of her access to the British camp. In an impassioned letter,[30] Nivedita explained her new thinking.

I have no interest in anything done by Government for India. To my mind, what a people do not do for themselves is ill done, no matter how brilliantly it seems. I keep on more and more seeing that what I once saw true for an individual is true for Communities. You may employ artists to teach Baby painting and they may touch up her work so that it seems marvellous, but one little scrawl that is really her own is worth thousands of such pictures. And so with countries. What they grow is good: What is done for them is a painted show. *I am doing nothing* FOR India. I am learning and *galvanizing* . . . India was absorbed in study: a gang of robbers came upon her and destroyed her land. The mood is broken. Can the robbers teach her anything? No, she has to turn them out, and go back to where she was before. Something like that, I fancy, is the true programme for India. And so I have nothing to do with Christians or Government agencies, as long as the government is Foreign. That which is Indian for India, I touch the feet of, however stupid and futile . . . Oh! India! India! Who shall undo this awful doing of my nation to you? Who shall atone for *one* of the million bitter insults showered daily on the bravest and keenest, nerved and best of all your sons?

How silly I think it now to do anything *in England* for India I cannot tell you! What utter waste of time! Do you think ravening wolves can be made gentle as babes? Can be made polite and sweet as little girls? That is what work in England for India means . . . People must come to England, people like Swami, Dr Bose, Mr Dutt, and must show in England what India is and can be. They must make friends and disciples and lovers by the millions . . . Oh Yum, in India now, we want, what do we not want? We want the slow-growing formative forces put well to work. Do not think I can be forgetful of the planting of trees, the training of children, the farming of land. But we want also the ringing cry, the passion of the multitude, the *longing* for death. And we cannot do without these . . . All we have to do is to float with the tide, *anywhere* anywhere it may take us . . . My task is to see and to make others see. The rest does itself. The vision is the great crisis.

Nivedita had finally come to realize the absolute nature of British domination. She, who had been denounced by Swamiji in the early months of her stay for still harbouring loyalty to the British flag, was now vituperative in her denunciation of the British colonial system. Perhaps her close association with Jagadish Chandra Bose and her first-hand knowledge of the deep injustice he suffered at the hands of the college authorities had made her bitter. This was the beginning of her obsession with Indian nationalism. She as a foreigner was hardly in a position to berate a colonized people and jolt them out of their apathy like her Swamiji did, or ridicule their outmoded religious practices and superstitious social norms. Instead, she believed that India's rich diversity, which was bewildering to the British, could give momentum to the anti-imperialist struggle. These idealistic and as yet undefined thoughts churned within her as she was poised to take a stand of her own, away from her guru's guidance.

However, there were compelling reasons that made it difficult for Nivedita to take the plunge and return to India immediately. She had now embarked on her writing career in right earnest, encouraged largely by her 'godfather' R.C. Dutt. He had followed her to Norway hoping to snatch some quiet time in which he could complete his own project of writing the economic history of India. Dutt urged her to put into a book her reflections on Indian society, the life of the women and other observations, which had consistently formed part of the lectures she had delivered. This led to Nivedita beginning her *The Web of Indian Life*, one of her best-known works. Dutt insisted she complete her work before she left England, which he could then help getting published and in which there would be money for her school. Nivedita was also inspired by his punctilious discipline, his writing by candlelight into the early hours of the morning during his stay in Norway.[31] She increasingly became convinced that the right moment in her writing career had come. As she wrote to Yum, 'How curious this is—that one may knock and knock at the wrong door—but there is never any answer till one comes to the right. I think of this because years ago I could write as well as I do now—but now I could fill my whole time with work that people would be glad of.'[32]

Still, pressures kept mounting for her return. Sarada Devi wrote to her 'baby daughter' (*khuki*) as she called Nivedita, 'I long for the day and the year when you shall return . . . May He fulfil your desires about the women's home in India, and may the would-be home fulfil its mission in teaching true *dharma* to all.'[33] This letter was written at the behest of Josephine MacLeod who had arrived in Calcutta in January 1901 on the way to Japan, and felt impatient with Sara for advising Nivedita not to return to India before completing her book. But Sara understood Nivedita and her intellectual needs well. She realized how Nivedita's stay in Norway had inspired her to think of a revival of ancient Indian literature by retelling the stories of the Mahabharata in modern idiom. Sara wrote, 'She [Nivedita] hopes to make it the ruling impulse in the new current of national consciousness. This feeling dawned, I believe, on her especially in Norway, where she found the Norse renaissance was brought about by the revival of the Saga literature. Think what the Mahabharata, with the teaching concerning action of the Gita can do for any people!'[34] It was finally left to R.C. Dutt to write to Vivekananda, praising Nivedita's work in England and requesting him to extend her stay to complete her work. Vivekananda was quick to reply,

> I am so glad to learn from a person of your authority of the good work Sister Nivedita is doing in England. I join in earnest prayer with the hopes you entertain of her future services to India by her pen . . . I am under a deep debt of gratitude to you, Sir, for your befriending my child, and hope you will never cease to advise her as to the length of her stay in England and the line of work she ought to undertake.

He also wrote to Nivedita reassuring her that she must stay as long as she thought necessary. To Christine Greenstidel, his disciple in America who was to finally take over the reins of the school in Calcutta, he wrote, 'Margot is doing splendid work in England with Mrs Bull's backing. Things are going on nicely.'[35]

From the time of his return to India late in 1900, Vivekananda's health had steadily deteriorated, with diabetes, general dropsy, breathing problems, failing eyesight in one eye and a growing realization that his days were numbered. But this did not dampen his resolve to complete all his unfinished tasks. Sad to learn that during his absence from the country, his trusted disciple Mr Sevier had passed away, he rushed off to Mayavati soon after his return, to condole with Mrs Sevier, unmindful of the arduous journey. He returned overjoyed with how exquisite the ashram had become, with beautiful roads, extended gardens, fields, and orchards surrounded by large forests. In March, he took a group of relatives, including his mother, on a long promised trip to east Bengal, visiting places of pilgrimage and performing the required rituals. Life in his Math on his return, continued at a slower pace, tending to his pet animals and kitchen gardens. The gastronomical expert that Swamiji was, he wrote to Christine raving about the delectable mangoes of the season, arguably the best fruit in the whole world, and the hilsa fish, swimming up the river, which were far superior to the ones he had tasted in America. Josephine entreated him from Japan to travel there, even arranging a cheque to support his travel. He declined, claiming that his flesh was weak although his spirit was willing.

Vivekananda now set his heart on making amends to win the confidence of all the orthodox people of the villages surrounding Belur Math who had felt alienated by the Ramakrishna Order for their novel ideas, liberal ways of living, their modes of work and non-observance of customs regarding caste and food. He was especially mindful of the calumnies that had been spread about his character for having befriended Western women disciples. While the Swami preached liberal ideas in social matters, he chose to follow the most orthodox norms for celebrating in Belur, in the autumn of 1901, all major religious festivals. Under the supervision of Sarada Devi, the festivities began with Durga Puja, followed by Lakshmi Puja and ending with Kali Puja. Large numbers of the poor were lavishly fed with prasad and special invitations sent to some of the Brahmins and pandits of Belur and Dakshineswar to join in the Puja. He also satisfied a long-term wish of his mother by offering puja at the Kalighat temple following conventional strictures of bathing in Adi Ganga, rolling thrice on the ground before the deity and performing puja before the purifying fire in the presence of his mother. He was agreeably surprised to find that the temple priests at Kalighat, unlike those in Dakshineswar, showed greater tolerance in warmly greeting him and not raising objections for having crossed the seas without doing penance. Slowly word went round among the orthodox members of the Hindu community that the Ramakrishna Order was committed to the prescribed conventions of the Hindu religion.

Deeply satisfied by the 'grand Pujas' held at the Math,[36] Vivekananda now felt tired, his prolonged illness sapping his energy. He had a great craving to collect around him his dearly loved disciples. He welcomed the news that Nivedita accompanied by Mrs Bull would be returning to India in January 1902. He invited Christine to come too and sent a cheque to support her travel, along with an invitation from Mrs Sevier, with whom she could stay for a while in Mayavati. Josephine, accompanied by her Japanese friends, was due to leave Japan for India in December. The Indian National Congress had its session in Calcutta in the winter of 1901 with scores of delegates, including Bal Gangadhar Tilak, visiting the Belur monastery to meet the Swamiji, whom they regarded as a patriot-prophet. Gandhi on his first visit to Calcutta, not wishing to miss the opportunity, went on foot with great enthusiasm to Belur Math only to be disappointed since Swamiji was then recuperating in his Calcutta home.[37]

The arrival of Josephine, Vivekananda's favourite Jo Jo, in Calcutta in January 1902 cheered him up considerably. She was accompanied by Okakura Kakuzo, better known in Japan as Tenshin, who was head of the committee for the Restoration of Old Temples, and one of the founders of the Tokyo School of Art, of the Nippon Bijutsuin (Japan Academy of Fine Arts) and of an art journal of traditional Japanese art. Along with him came Hori, a twenty-five-year-old zealous Buddhist priest from the ancient Japanese shrine, Nara. Charmed by Swamiji, Okakura exclaimed to Josephine, 'Vivekananda is ours. He is an Oriental. He is not yours.'[38] Okakura had arrived to travel in India and to personally invite Swamiji to attend the Congress of Religions that was to be held in Japan. He was also keen to acquire some land near the Mahabodhi Temple in Bodh Gaya, where a rest house could be built for Japanese pilgrims. At his invitation, Swamiji readily agreed to accompany him to Bodh Gaya, since he had already planned to visit Benares for health reasons, which would be on the way. Accordingly, they set out on 27 January.

In the meantime, Nivedita, accompanied by Mrs Bull and R.C. Dutt, left for India by the *S.S Mombasa*, which set sail from Marseilles on 4 January 1902. On their arrival in Madras, they were warmly welcomed in a civic reception organized by Subramania Iyer, Editor of *The Hindu*. Dutt introduced Nivedita as 'a lady who is now one of us, who lives our life, shares our joys and sorrows, partakes of our trials and troubles and labours with us in the cause of our Motherland.'[39] *Amrita Bazar Patrika* in its report commented that Miss Noble was 'one of the most eloquent living English women.'[40] By the beginning of February, Nivedita and Mrs Bull reached Calcutta having taken a train from Madras. After meeting Josephine, who had come down from Benares to receive them, they stayed at the residence of the American Consul General, their old friend. They were greeted by welcoming letters from Vivekananda, who was still in Benares. To his 'daughter' (Nivedita), he wrote as a 'loving father' that he was 'overjoyed' that she had come with 'unimpaired will and recuperated health.' He cautioned her to trust no one but Swami Brahmananda with regard to certain financial arrangements at the Math, about which he had written earlier seeking her help. For her, his advice was:

Do just as the 'Mother' directs. I would help you if I could, but I am only a bundle of rags and with only one eye at that; but you have all my blessings—all—and more if I had. All my powers come unto you—may Mother herself be your hands and mind and if possible along with it infinite peace . . . If there was any truth in Shri Ramakrishna, may He take you into His leading, even as He did me, nay a thousand times more.[41]

As she awaited the return of her 'Father', Nivedita met the future 'father of the nation' and the 'Mahatma', Mohandas Karamchand Gandhi, who visited her at the American Consulate. Taken aback by the splendour of the Chowringhee mansion, Gandhi wondered whether there could be any meaningful conversation between them. He, however, did not fail to express admiration for her love of Hinduism.[42] Gandhi confessed in a note written after her death that he had been unaware that Nivedita was a guest at the American Consulate. Looking back, he cherished with gratitude his meeting with the one who had loved India so well.[43]

Vivekananda returned to Calcutta in early March, relieved that despite his apprehensions, Okakura and his Japanese friend had found no difficulty gaining access to the sanctum sanctorum of the Hindu temples in Benares. He reasoned that it must have been by dint of their being Buddhists, Buddhism being regarded as akin to Hinduism.[44] Meeting her Guru after a gap of sixteen months, Nivedita noted with concern that Vivekananda's health was now deteriorating fast. But he still had dreams that he shared with Nivedita and Mrs Bull, when they visited him in Belur on 22 March, about establishing a Math for women on the banks of the Ganga near Calcutta. It would follow the same structure as the Math for men. The Holy Mother would be its centre of inspiration and spiritual guide. Brahmacharinis and women teachers would be trained there, to work for the regeneration of women in India.

Soon after their arrival in India in February, despite the absence of Vivekananda from Calcutta, Mrs Bull had not delayed a moment in formally reopening the girls' school at Bosepara Lane, Baghbazar on Saraswati Puja. However, in reality, it was only when Christine Greenstidel arrived from America in March to take over the running of the school that it could be steered in a fruitful direction. Nivedita herself acknowledged that Christine was able to contribute to the school with her single-minded dedication which she herself found difficult among her many distractions. Further, Christine could offer total obedience and devotion to Vivekananda with her sweet, docile manner, that Nivedita herself was unable to due to her feisty, argumentative nature. 'Perfect in sweetness and perfect in trustworthiness and so large in her views!' is how Nivedita summed up Christine.[45]

One key reason Nivedita found herself unable to dedicate her energies solely towards Vivekananda's cherished projects was her mounting desire to plunge headlong into India's nationalist politics. She was already familiar with Okakura's manuscript 'Ideals of the East', which Yum had sent to her to edit.[46] The concept that Asia is one, rooted in its traditional inherited culture and while receptive to new cultural thoughts carried by the winds of change, could never be swept off its feet, appealed to her greatly. She had suddenly discovered someone voicing her innermost thoughts. Nivedita believed in the need for the Indian people to know themselves, to discover the wonders of indigenous art and cultural traditions, read anew traditional epics and literature and revisit priceless heritage sites of architecture. To articulate a new vocabulary of pride and confidence that would strengthen the soul and bring victory in the ultimate confrontation with colonial domination, Indians had to desist from borrowing from foreign sources for cultural inspiration. Nivedita felt these thoughts had to be disseminated as an immediate measure so that they could galvanize action against imperialist rule. Enunciating her dream, Nivedita wrote: 'Love of Country—love of Fellows—Pride of birth—Hope for the Future—dauntless passion for INDIA—and there will be such a tide of Art, of Science, of Religion, of Energy as no man can keep back. Instead of dolts— heroes—instead of copyist—original geniuses. All this one could create—all these must be created. Will it be done?'[47] She was in search of an inspiring personality who would serve as a pivotal point around whom such a movement could be launched. In her impulsive rush, Nivedita felt that Okakura would be just such a personality. She gushed to Yum, 'I long to see him [Okakura]—I care nothing for his knowledge—or his prestige—or anything. I want to sound his will—to measure the depth of his soul—to hear from him at what point a people's thirst for Life should cease. I *think*, I trust, I shall have an answer that so far I have failed to get from the successful.'[48]

Okakura returned to Calcutta around the same time as Vivekananda, in early March. From her very first encounter with him, Nivedita felt increasingly convinced that destiny had brought her close to a man whose ideas matched her own. With him, she felt she could take a new turn in her life towards awakening a hapless people. From her idealistic position of trying to mould a people with her mantra of nationalism, she hoped to move in the direction of planned action. Okakura's samurai background, his distinguished family's history of turbulence and bloodshed gave him, in Nivedita's eyes, the right stature of a leader who could inspire the youth to action. With the cry of Kali, bloodshed and death on her lips, she found Okakura no less resolute, having watched as a child the decapitation of his uncle.[49] Okakura's desire to travel around India seemed the right note on which Nivedita could begin networking and getting in touch with secret groups and associations who were restive and waiting for meaningful action against the foreign government. She introduced Okakura to the key leaders of the day, including Rabindranath Tagore, C.R. Das and Bipin Pal, as well as key militant leaders such as Pramatha Mitra of the Anushilan group, who were impressed with Okakura's proposed Asiatic Federation.

Surendranath Tagore recounted his first meeting with Okakura at a party hosted by Mrs Bull. Clad in a black silk kimono, with straw sandals, the elegant figure sported in his hand a bamboo-and-paper fan as he smoked endlessly. Considering Suren to be a true nationalist, Nivedita was keen that he should have an exclusive meeting with Okakura and whisked away the two from the party to a small anteroom where Okakura offered him a cigarette and posed the question: What are your dreams for your country? Seeing his hesitation, Okakura remarked how pained he was to see despondency in the youth. It then struck Suren how Nivedita wanted Okakura to rouse and inspire the youth.[50] She now dreamt of a major role for Suren to befriend Okakura and accompany him on his travels around the country. Okakura had already travelled to places of Buddhist interest with Josephine after his visit to Bodh Gaya and Benares with Vivekananda. He also accompanied Oda, the newly arrived emissary from Japan, to Bodh Gaya again to pursue the matter of acquiring land around the shrine. Now with Surendranath, elaborate plans were drawn up of visiting western and northern India. There is also a reference in Nivedita's letters to plans to visit Nepal for which passport clearance was awaited. However, there is not enough evidence to prove if Okakura's travel interests were solely guided by the networking objectives with secret societies working towards India's incipient freedom, as Nivedita wished. He was equally curious to visit India's historical and archaeological heritage as a keen student of antiquity.

Vivekananda knew well how his 'child', Nivedita, could be swayed on impulse and could forcefully persuade others to her point of view. Her close interaction with Okakura for the next seven weeks, since they were both staying at the American Consulate on Chowringhee in Calcutta, did not go unnoticed by him. Although he had welcomed Okakura for his cultural commitment to the Arts, he was sceptical about how as a foreigner he could ever acquire any definitive role in India's freedom struggle. Vivekananda had a fundamental difference with Nivedita's ideas.[51] The need of the hour for Vivekananda was 'man-making', preparing the ground for freedom, with education and creating awareness for social development, removal of poverty and the many obstacles to progress. Freedom for him would be premature without the ground being properly prepared for self-rule. Vivekananda felt that Nivedita's new programme of getting involved in political matters might jeopardize his life's work at the Ramakrishna Mission. He asked Nivedita to choose between one and the other as she was already under police surveillance.[52] Nivedita had anticipated her guru's displeasure if she chose a different path, but her mind was made up.

Vivekananda could also sense the mutual attraction between Nivedita and Okakura and feared that temptations might arise in their interpersonal relationship. When he had sounded Okakura about his commitment to brahmacharya in the service of country and people, Okakura's answer had been that he was not ready yet.[53] Chastity became one subject on which Vivekananda dwelt at length with Sara Bull when she called on him at the Math in April. He spoke of the value of chastity in building the disciplined character of Indians, in particular to rebuild the great Indian nation he envisioned. The power and vision accrued from his own life of chastity stood as an example to the younger generations. But he also struck a note of caution when he wrote in what was to be his last letter to her, on 18 June 1902,

> In my opinion a race must first cultivate the great respect for Motherhood, through the sanctification and inviolability of marriage, before it can attain to the ideal of perfect chastity . . . So until there is developed in Japan a great and sacred ideal about marriage (apart from mutual attraction and love) I do not see how there can be great monks and nuns.[54]

For Nivedita, however, the die was cast. She accepted Okakura as 'the goodest of your good gifts'[55] from Josephine, who had discovered him in Japan and invited him to India. She persuaded Yum to finance his travels and even provide additional funds he needed for occasional bribes.[56] Vivekananda expressed his unhappiness to Josephine when they met for the last time in April. There was finality in his announcement that he would not live to see his fortieth birthday. He explained, 'The shadow of a big tree will not let the smaller trees grow up. I must go to make room.'[57] Josephine was deeply pained and distressed enough to contemplate leaving, 'cutting the connection forever'.[58] It was Nivedita who comforted her and asked not to take Vivekananda's reprimands to heart since 'his ups and downs are the tides of receding illness on the shores of nerves'.[59]

In the meantime, news of her daughter's surgery made Sara decide to leave immediately, to be at hand for Olea's recuperation. Josephine, too, decided to join Sara and left for Bombay directly from Mayavati, where she had been visiting Mrs Sevier. On 20 April, they both set sail for England.

In April, Okakura left with Suren on their extensive travels. Nivedita stayed on for a while in the Consulate in the company of Christine and Bet, her old nurse from England, who had decided to join her. Describing 'the sweetest parting ceremony' they had, Nivedita spoke of the drop of brandy she and Christine had in their mugs, since 'the parting cup must be of wine'. After dinner, each sang—Oda with a lovely chant of prayer; Hori with a Japanese *fugiwara* song that sounded like a Gregorian chant; Christine, a German parting song; the Chieftain (one of many code names used by Nivedita to refer to Okakura) a grand hurly burly of demons and dragons; while she ended with a salutation to Shiva Guru and Hari Om.

Alone in the apartment the day after the departure of Okakura, Nivedita was lost in thought. The last six weeks in the company of the Banner-Chief (another name for Okakura) had deeply moved her. Acknowledging that 'it is a great voice that passed out of my life last night' she realized how 'the kinship to every longing of my own soul has been growing on me of late'. She felt 'alone and yet not alone, for another's heart and brain and eyes have been at my service for six weeks and my vision is not my own now it includes that also'.[60] Trusting Okakura, Nivedita accepted the wisdom of his judgement to keep Swami in the dark about many of their plans. She agreed with Bet's observation that Okakura's fearlessness matched her own and was convinced that he was poised to take 'a leap in the dark'.[61]

The heat of the summer made it imperative to seek comfort in the cool environs of Mayavati Ashrama. On 5 May, a large group comprising Nivedita, Christine, Bet and Sadananda, accompanied by Okakura and Suren, who had returned, left for the hills.

However, this trip did not prove to be very rewarding for Nivedita. In her commitment to help Swarupananda in Mayavati with the publications of *Prabuddha Bharata*, Nivedita was left with little time for her own writings. Also, Swarupananda's control over her writing left her fuming. She complained, 'I cannot spend my time writing for the PB if his high and mightiness is to sit on what I do and pronounce it impossible. You see, he does not know how to *give* Freedom.'[62]

Additionally, Okakura's behaviour had been erratic. He decided to leave suddenly and was apparently proving to be 'an incongruous element' with the ashram. Nivedita felt that his departure resulted in 'unspoken relief on both sides'.[63] The news reached Swami, who, without mincing words, wrote to Christine on 27 May, 'So the place did not suit Mr Okakura; why? Was it not sublime enough for him? Or Japanese do not like sublimity at all? They only like beauty. How is Margot? Is she still there? Or gone away with Mr Okakura?'[64] Nivedita had of course stayed on in Mayavati till the end of June, coming away with a feeling that her visit had been 'a waste of time, as far as work went'.

Nivedita was confused and in despair as her love for Swami and now for Nigu (another name used for Okakura in her correspondence to Yum) tore her in different directions. Trying to explain her dilemma, she wrote that he (Swamiji) was so ill that even at the cost of being insincere or inconsistent she had to be 'soothing' to him. She had to guard him from any knowledge of her friendship with Okakura, which was sacred to her, 'lest He destroy it'. Indeed, she thought it would be better if Swamiji were not in India so he could be spared such eventualities. About Okakura ('The Other'), she felt in despair that he should perhaps 'go home'. She could continue to act as a translator or editor for him should he so desire. Nivedita was now convinced about the wisdom of her Master's logic that the 'best intimacy with everyone is to become wholly impersonal, to give every thought and every moment to the task in hand'.[65] She obviously felt vulnerable in the company of Okakura, to whom she was very attracted, and found it difficult to believe that he could remain totally detached. In her lament to her confidante Yum, Nivedita wrote: 'Oh, Oh, Oh, if men could but exist who were one great breath of work! This dear sweet Rishi-soul [Okakura] is utterly inadequate—and the one person who is adequate [Swami] is obnoxious to every other man with whom I am associated.' She wondered whether like her, Okakura would be able to hold on to work 'without any association or even personal friendship. Is he? Will he? Why should he?' she asked rhetorically.[66] Ultimately, Nivedita conceded, 'I feel that if Nigu had been a woman or a child, I could have had with him the most exquisite friendship. As he is a man, I do not feel that I could dare, or perhaps rather *ought* to dare, to indulge this possibility so completely. It is really a common mind and interest that produces the bond between Our Work, but you know what Hindu society is!'[67] She was always conscious that her every action was subject to the censoring gaze of monks and others in the conservative Hindu community.

On her return from Mayavati, Nivedita settled into the house that had been secured for her at 17, Bosepara Lane, adjacent to the school. Christine, who had been sent to Mayavati to get strength and stamina before she undertook her work in Calcutta, was now asked by Vivekananda to join Nivedita in the school. On 28 June, as Nivedita was getting ready to go to Belur to meet Swami, she was pleasantly surprised to receive his gift of a large deerskin prayer mat and hear that he himself would be coming since he had some business to attend to in the city. Arriving early in the morning, he went through the whole house, examining with interest every detail, including the learning tools that Nivedita had brought with her, such as some dancing Lucknow dolls, a microscope, a magic lantern and a camera. He asked her to visit him at the Math the next day with the microscope. When Nivedita shared with him her dreams of starting a university for the education of Indian women rather than working in the school, Swami did not disagree, since he was now in the mood of withdrawal, giving only his blessings.

The 29th of June turned out to be one of the last days that Nivedita was to spend meaningfully with Swami, and she alluded to it with great nostalgia in many of her letters. Setting off early and reaching Belur Math by eight thirty in the morning, she stayed on till five and had the opportunity of sharing precious and candid moments with her Swami. She had the satisfaction of obtaining his understanding and receiving his blessings for the course of action she was about to take. Nigu (Okakura) figured in their talks and Nivedita was immensely relieved to find that Swami held no bitterness. On the contrary, he said 'he *loved* that boy'. To Nivedita '*that* was the blessing'.[68] He also revised his opinion about homes for widows and orphans in India, saying it would be folly 'doing more harm than good. Missionaries did it—but they bought them and frightened them. Behind them were money and the sword'. At this, Nivedita interjected saying that was why she strongly felt that the pressing issue was freedom and only '*then* all questions of Education'. Swami replied, 'Well Well Margot! Perhaps you're right. Only I feel that I am drawing near to death—I cannot bend my mind to these worldly things now!'[69] Nivedita also made many 'tender reproaches' to her Swami and he admitted how sorry he was. She did not fail to point out, for instance, how 'wrongly' he had acted in complaining about her before Sadananda while they were in Mayavati. Swami's answer was that Sadananda, too, had been over protective and jealous about her since 'he loves you Margot and wants to follow you about like a dog'.[70] Addressing Nivedita on that day as 'our little Margot', he shared his deep sense of relief about the successful settlement of the lawsuit about his family property, which had been hanging over him for three years. He felt he could now leave with everything in order. By the evening, he felt tired and gave Nivedita a 'beautiful blessing', holding her head and twice blessing her in a 'caressing way'.[71] Nivedita pleaded with him not to misjudge her and, even when he doubted and disapproved, never to make up his mind apart from her. Vivekananda mentioned that a great tapasya[72] was coming over him and death drawing near. At these words, the house gecko cried out.[73]

On 2 July, Nivedita was to return again, staying for the morning meal consisting of boiled seeds of jackfruit, boiled potatoes, plain rice and ice-cold milk, which Vivekananda insisted on serving himself, fanning her all the time and at the end of the meal pouring water over her hands and drying them with a towel. 'It is I who should do these things for you, Swamiji! Not you for me!' Nivedita protested. Startling in its solemnity was Vivekananda's reply: 'Jesus washed the feet of his disciples!' Reflecting on the incident, Nivedita remembered how it was on the tip of her tongue to say that it had been the last occasion for Jesus. Sadly, she realized that for him, too, the last time had come.[74] On the morning of 5 July, Nivedita received a cryptic note from Belur Math: 'The end has come. Swamiji has slept last night never to rise again.' With a deep sense of thanksgiving, she wrote, 'With the laurels green,—with all things in order—with the shield undimmed—he went.'[75] He went out—as one drops a loose garment. Without a struggle. "Conqueror of Death". But he has NOT left us.'[76]

Recounting Vivekananda's last moments on the day he died, Nivedita wrote that he had sent a message to Calcutta that he had never felt better.

He was at the Chapel till noon. Then he gave a Sanskrit lesson to the boys for three hours, and talked to many people with SUCH sweetness all the afternoon. At half-past four, his message reached Calcutta, he drank a cup of hot milk and water and set out on a two miles walk—coming home, he sent everyone away, that he might meditate alone—the evening meditation at sunset. And strange to say—quite contrary to our usual custom, he sat through that meditation facing the north-west. After an hour or so, he turned round and lay down, calling a boy to massage and fan him. Suddenly there was a trembling—a crying as if in sleep, a heavy breath, then a long pause—another breath, and that was all. Our beloved Master was gone from us forever. Life's evensong was over, Earth's silence and Freedom's dawn was come.[77]

Nivedita's prayer was that he might be lost in 'Existence-Knowledge-Bliss', which he had so often spoken about, and freed from the memory of the torture of life.

In a detailed enumeration of certain inexplicable experiences she had on the day of Swamiji's cremation, Nivedita wrote to the inconsolable Josephine. Seeing the cloth that Swamiji had worn on the last day that she saw him, Nivedita asked Swami Saradananda whether it was to be burnt too. Although it was offered to her immediately, she hesitated, since she neither had the scissors to snip off a portion of the cloth nor was it seemly to do so. Later, at six in the evening, the cremation took place under the banyan tree at a spot already decided by Swamiji. Nivedita felt 'as if I were twitched by the sleeve. I looked down and there, safe out of all that burning and blackness, there blew to my feet the very two or three inches, I had desired out of the border of the cloth. I took it as a Letter from him to you, beyond the grave . . . When I told Girish Babu [Girish Ghosh], he said quietly, "I have heard many stories like that!" To him it was very natural—for Swami—our Swami—is *not* dead'.[78] Nivedita posted this piece of cloth and the incense burner, which was on Swami's bed, to Josephine to be kept as precious mementos.

In the days following Swamiji's passing, the Math sank into deep mourning. Nivedita felt the time had come for a parting of ways. She admitted that she did not feel the same sense of desolation as she had two years ago in Brittany when her Master had snapped the closeness of their ties.[79] The monks were candid in their disapproval of Okakura and his methods, and felt he would lead to 'utter ruin'. Nivedita, on the other hand, was not willing to let go of Nigu and the path of aggressive nationalism, which had opened up new vistas for her.[80] In the meantime, to the great alarm of the monks, newspapers announced that Nivedita had become the leader of the Order of Ramakrishna on Vivekananda's death. She rushed to make public denials. In a letter to the editor of *Statesman*, she clarified that as a brahmacharini or novice, and not a sannyasini or fully professed religious leader, without any pretensions to Sanskrit learning, she would happily be absolved of any duties to the Order, pursuing instead her own social, literary and educational work, entirely outside their supervision. She added, 'To my own mind, no mistake could be more deplorable than that which assumes that the Hindu people require European leaders for their religious life. The very contrary is the case.'[81]

Swamiji had clarified that any political association might imperil the work that he stood for. The monks felt therefore that she ought to respect his judgement. Nivedita, however, was quite decided that 'I *cannot* do differently from this. I have become the idea and could die more easily than submit!'[82] On 18 July, she wrote a formal letter to Swami Brahmananda, offering to dissociate from the Ramakrishna Order and be allowed complete freedom to pursue her own goals. She continued to believe that Swami Brahmananda had nevertheless not 'taken his heart away from me'.[83]

Nivedita felt the moment had come for her to strike out on her own. She realized that the education of a few girls could hardly serve the larger purpose of securing the freedom of an enslaved people. She asked, 'Is it not rather by taking the *national* consciousness of the women, like that of the men, and getting it towards greater problems and responsibilities that one can help? I think my task is to awake a nation, not to influence a few women.' Okakura's message had merely reinforced her own beliefs and given 'edge to her sword'.

Nivedita realized at the same time 'the hopelessness of the task' and her 'own utter inadequacy'. She reasoned that there was perhaps a divine design to why her Master had been withdrawn just then. Did he not mention repeatedly that when a great man has prepared his workers, he must go to another place, for he cannot make them free in his own presence?[84] Uncertain of whether Mrs Bull would approve of her plans, she decided to keep Josephine informed but requested her to destroy her letter.[85]

To herself, she admitted that she scarcely now felt a touch of sorrow. Her Master's departure from the world had come as his great Victory—'so pure—so flawless'.[86] She began considering the suggestions that were made to write the life of her Master. Any such account, she decided, would have to be 'so simple, so great— so full of the throb of India—and yet so unmistakably the story of an Avatar'.[87] She asked Yum for her old letters, which contained scenes and words of Swamiji, which would help her in her task.[88] It was in 1906 that she began writing serially for *Prabuddha Bharata* her much acclaimed book *The Master as I Saw Him*.

The stress of the previous weeks took a toll on Nivedita's health and she fell ill in August. The monks, Brahmananda and Saradananda, helped her regain her strength on a diet of chicken and eggs. Nivedita was relieved when Okakura returned from his wanderings and they found time to meditate together in the chapel. Nivedita ascribed his sudden return and also the news that he had successfully acquired the land in Bodh Gaya to Swamiji's blessings. She still felt that Vivekananda held control over her life. 'I feel that it was Swami who brought him back Last Friday—and will bring him again when He wants me to see him. Isn't that right?' she asked Yum.[89] Despite periodic misunderstandings she had with Okakura and the fear that they may not even meet again, Nivedita rallied round soon enough to pin her hopes on his providing inspiration to the youth in underground activities. Suren Tagore remained his close supporter and collaborator in his travels. Although in her letters, which she knew were being surveilled, Nivedita did not elaborate on the exact nature of their work, she did mention her satisfaction with comments such as 'he is away, doing work that only he can do'.[90] Elsewhere she praised him saying, 'Nigu is indeed a great genius. He and Suren have seen India and returned. What have they not done? Everything. We can see our way now.'[91]

Perhaps Okakura's main contribution to Nivedita's plans was to have prepared the ground for her to travel with her lectures, locating places she might visit, firming up houses where she could stay and networking with people she might meet in her larger design of an inclusive nationalism. Nivedita reported that the young boys with whom she had a strong rapport since the days of the plague when they worked together, worshipped him. They regarded him as a *khalki* avatar and often referred to him as Krishna. Sadananda, always by Nivedita's side, shared her admiration and paid him daily obeisance.[92] In Calcutta, Okakura was in close touch with Sarola Devi, who was actively engaged in training the youth in martial arts and preparing them for militancy. Although Nivedita was involved in this group initially, differences arose between them, with her asking the young men in her group to stay away. She was to write how totally disillusioned she was about the whole Ballygunge connection with Sarola, who, despite all her Brahmo misgivings of the past, now preached Kali worship, acting as 'vice regent of the Mother' and trying to organize all into her 'army'.[93] Sarola wrote to Nivedita requesting her to return her letters to Vivekananda, saying how she was not the 'uninformed inexperienced girl' of three years ago when asked to join Vivekananda's movement. Now she was 'matured, experienced . . . able to face anything and anybody in the world'. Accusing Nivedita of having 'irritating indications of superior European airs and imperiousness' she threw down a challenge before her.[94] Nivedita grew increasingly worried about the consequences of their reaching out to various groups training in martial arts, reading revolutionary literature and biding time by remaining underground until they could surface for some definite action. She feared for Okakura's safety and wished he were safely back home.[95] Already, on his instructions, she had torn up all of Josephine's letters to him.[96]

Okakura's book *Ideals of the East*, revised and edited by Nivedita, was produced in 1903 by the reputed publisher John Murray in London. In her introduction, she described Okakura as the foremost living authority on oriental archaeology, opposed to the pseudo-Europeanizing tendency that was so fashionable then in the East. Okakura saw Asia not as geographical fragments but as a united living organism. His book famously began with: 'Asia is one: the Himalayas divide, only to accentuate two mighty civilizations, Chinese with its Communism of Confucius and India with its individualism of the Vedas'. His vision was of an Arab chivalry, Persian poetry, Chinese ethics and Indian thought, all speaking of an ancient Asiatic peace, in which grew up a common life with Asiatic races forming a single mighty web. In contrast, the great mass of Western thought seemed 'perplexing' with the 'scorching drought of modern vulgarity parching the throat of life and art'. These were the very thoughts that Nivedita cherished, of finding a web of cultural continuity among the far-flung regions constituting India.

In July 1902, Nivedita worked on revising Okakura's second book, a shorter work called *Awakening of the East*, which was even more vocal in criticizing the imperialist West for exploiting a subjugated people. It spoke of the vast suffering endured by a people where 'the Oriental has become a synonym for the effeminate, the native is an epithet for the slave'. The glory of Europe had been achieved through the 'humiliation of Asia', with industrial conquest and moral subjugation, where ancestral ideals, family institutions, ethics and religions had faded away in contact with the so-called culture of the West. At the end of the book, there were two invocations, which echoed Nivedita's voice and might have been added by her. One was to the Sword and began with 'Om to the Steel of honour! Om to the Strong! Om to the Invincible! India worships thee in Kali-dread, mother of relentless mercy; Japan worships thee in Fudo—grand vision of unflinching pity.' The second invocation was an overt call to arms: 'The hour is coming when the mailed hand of revolt shall strike behind the thundercloud of Religion in the blaze of national fervour.'[97] Nivedita gradually came to realize the folly of sending this book for publication, for she wrote, 'Nigu's second book will be enough to send us all to prison. He is a reckless child. He sees this now too.'[98] Eventually *The Awakening* was published in 1938 long after Okakura's death, after being discovered by his grandson among his papers. Released just before the Second World War, the book proved inspirational to Japanese soldiers who were to militarily engage the Allies on the Asian mainland.

Ill health and nervous exhaustion now made Okakura turn to Nivedita for recovery. For the first time, she felt guilty at having perhaps pushed him too hard and thrust upon him a responsibility that he was not prepared for. The concern of Sadananda coupled with her own anxiety made her decide to move him into her own house as quietly as possible, so that his presence remained unnoticed. Arranging for him to lie on a long basket sofa in the sitting room, they took turns to nurse him back to health providing soups and massage, rest and comfort so that he would be fit to take the sea voyage back to Japan in October. Diagnosed by a doctor with malaria and neuralgia of the head, Nivedita spent long hours into the night bathing his head, fanning and massaging him. It was in such moments of gentle care that Okakura, lying ill, confided that for the first time he felt as if he was at 'home' and 'whole fields of love, of which he had been unaware' had opened out to him. While narrating these events to Josephine, Nivedita mentioned that

she had, however, maintained a discreet silence with Mrs Bull.[99]
Nivedita did not know how to respond to Okakura's protestations
of love. His message made her look at life afresh. Recognizing the
'hunger out of which such words were spoken,' Nivedita felt that she
began 'to understand wealth and desire for the first time in my life
and yet I dare not say it was irreligion either' for in Nigu's splendid
message '*this* was the highest spirituality—to say otherwise was
to him a deadly crime. I understand now Swami's three rooms in
European style—His food—and many other things. I myself seem
utterly detached from austerities.' Laying bare her soul, Nivedita
engaged Josephine in a frank discussion on the definition of pure
and impure.

> The union of the sexes is not impure—how could it be? It is
> forgetting that all-is-One that constitutes impurity . . . In the
> end we see that pure and impure are two expressions of the
> Kindergarten, by which we rise to the other and find Freedom
> even from this subtlest and strongest of temptations. We don't
> *want* the union, etc. not because it is impure but because it is a
> new load to carry—it binds into a single form that which knew
> itself as light and air. But it is not in itself any more impure than
> seeing and hearing and tasting. A man is neither more nor less
> pure by having a wife—but he is *bound* by it. He has used more
> of his force for the Earth so to speak, and has less for the Sky. As
> for Sri Ramakrishna's wife—that was at least as perfect celibacy
> as Swami's.[100]

Nivedita explained that Nigu had been 'so lovely—talking things
out and understanding and explaining my own ideas to me'.[101]
But she was on the whole relieved that Okakura had to leave in
October, as she was increasingly eager to have him away. Nor did
she desire to visit Japan as had been discussed earlier, preferring to
send instead a worthy disciple like Saradananda.

An alarmed Josephine wrote back to Nivedita about a possible 'physical awakening', which had made her enter people's bedrooms to give massages.[102] She reminded her of Swamiji's stern strictures on the subject. Nivedita's response was swift. Feeling 'absurdly shocked and hurt,' she proceeded to explain that the groans of an ill Nigu woke her up and she got dressed to come to his side. She recalled mentioning to Swami in the context of a similar discussion how careful she had always been, inventing safeguards to protect herself. Indeed she felt confident that her own standards were 'far stricter and impose far more pain than even His', However, if at all she had erred it was because of a 'failure of judgment, and never of temptation'. She felt enriched by each experience, whether of 'stern negation' or 'sweetness and indulgence', since it made her see 'things from a larger and truer point of view' and ended in a 'more complete revelation of the ideal to others'. Whereas a few years ago she had a childlike innocence, she now felt endowed with a mother's compassion and affection. Realizing that her almost daily letters to Yum had helped unfold 'the novel' of her life,[103] she declared that she was 'thankful for every look that has been granted me into the abyss of life'.[104] Looking back, she reaffirmed that the brahmacharya, which her Master had given her to guard until the end of life, had remained unbroken, though thoughts of human intimacy and affection had sometimes crossed her mind, for which she felt no guilt as she had 'done right—and all is well'.[105] Nivedita reminded Josephine of the 'torture and confusion of mind' that both of them had gone through because 'Swamiji was a *man*, and could see women only from the outside . . . He lived as if women were minds, *not* bodies'.[106]

Nivedita had emerged a mature person after her encounter with Okakura. Her frank analysis of the man-woman relationship showed that she did not fight shy of discussing the physical attraction that must exist. Unlike her guru, who recoiled from the issue, Nivedita went on to explain that celibacy, which she had embraced, ensured freedom to devote oneself to spiritual matters which householders would find difficult as they were bound to earthly requirements. In long discussions with Okakura, which she alludes to in her *Letters*, she came to acknowledge that by embracing total austerity many pleasures of life would be denied. Although her Swami had enjoyed good food and good living, he had been equally happy when deprived of these. This ability to live with extremes tested one's self control and was exceptional. However, as she had pledged herself to a brahmachari's life, she was going to respect her choice. Contrary to some opinions that she was 'spurned in love', it was her immense strength of character that made her distance herself from Okakura; she consciously decided not to meet him again even when she travelled to America later.[107]

As 'the spell of dear Nigu' slowly lifted,[108] Nivedita was reminded that her Swami had once remarked that it was in her impulsive nature to be seized by an issue at a time, to which she gave her entire attention, until it was replaced by another. On that fateful Sunday before his death, he had exclaimed: 'Well, Margot, I see. This is the period of your such and such a conviction! You have had your Brahmo conviction and your Tagore conviction and now you have these convictions. And they will pass as the others did.'[109] And so it did. She realized that 'Nigu must be left free, to do what he can. I shall always feel a love and tenderness for him, which cannot change. But I think India is going to need no helping.'[110]

Nivedita's horizon had now expanded. She was at last free to expand on her dream of nationalism independent of the guidance of Okakura or the restraint of her guru. She was released from the Ramakrishna Order and able to travel within India, establishing networks, meeting potential leaders, encouraging the youth to train themselves physically in anticipation of a movement, which seemed inevitable, and to read inspiring writings of revolutionary leaders.

In her lecture tours preaching nationalism and Vivekananda's national ideas, Sadananda accompanied her. She felt grateful that he served not only as a bodyguard but had also given her freedom, sharing her love for Nigu and calling him leader.[111] On 26 September, she spoke on Vivekananda at Bombay's Gaiety Theatre, to a thousand-strong audience, receiving a rousing reception. Succeeding days saw her giving lectures on 'The Unity of Asia', 'Hindu Mind in Modern Science', 'Indian Womanhood', 'Indian Woman as she strikes an English Woman' and 'How and Why I adopted the Hindu Religion'. Lectures followed in Nagpur, Wardha and Amraoti. At a prize distribution ceremony in Morris College, Nagpur, following a friendly cricket match, Nivedita's speech caused consternation among students, whom she berated for playing foreign games to the neglect of their own national games. Since it was the time of Dussehra festivities, she implored the students to celebrate the next day with a martial demonstration of swordplay and wrestling. Addressing the students who had been inspired to oblige her request, Nivedita mentioned that graduates were being churned out of universities but many of them were physical wrecks incapable of protecting themselves or their mothers and sisters. There was a need for robust and patriotic men who should feel a disgust at having to serve the authoritarian rule of an alien government.[112]

On 20 October, Nivedita reached Baroda, giving lectures for three successive days and meeting the Gaekwad of Baroda. Her interaction with Aurobindo Ghosh, then in the employ of the Gaekwad, marked the start of an important association with far-reaching implications in the revolutionary movement. After visiting the Ellora caves, Nivedita returned to Calcutta. Again, in December she set out for Madras, from where she began her lectures in south India. On the way, Nivedita halted in Bhubaneswar, on the outskirts of which, at Khandagiri she decided to observe Christmas Eve.

Sitting at the foot of the Khandagiri hills below 'whispering trees', behind the 'solitary caves' and beside a log fire, Nivedita read passage after passage from St Luke's Gospel about the Wise Men of the East, the appearance of angels to the Shepherds in the fields and the Divine Incarnation that appeared to the disciples, from Peter to Mary Magdalen, after he had left, as a 'gleam here and there.' Sadananda and his nephew, brahmachari Amulya, later Swami Sankarananda, staff in hand and swathed in blankets, looked like shepherds who heard her intently. To all of them came the realization that the Resurrection was not a 'vulgar miracle' but a palpable Presence that was revealed not only to those who were the most spiritual but also to the most determined doubter. The days following death presaged a closeness with the 'risen life' which had 'an ethereal intimacy' more tender and sacred, and yet more elusive than perhaps what existed during the lifetime. Ever conscious of the presence of her guru, Vivekananda, who had at once been to her a King, a Master and a Father, Nivedita asked, 'Do I not remember that Swamiji saw 'a luminous ghost' in the week of Sri Ramakrishna's death? Do I not know how my own sleeve was plucked and a message sent through me, beside His burning pyre? Do I not know the truth of Resurrection?' In the cold December evening as Nivedita and the two monks sat huddled facing the hills, there was a comprehension that the 'very mythology of the Christian Faith becomes credible once more, re-fixed, reinstated when illuminated by the Wisdom, the Character and the daily life of this Eastern land'.[113]

4

Nationalism

Nivedita was now driven by her mission of generating awareness among Indians about the underlying oneness in their civilizational experience, despite external disparities. It was a misconception to think that the British, with English education, introduction of cheap postage and building of a strong infrastructure of roads and railways, had created India. The idea of India was to be propagated by homegrown efforts and not foreign examples. In her expressive words, Nivedita wrote, 'It is not by imitation of foreigners, but by renewed effort to self-expression—in other words, by movements of national revival—that nations rise. History is *ashirbad*, the promise that the nationality makes to each one of its children . . . History is the warp upon which is to be woven the woof of Nationality. Only in the mirror of her own past can India see her soul reflected and only in such vision can she recognize herself.'[1]

The lessons of Pestalozzi and Froebel in the field of education, which had formed a deep impression on Nivedita in her early days, could be applied to all areas of development. In this, she had found support for Vivekananda's views of national development along indigenous lines and now felt a great urge to articulate and elaborate on this ideal. 'The whole task now is to give the word "Nationality" to India—in all its breadth and meaning,' she explained.

India must be observed by this great conception. Hindu and Mohammedan must become one in it with a passionate admiration of each other. It means new views of history, of custom, and it means the assimilation of the whole Ramakrishna-Vivekananda idea in Religion—the synthesis of all religious ideas. It means a final understanding of the fact that the political process and the economic disaster are only side-issues, that the one essential fact is realisation of her own Nationality by the Nation.[2]

These thoughts, with which she found herself 'bubbling over'[3], found powerful expression in her significant book *The Web of Indian Life*. Her great satisfaction lay in the realization that 'it is not my book at all, but Swamiji's, and my only hope about it is that I may have said the things He would have liked said'.[4]

Ever since her arrival in India in 1898, Nivedita had slowly come to identify with the inner cry of its people. Her stay in a conservative Bengali locality, interaction with residents during plague, advocacy of education to girls and women, extended travels around the country, some with Swamiji and some in the course of her lectures, had given her a rare insight into the vastness of India and its cultural differences. But she could also see from the distanced, broader perspective of a Westerner the fundamental pattern of unity that lay below the surface of diversity. With a compassionate mind, she sought not to critique but to understand the societal and religious structure that bound the country. At the same time, she drew on her own knowledge and experiences of Western society to make relevant analogies placing her observations in context. Nivedita acknowledged that Prof. Geddes had taught her to understand Europe and indirectly given her a method by which she could also read her Indian experiences. In the six-word sequence of Place-Work-Family-Ideals-Thoughts-Action used by Geddes in his social analysis resulting in a synthesis of knowledge, Nivedita detected 'enough dynamite to make a nation'.[5]

Geddes had recognized Nivedita's keen vision and sympathetic and spiritual insight. Far beyond the simple underlying canvas of its material conditions, Nivedita could discern India's rich and varied embroidery.[6] According to her, there was a fundamental unity, which through centuries had been forged on folklore, mythologies, music and shared history, but had remained unnoticed and dormant. It was only by invoking this spirit of national unity that the exploitative British rule could be challenged and vanquished.

As Nivedita put it, 'The idea of Nationality will be the Sword of India . . . She will have to be ready and willing to fight.'[7] Vivekananda had stressed on 'man-making', character building and physical training, which would create an inner strength, shaking off the diffidence and inertia of centuries. Nivedita added to this her mantra of nation-making, which would set a direction and course to an awakened people in their ultimate movement towards freedom.

In his introduction to *The Web of Indian Life*, Rabindranath Tagore drew attention to the customary contempt and disparaging remarks of Western commentators on India, which had sapped the national morale. This 'vast accumulation of calumny against India' was the result of a superficial knowledge and a limited acquaintance with Indian languages. Nivedita, on the other hand 'had won her access to the inmost heart of our society by her supreme gift of sympathy. She did not come to us with the impertinent curiosity of a visitor nor did she elevate herself on a special high perch with the idea that a bird's eye view is truer than the human view because of its superior aloofness. She lived our life and came to know us by becoming one of ourselves. She became so intimately familiar with our people that she had the rare opportunity of observing us unawares'.[8] The Poet could recognize the sensitive understanding of Nivedita and commented,

The mental sense, by the help of which we feel the spirit of a people,
is like the sense of sight, or of touch—it is a natural gift . . . those

who have no ear for music, hear sounds, but not the song . . . And
Sister Nivedita has uttered the vital truths about Indian life.[9]

Nivedita's book begins with a chapter called 'The Setting of the
Warp', an account of her unique experiences of settling in a home in
Calcutta. She gradually understood life in novel surroundings that
moved in a rhythm different from what she had known. On the one
hand 'it was a world in which men in loin-cloths seated on door-
sills in dusty lanes, said things about Shakespeare and Shelley that
some of us would go far to hear'.[10] On the other, it was steeped
in tradition, with gongs and bells going off in 'family chapels' at
sunset announcing 'Evensong'. Eating and bathing, both functional
occupations in the West, assumed great sacramental significance
and were observed with discipline and rigour. 'It is a love with which
the day's life throbs. Without praying, no eating! Without bathing,
no praying!'[11] With a similar unchanging routine came the twelve
or thirteen great religious festivals or pujas where the festive spirit
and attendant music were reminiscent of Christmas decor with holly
and mistletoe and carol-singing. But the image of the deity so dearly
worshipped for the stipulated period, and to be immersed soon after,
led Nivedita to realize that the image after all was in itself merely 'a
suggestion offered to devout thought and feeling'[12] as was the altar
piece and the stained glass window in an Anglican church.

Perhaps what intrigued Nivedita most was the rhythm in an
Indian household, which was bound by protocol, protection a
loyalty. Here, strict gradations of rank and deference defined the
complex etiquette. For instance, contrary to Western norms, Indian
men did not rise when a woman entered nor did they hasten to
open the door through which she was about to pass. However, the
relationship between an elder and younger sister, with a different
word for each, conveyed a 'whole world of sweetness' as did
addressing a cousin as brother or sister and elders of the community
as Aunt or Uncle. This was 'an emotional training of extraordinary

kind' producing 'an ultimate sense of kinship to the world'.[13] The 'special delicacy of affection and respect between the husband's father and his daughter-in-law' or with other men in the Hindu woman's life displayed 'more healthy human intercourse than in those of thousands of single women, living alone, or following professional careers in the suburbs of London and other Western cities'.[14] Nivedita reflected that the 'culture of the home' with harvesting, seed sowing and family gatherings must have been at the beginning of religion and she noted how the ties of family affection and loyalty had continued into later times. She was most touched, for example, to be told by Jagadish Chandra Bose about the rousing welcome he had received during a visit to his ancestral village he had left twenty-eight years ago in pursuit of higher studies. From far and near, people had gathered to 'bless and welcome and offer salutations' in the spirit of an old Indian civilization paying homage to 'learning and the learned man'.[15]

Nivedita saw the 'Eastern woman' as the product of an ethical civilization, 'more deeply self-effacing and more effectively altruistic than any western'.[16] The central position of the mother in relation to her children, and later as the mother-in-law, and in advanced years as she 'mothered' her spouse and was addressed as the 'mother of her sons,' fascinated Nivedita, who found a parallel in the role of the lady abbess in a church, who functioned with a blend of sweet indulgence and strict discipline. At a time when Western education was fashioning a 'new woman' highlighted for instance by Tagore in his *Shesher Kobita*,[17] more versed in romantic English novels than in Indian literature, more attracted to Western consumerist fashion than to household responsibilities, Nivedita's focus on traditional values held an important message. She felt that the British had Europeanized India rather than modernized her.[18] Describing Indian society, Nivedita not only focused on the role of the traditional woman but also mentioned parts of India such as the Malabar, where the matriarchal system ensured that the right of inheritance came through the mother. This incredible variety made her conclude in her *The Web of Indian Life*, 'Thus far from India's being the land of the uniform oppression of woman by a uniform method, it represents the whole cycle of feminist institutions. There is literally no theory of feminine rights and position that does not find illustration somewhere within her boundaries.'[19] One of Nivedita's most profound observations was her equation of wifehood and nunhood. The Indian bride came to her husband much as a Western woman might enter a church. Their love was a devotion to be offered in secret and a life to be led in a veiled and cloistered environment—one of actual seclusion. The inviolability of the marriage tie had nothing to do with attraction and mutual love. Once a wife, always a wife, even though the bond was shared with others. Although this was certainly not an arrangement of equality, she felt the sanctity of an impersonal life equalled the sanctitude of religious celibacy. Perhaps in justification of the life that she had herself chosen, Nivedita concluded that the Indian bride, as also the nun, upheld the ideal of the finite merging with the infinite. As she explained in a letter, the vows of nunhood and wifehood implied a daily faithfulness of word, thought and deed. 'The husband is a motive of *self-consecration*, just as the altar is . . . the love of the body must be, of course, but it should be the *result* of the love of the mind, not the cause.'[20] Nivedita believed that the integrity of a person was tested on adherence to vows undertaken, whether of a celibate nun or a wife dedicated to the husband. Her friendship with Okakura ended when she realized that her commitment to celibacy within the framework of a close friendship was not matched by Okakura's expectations in the relationship.

In the national life of India, society was framed by ideals and methods, which sprang directly from the soil. The correspondence with its environment resulted in stability, which would be inconceivable to persons who flattered themselves as 'favoured members of most favoured nations'.[21] However, this had its own drawbacks. The inbred habit of community life made the Indian mind content with the sufficiency of home and not eager to explore the world outside. There was a need therefore to shift the centre of social gravity from the exclusive focus on the family to the civic and national life of the larger community. The intellectual atmosphere of India had to be saturated with fresh ideals in which its women could participate on par. India had to complement its traditional proficiency in literature with an assimilation of scientific ideas and mechanical skills of the West. However, this process had to be initiated carefully. Already, Nivedita feared that the country had become 'a host to the parasite of European trade' and was losing many of her handicrafts to machine-made goods of the colonial state. A 'dynamic orthodoxy' could ensure a flexibility to welcome some change but maintain respect for existing conventions. Above all, 'the fundamental task of grasping and conveying the inspiration of the West must be performed by Easterns for Easterns and not by foreigners'.[22] The national idea had to develop from within in full congruity with all national religions, forgetting past feuds and uniting in a common glorification of India and the whole Indian past. [23]

Nivedita dwelt at length on the unseen but all-pervasive influence of the Indian epics—the Ramayana and the Mahabharata—in the national consciousness, similar to that of the Icelandic sagas or the Greek epics. The continued narration, depiction and interpretation of Indian epic tales through the ages had resulted in considerable popular appeal since they appeared as opera, sermon and literature all in one. What moved Nivedita most was the Bhagavadgita, the divine sermon delivered by the charioteer Krishna to the doubting warrior Arjun on the battlefield at Kurukshetra. As she wrote, 'That place which the four Gospels hold to Christendom, the Gita holds to the world of Hinduism, and in a very real sense, to understand it is to understand India and the Indian people.'[24] Only slightly longer than the Sermon on the Mount and shorter than the Gospel of St Mark, the Gita, Nivedita concluded, was unrivalled as a sacred writing of mankind which was at once 'so great, so complete, and so short'.[25] She felt that though it was central to Hinduism, the Gita had a universal message. Nivedita wrote that 'the voice that speaks on the field of Kurukshetra is the same voice that reverberates through an English childhood from the shores of the Sea of Galilee'.[26] The divine voice declared that by worshipping God and doing at the same time the duty of his station every man may attain perfection. 'Better for one is one's own duty, however badly done, than the duty of another, though that be easy.' Nivedita sought to explain the logic behind the caste system by referring to this verse of Gita. She knew of the great evils that had accrued from caste differences and mindless superstitions such as 'don't touchism' that had created deep chasms in Indian society. Reiterating her Master's belief that caste laws had crystallized with the Aryan and non-Aryan divisions of society, Nivedita believed that it had helped retain the dignity of tradition. She thought it was in a sense a 'noblesse oblige' or an 'honour' that had to be protected.[27] The main argument of the Gita, that man had always the right to work with no right to its results, Nivedita pointed out, echoed the dictum of Stoicism—'Thou hast no right to success if thou art not also equal to failure.'[28]

Nivedita considered the Gita to have an overwhelming vitality for the emerging nationalist movement. It was, in many ways, a battle cry proclaiming that spirituality lay not in a retreat from the world but in a burning fire of knowledge that destroyed bondage, consumed sluggishness and egoism and penetrated everywhere. The rousing message of the Gita coupled with the eclectic doctrine of Ramakrishna, Nivedita believed, would mould a people into national consciousness. 'The final differentia of Hinduism,' she concluded, 'lay in the acceptance of the doctrine of the *Ishta Devata*, i.e. the right of every man to choose his own creed and of none to force the same choice on any other. At last then Indian thought stands revealed in its entirety—no sect, but a synthesis; no church but a university of spiritual culture.' For her, as an idea of individual freedom, it was among the most complete the world had known. She explained further that it would be foreign to the genius of Hinduism to require an oath of conformity to any given religious tenet whatsoever, just as 'it would be to the habits of an Oxford don to require adherence to the doctrines of Plato as against those of Aristotle'.[29]

The Web of Indian Life, which Nivedita had begun in England in 1901, was finished in September 1903. She was keen that the published book receive publicity with newspaper announcements. In a suggested draft to Mrs Bull, she mentioned, that 'Sister Nivedita had attempted to set forth some of the essential elements of that National idea which she would hold to be nascent today in India . . . The modern era has imposed upon India the necessity of developing the national thought-dimension, as it were.'[30] She believed that she had expressed Swamiji's thoughts in the book and hoped dearly that Yum would feel the same.[31] She was encouraged to hear that Yum had actually bought the *Web* by the dozen[32] and that Rudyard Kipling and Flora Annie Steel were 'warm about the book'.[33] When the reviews appeared, barring some venomous attacks from missionaries in the American press and disparagement in the *Englishman* that it was a political pamphlet in disguise, there were some favourable reports where the book was not considered a mere rhapsody on the customs of the 'Orient'. Explaining the gist of the book as 'nation-making-consciousness,' Nivedita reiterated that 'the book is *constructive.* Custom is interpreted in consonance with self-respect. Religions are described in demonstration of unity. The education of woman in the modern sense is considered in relation to the common weal.' Hindu and Moslem were 'both necessary and mutually supplementary' and not 'antagonistic'.[34] As she wrote elsewhere, the 'real theme of my book is the essential unity of the Hindu and the Mohammedan and their great and united future,' which was Swamiji's considered opinion.[35] She was reassured when a Muslim gentleman from Bombay called on her to thank her for having expressed so clearly what they felt about their motherland. Her brother Richmond complimented her on having produced 'a standing monument of your work in India'.[36] The intellectual Gerald Nobel, an old family friend of the Leggetts, who had befriended Swamiji on many occasions, wrote that though he did not share every opinion of hers, he felt the *Web* was a 'fine and splendid book' which 'she has written of Hindoos as a true friend does of friends'.[37] Perhaps the best compliment that Nivedita received was when an Indian editor wrote to her that in his mind the book was 'as great an event as Swamiji's visit to the West'.[38]

In 1894, Rabindranath Tagore had been euphoric[39] that he was at the dawn of a new age. He had exclaimed: 'Whither departed that darkness, that confusion, that somnolence . . . whence appeared so much light, so much hope, so much music, so much diversity?'[40] This was the *nabayuga* or new age, also described as the 'Bengal Renaissance'.[41]

Although it has been debated whether this age was indeed one of rebirth or merely a break with the past,[42] it was indeed an age when contact with the West proved transformational, with significant changes. But these changes were not unilinear—there were contradictions, ambivalences, oscillations of positions between reformists and revivalists—all of which is reflected in the intellectual history of the times, captured in literary writings, essays, diaries, letters and speeches of key personalities. Western education had doubtless opened up the possibilities of a better livelihood and a more egalitarian social organization. In Bengal, the introduction of a consolidated rule of law and the spread of print culture gave rise to a new kind of civil society, where voluntary associations of individuals, irrespective of their caste and community identity, could be formed.

Western education and the British model of development had been hailed for their Utilitarian principles. On the political front, the Moderates were hoping to transplant European nationalism to the Indian soil.[43] They agreed with the British that India lacked all the classic ingredients like unity of race, language and creed, to form a nation. There remained only the unity of history which the British had imposed in the last hundred or so years. Simultaneously with these ideas there existed a genuine attachment to a whole range of inherited values and ways of life, which seemed to have come under threat and needed to be fiercely defended.

Slowly frustration set in among the educated middle class with petty clerical jobs and the stereotype of effeminacy labelled on them. Empty imitation of the Western model proved so ludicrous that Michael Madhusudan Dutt was provoked to write his satire, *Ekei ki boley sabhyata?* (Is this called culture?) Tagore too had come to realize that the euphoria about Western values was already wearing off. In his essay 'Byadhi O Pratikar,' he wrote,

> We were spellbound by Europe. We contrasted the generosity of that civilization with the narrow-mindedness of our own, and applauded the West . . . The time has come now to discuss this change because an element of doubt has certainly crept in. We seem to be sitting undecided at the crossroads of ancient India and modern civilization.[44]

In the midst of this, Ramakrishna's simple message of the parity of all forms and paths of religions appealed greatly to the Bengali middle class. Equally encouraging was the message of Vivekananda that through physical fitness, Indian men could counter the stereotype of being effeminate and Indian women of being *abala* or helpless. Vivekananda inspired Indian youth to a robust life of dedication to the cause of nation-building, and it was her Master's thoughts that Nivedita so skilfully penned.

The restive mood in India at the turn of the century intensified with the policies of Lord Curzon, who had come to India as Viceroy in 1898. His efforts to slowly bring all institutions under government control were viewed with suspicion. He had earlier brought under official authority the Calcutta Municipality under a plea of efficiency. He now sought to do the same by the Universities Act of 1904, bringing the entire system of higher education under government supervision. The pomp and meticulous precision with which he organized the Delhi Durbar in 1902 to celebrate the succession of King Edward VII and Queen Alexandra as Emperor and Empress of India, at a cost of over two million rupees, was viewed in the country as wasteful expenditure. The dazzling display was so lavish that it was not only unmatched by the preceding Durbar in 1877 but also was to be by the succeeding one in 1911. Particularly distasteful was the pride of place given to the Bengal Lancers in the ceremonial parade during the Delhi Durbar, when they had been found guilty of rape and murder of Indians and were facing disciplinary charges. Much to Curzon's disappointment, Edward VII was unable to attend the Durbar but sent in his place his brother, the Duke of Connaught.

To articulate rising popular discontent, the Indian National Congress provided a platform for public protest. Founded in 1885 it was dominated by Moderate leaders like Gopal Krishna Gokhale, vesting its hopes in formal methods of agitation—pleading, protesting and petitioning the government with popular grievances. Nivedita took a keen interest in all these developments and was kept well informed about them by friends like S.K. Ratcliffe of the *Statesman*. However, in the initial years of the twentieth century she was busy with the school, which had reopened in February 1902. It began functioning in earnest in January 1903 when Bet, Nivedita's nurse from England, came to support her; later in March, Christine Greenstidel too joined them. The school had printed a notice hammered on the door that read 'The House of The Sisters: Calls—Classes—Library'.

Nivedita's school[45] had in all forty-five girls, who were taught according to kindergarten methods whereby all knowledge was grounded in play and observation. The curriculum included Bengali, English, arithmetic, geography and history. Alongside these were introduced clay modelling, brushwork, mat weaving, paper cutting, sewing and games. Nivedita introduced innovative methods of teaching with magic lantern slides, hoping to build up the geographic sense of her students by projecting pictures of maps, of architectural places in Europe and different costumes of people. With the help of Jagadish Chandra, she secured some laboratory apparatus for science lesson to demonstrate how to ignite fire from oxygen.[46]

Saralabala Sarkar, one of Nivedita's early students, has recorded how Nivedita worked hard to make studies interesting for her students. For instance, young girls were initiated to counting with the help of tamarind seeds, learning the difference between odd and even numbers. Art classes were held with the participation of all, including Christine. There was much appreciation for any original work of a student, however rudimentary it might be. Nivedita encouraged students to perfect the traditional drawing of *alpona* or free-hand floor designs. She treasured a particular alpona of a lotus with many petals surrounded by tiny jasmine blossoms, receiving with pride the praise that came from the famous art connoisseur Coomaraswamy.[47] Recounting stories of valour from India's medieval history, Nivedita often became so involved, as for instance while speaking of the sacrifice of Rani Padmini, that some 'people went so far as to call her mad'.[48] She tried hard to learn the Bengali language, which she could not quite master. However, she was insistent that her students made no compromise while speaking it. Sarkar mentions an amusing incident when a student drawing on a slate said to Nivedita that she was trying her hand at line drawing. Disappointed that her student did not know the Bengali word for 'line', Nivedita was finally assuaged when another student brought to her attention the equivalent Bengali word, *rekha*.[49]

She sent a long wish list of books to Mrs Bull that included James Fergusson's *Indian Architecture*; Lubki's *History of Art*; *Old Chronicles of Crusades*; works of William Morris; Homer's *Odyssey* in prose by S.H. Butcher and Andrew Lang; the Norse sagas; *Don Quixote*; a prose by Dante; histories of Buddhism; travels of Hiuen Tsang; biographies, an atlas and the English dictionary, which reflect the wide range of education she wished to impart.[50]

Meticulous records kept on each student detailed their attendance, caste background, general conduct, deportment, ability with languages, drawing and artistic interests. At a time when book learning was forbidden for girls in conservative families and contacts with foreigners avoided, it was quite a revolutionary initiative. There were only a few girls' schools at that time. Mahakali Pathsala, which had been visited by Vivekananda, ran along orthodox lines while the Victoria Institution for Girls founded in 1871 by the Brahmo reformer Keshab Chandra Sen was more liberal. Victoria invited Nivedita to teach, an offer she declined since she sought to devote herself to children of mothers completely without education. Remarkably, she was able to bring children from several castes into the school, ranging from Brahmin and Kayastha to Gowala and Kaibarta. Many child widows found a new purpose in life and pledged to devote themselves to the school. Sudhira Devi, who had taken a vow to never marry, proved to be of invaluable help to Nivedita as an administrator of the school.

Irregular attendance and child marriage hampered the progress of studies. Nivedita kept hoping that in some of the promising girls enough common sense could be instilled to resist early marriage. Nivedita and Christine felt encouraged to begin a women's section, which was opened in November 1903, which functioned from 12 p.m. to 4 p.m., enabling women to attend after finishing household chores. Arrangements were made to provide a carriage to bring the women to school. Belur Math agreed to send Swami Bodhananda once a week to teach the Gita. Labanyaprabha Bose, sister of Jagadish Chandra, offered help with teaching, reading and writing. Christine took on the responsibility of teaching needlework and sewing twice a week while Nivedita conducted teachers' training classes for the senior girls. Mrs Bull, on her return from Japan was present at one of the meetings for women students held in October. She regaled them by playing the harmonium, which as an accomplished pianist, she did with excellence. As the students in both the children's school and the women's section increased, 17, Bosepara Lane proved inadequate. Accordingly, the old house at number 16, where Nivedita had earlier stayed after her arrival from England, was rented. Nivedita and Bet lived at number 16 while Christine stayed in Nivedita's place at number 17.

Nivedita took great pride in her home and school, which she maintained with an austere yet simple aesthetic. She designed some of the furniture such as her writing table and shelves, which she sketched in her letters to dear friends like Josephine. She wrote to Mrs Leggett on 9 April,

> I wish you could see our little house. I really think you would be charmed with it. Our first courtyard is quite a vision of red brick and green plants, and we keep it exquisitely clean and have two or three good airy rooms. Sometimes, after dark, ladies come in to see us, and they sit down in basket chairs with cushions, while we often sit on the floor to talk with them. I know they like it, and they are so fine they never show the least surprise or shyness about foreign ways. And when we go to them they give us their things—a mat, or a stool, or what-not, with such quiet dignity! We are just living here quietly, and letting things grow about us.[51]

The courtyard of the house was often used to hold *kathakautha* or presentations of folk tales and religious texts through songs and recitation, which were usually attended in large numbers. The success of their initiative surprised even Nivedita, who wrote to

Josephine, 'It is unheard of that married Zenana ladies should leave their homes and come to lessons at the house of a European. But they do it, and there never was a moment's difficulty.'[52]

Girish Ghosh, the theatre personality who was a friend of Nivedita, requested her to allow a visit to her house of two women of 'un-virtue' since he wanted to educate them. Describing this experience, Nivedita wrote how bored the women must have been with pictures from the story of Beatrice and Dante. She was amused to see the 'contempt' with which they viewed the austere bedrooms of the house. On a more serious note, Nivedita spoke of 'the occasional virtue of the un-virtuous' since 'one who has *given*, however mistakenly, has not fallen, never-never-never. He who *takes* has. Selfishness is the only sin. . . *Only* Jesus could understand Mary Magdalene. Remember that. He alone. There was no other great enough for that'. Nivedita was slowly discovering that even many respectable householders were courtesans. Endless sexual appetite directed even at one human, Nivedita felt, amounted to cannibalism. 'Sex is the faculty of gobbling up human beings, just as hunger is of good, and thirst of drink; it is moral cannibalism.'[53]

Nivedita's school received mention in Ramakrishna Mission's Bengali monthly *Udbodhan* and was generously reviewed by Ratcliffe, Nivedita's close friend and supporter. He wrote:

As conducted by Sister Nivedita and her colleague, the school involved no uprooting from familiar surroundings . . . The principle was, as Sister Nivedita herself expressed it, by means of familiar factors of her daily life so to educate the Indian girl as to enable her to realize those ends which are themselves integral aspirations of that life. There was no attempt to convert her to any religious or social system alien from her own; but rather, by means of her own customs and traditions, to develop her in harmony with Indian ideals, the teachers themselves following those ideals as far as they could be made practicable.[54]

The school, named by Nivedita as the Ramakrishna School for Girls, was also known by many as the Vivekananda School or the Nivedita School.[55]

Another idea cherished by Nivedita was to open a boys' home where students would be in residence for six months and spend another six months travelling the country, gaining vital knowledge and experience to make them worthy monks. Although this idea was never realized, she did arrange in April 1903 for a group of boys, which included Rathindranath, Rabindranath Tagore's son, to go on a pilgrimage with Sadananda to the Pindari Glacier in the Himalayan region.

Although Nivedita had designed the course and remained involved in all the activities of the school, she felt that it was actually Christine, with pleasing manners and a methodical and disciplined working style, who had contributed to the bulk of the school's success. Nivedita herself had been torn in different directions after her return from England in February 1902. On the one hand was the death of Swamiji a few months later and her break with the Ramakrishna Order, and on the other was total obsession with the ideal of nationalism, articulated in her book *The Web of Indian Life* and voiced in several lectures and articles. She became intensely involved with Okakura, who appeared as the ideal spokesman of her mantra of nation building. Over time, she realized his romantic involvement and fought hard to keep the relationship impersonal. In all this time, the school had the undivided attention of Christine.

One senses a certain remorse in her belief that Christine perhaps fitted Swamiji's ideal much more than she did. Nivedita felt,

All the things that Swamiji dreamt for me *she* is fulfilling. The woman's work is a wonderful success. But SHE is *more* wonderful. Her whole time is given to study, work and visiting. She lives *here*, without fuss, without complexity. I look at her in a vain envy, and feel that I never knew my own measureless inadequacy

before. She has never been burnt up with the fiery longing to be
and do the right things here, as I have.

With remarkable candour, Nivedita assessed herself in comparison
to Christine.

> The contrast is there—and is complete. She is the Eastern
> Woman and Nun, without seeming to love it as an ideal, or
> even to think of it—and all my love of it is thwarted and baffled,
> and I am nothing but an impulsive publicity-seeking fool . . .
> In me, sweetness wars against strength, and strength against
> sweetness—and I am not sure that my whole life is not indolence
> and self-indulgence.

There was clearly an internal struggle going on within Nivedita as
she sought to conform to the image of a docile, committed, celibate
nun that society expected her to be and the alive, impassioned,
questioning individual that she actually was.

At this moment of candid introspection, she sorely missed
the guidance of her Master. 'Alas—the visible token is gone—and
only the ache in the heart is left for a mariner's compass, with
which to direct one's course through the ocean of complexity.'[56]
She reminisced: 'Ah for the touch of a vanished hand—and
the sound of a voice that is still.'[57] On 4 July 1904, which she
remembered as 'the great Night of Swamiji's departure' two years
ago, she complimented Josephine for her imaginative way of
commemorating the Swami. Josephine had got the famous French
designer René Lalique to make a reliquary locket of embossed glass
and sapphire, enclosing a strand of Vivekananda's hair to be worn
round her neck. Nivedita added that she could never bring herself
to wear such an amulet. Instead she would prefer to place it on the
wall and kneel to look at it.[58] She later wished Lalique would help
design some medals in the name of Swami Vivekananda, which

Sister Nivedita in her study

The 20-paise stamp
issued by the Government of
India in 1967 on the centenary
of Sister Nivedita's birth

Swami Vivekananda in London, 1896

At Mayavati Advaita Ashrama. From left to right: Sister Nivedita, Mrs Sevier, Sister Christine and Abala Bose

Mayavati Ashrama, 2016

Sara Bull

Josephine MacLeod, or 'Yum'

Swami Vivekananda and his disciples in Kashmir. From left to right: Josephine MacLeod, Sara Bull and Sister Nivedita

Portrait of Sarada Devi taken at Sara Bull's request in 1898.
Seen here with Sister Nivedita

Sister Nivedita with Gopaler-Ma

The national flag with a vajra, conceived by
Sister Nivedita and embroidered by her students

The iconic painting *Bharat Mata* by Abanindranath Tagore.
Inspired by Sister Nivedita, it was the first of its kind

Jagadish Chandra Bose with
his scientific instruments

Okakura Kakuzo

Sarola Devi Chowdhurani

Sri Aurobindo

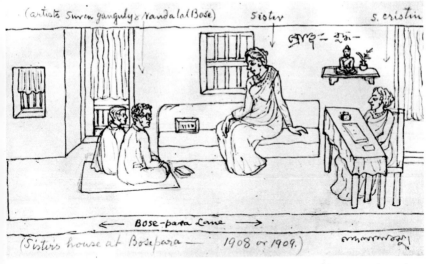

A sketch by artist Nandalal Bose, depicting how Surendranath Ganguly and he were made to sit on the floor while Sister Nivedita sat on the couch

Sister Nivedita Girls' School

A sketch of Bosepara Lane where Nivedita lived, by artist Rathin Mitra

A sketch of Roy Villa, Darjeeling, where Nivedita passed away, by Rathin Mitra

Bas-relief plaque of a lady with a lamp at the J.C. Bose Institute

she could present to her students from time to time. She sketched some of her thoughts, which included a thunderbolt motif.[59]

Nivedita was not one to remain pensive for long. Her restless spirit could not remain satisfied with only the quiet discipline of school life; she once again wished to connect with Indians through a larger and more political platform. She had written to Josephine that only 'women-making' and the training of ten to twelve girls could hardly make much of a difference. She asked, 'Is it not rather by taking the national consciousness of the women like that of the men and setting it towards greater problems and responsibilities that one can help? I think my task is not to influence a few women but the nation.'[60] Nivedita felt the charged atmosphere of the time had begun to grip the 'political side of my brain'[61] as she found the 'lava-like mass of molten thought and passion irresistible—overwhelming'.[62] With Christine's total involvement in the school, Nivedita felt that she was set free for 'bigger things' for which she had 'the force and fire'.[63] Nivedita had been an active crusader for Irish home rule in England. She felt the need for a sustained strategy against the imperialist government that included awareness-building campaigns among the youth as well as concerted action from the Indian National Congress to mount pressure on the British government. On Sundays, she held breakfast meetings, in which over brown bread and Quaker oats, there would be animated interactions with journalists, stage personalities, politicians and budding activists on the significant issues of the day.[64] The meetings were held in the study on the upper floor of her house where a rare statue of Buddha adorned the table and on the walls were an ivory crucifix and a photograph of Vivekananda. The visitors sat on straw mats protected from the blazing heat by straw blinds, participating in lively discussions over cups of coffee.

The Indian National Congress had in its first twenty years followed Moderate politics.[65] It would meet at the end of each year for three days in what became a grand social occasion as well as a political assembly where a similar set of resolutions was passed dealing with three broad types of grievances—political, administrative and economic. The Moderate leaders, anglicised in their personal life and successful men in their professions, displayed an ambivalent attitude when criticizing specific policies of the British administration. They even expressed a belief in the 'providential' nature of British rule. The Moderate politicians did not necessarily appeal to the hardened bureaucrats of British India but to the presumed liberal-minded public opinion of the land of John Stuart Mill and William Ewart Gladstone. They pointed out, as Dadabhai Naoroji did, that British policies in India had caused an uncharacteristically 'un-British Rule'. Hope was expressed in the Council reforms and the 1892 Council Act obtained concessions for Congress leaders to be elected to the new local and imperial legislatures.

Nivedita developed a friendship with Gokhale, the Moderate Congress leader. Reposing faith in him, she wrote in an encouraging letter: 'It is an infinite joy to me to know that a Mahratta is loved in Bengal as you have caused yourself to be, by our first men here and when that love is joined with such respect for your intellect and such implicit confidence in your courage and disinterestedness, it is beyond all price.'[66] Nivedita congratulated Gokhale for his 'manly speech'[67] to the Viceroy as a member of the Viceroy's Legislative Council, to which he had been nominated. Repeated famines had kept the focus of debates on economic matters and Gokhale's speech on the budget expounded the nationalistic economic theory on the floor of the Imperial Legislative Council for the first time. Naoroji's doctrine that there was a steady drain of wealth from India served as a radicalizing force while R.C. Dutt's resolution in the 1899 session of the Congress focused on the excessive land revenue burdens that had brought on abysmal poverty.[68] To Nivedita economic issues, though important, were not the key driving force to awaken an

apathetic people. Hoping to shake Gokhale off his sedentary style
of politics to a more animated, active stance she wrote to him,

> I *wish* I could infect you with my view of the whole thing . . .
> There is a great festival of struggle and growing life before us.
> When one feels baffled and sad, it is because one has failed to
> find the true lines of action, along which the fire leaps to the
> blaze . . . Do not let us spend our effort longer in trying to reform
> abuses; *let us make life.*[69]

Although the Congress had fallen into the doldrums in the 1890s
and Curzon assessed in his note to Secretary of State Hamilton
(18 November 1900) that it was tottering to its fall, it represented
only a fraction of the national sentiment. It did not reflect the
widespread resentment against the Raj that had been steadily
building up at this time. A chain of samitis or youth organizations
had been set up in many parts of the country, all aimed at offering
civic and political education to the youth and raising awareness
about pressing issues. When Okakura had travelled with Suren
Tagore through the country, he had established contact with
many of these organizations. In southern India, Tilak, the
outspoken nationalist leader, had inspired the opening of many
such youth organizations where young men would meet to hear
about the lives of Giuseppe Mazzini and Giuseppe Garibaldi, read
rousing speeches of Vivekananda, listen to the logic of righteous
war in the Mahabharata and ponder on the commentary of the
Bhagvadgita. There was also focus on bodybuilding and physical
training to create potential soldiers for the impending struggle
for the motherland. Many groups emphasized the promotion of
indigenously produced goods, such as Lakshmi Bhandar, opened
in 1903 by Sarola Devi, who was also the key inspiration behind the
training of young men in martial arts invoking the name of Kali,
the divine mother. In 1902, Satish Chandra Mukherji founded the

Dawn Society with the express idea of promoting ethical, moral and patriotic principles through the Society's journal *Dawn* and the National Council of Education, which it actively supported in 1905. The Society imparted technical training to promote the use of products of indigenous industry. The students of the Society started a Swadeshi Bhandar as early as 1903, anticipating many of the programmes that the Swadeshi Movement was to later support and advocate. Nivedita was actively associated with the programmes of the Dawn Society, imparting lessons to the youth to realize their rich heritage and instil courage and self-confidence to undertake whatever challenges presented themselves. Self-help, use of indigenous languages, utilization of traditional, popular customs and institutions like the village fair or mela and increasingly an evocation of Hindu symbolism were adopted as the means to reach out to the wider public.

Another society of great significance was the Anushilan Samiti set up by Satish Chandra Basu in March 1902. Initially, a physical culture club in north Calcutta, it shifted to Cornwallis Street after being reconstituted with several prominent members. Among these were Promotho Mitter, barrister, who was President of Anushilan, and Jatindranath Banerjee, initially trained in the army of the Gaekwad of Baroda and sent by Aurobindo Ghosh as an emissary to network in Calcutta. There, Jatindranath set up a riding club that imparted military training to Anushilan seniors. There were also Barindra Ghosh, younger brother of Aurobindo, with whom Jatindranath eventually fell out, and Aurobindo himself, who in time left Baroda to control activities of the Samiti. Along with the famous barrister C.R. Das, he functioned as the vice president. Surendranath Tagore functioned as treasurer of the Samiti. Nivedita joined this group, supplying it with a rich collection of European revolutionary literature, which included her personal collection of books on the Irish Revolution, the history of the Revolt of 1857 (then known as the Sepoy Mutiny), the American War of Independence, the lives of Mazzini and Garibaldi and books on the Indian economy written by R.C. Dutt and Dadabhai Naoroji. In 1902, a central revolutionary council of five was set up with Aurobindo in which Nivedita was included. It was later disbanded. In 1905, a branch of Anushilan Samiti was set up in Dhaka by Pulin Bihari Sen and many smaller branches also sprang up in the towns of both east and west Bengal. In time, the mouthpiece of the Anushilan group became the journal *Jugantar*, which came out in March 1906. Soon a group named Jugantar Party was formed; it was headed by Aurobindo's younger brother, Barindrakumar Ghosh, and included Bhupendranath Dutta, Vivekananda's younger brother.

Perhaps the first systematic critique of Moderate politics was offered in 1893–94 in a series of articles titled *New Lamps for Old* by Aurobindo Ghosh, then living in Baroda under the employment of the Maharaja of Gaekwad. Having returned from England with an Anglicised education and upbringing, he began to react sharply to the colonial regime. Rejecting the model of slow constitutional progress advocated by the Moderates, which he termed as mendicancy, he urged a closing of ranks between the middle class, which the Congress represented, and the rural masses whom he sought to enthuse through revivalist Hindu imagery. Bankim Chandra's *Ananda Math* with its cry of 'Bande Mataram' and glorification of the Goddess Incarnate, the motherland, inspired Aurobindo's own writing of *Bhawani Mandir* (1905). He had also been deeply impressed by Nivedita's *Kali the Mother* with its stark depiction of the brutal realities of conflict.

In Bengal, disillusionment with the Congress also came to be steadily voiced by Ashwini Kumar Dutta, a Barisal schoolteacher, who dedicated himself to social work in his district with a unique mass following. Rabindranath Tagore, already Bengal's leading literary figure, not only voiced his mental anguish in his literary works but also directly spoke against Congress mendicancy, calling for self-reliance or *atma* shakti, which would lead to the growth and development of swadeshi enterprise. He also called for mass contact programmes through melas, *jatras* or travelling shows and the use of the mother tongue in both education and political work. The Bengali bhadralok was also turning to indigenous enterprise, such as Prafulla Chandra Ray's Bengal Chemicals set up in 1893. Satish Mukherji through his Dawn Society and Rabindranath Tagore through Ashrama, his school in Santiniketan, were experimenting with new homegrown forms of education. Already Vivekananda's message of a man-making mission, of finding purpose in life by invoking the divinity that lay within, articulated at various platforms by Nivedita was enthusing the youth. As Max Müller put it, Vivekananda's Neo-Vedantism 'spread like burning alcohol in the veins of his intoxicated nation'.[70] In other words, Bengal at the turn of the twentieth century was like a volcano waiting to erupt and Curzon's plans to partition Bengal brought on an unprecedented explosion.

The proposal to partition Bengal, a state considered administratively unwieldy, had been under consideration for a while. But the urgency given to the move by Curzon was prompted by the desire to split up educated Bengalis and reduce them to a minority in each of the two parts: West Bengal, which along with Bihar and Orissa would constitute Bengal, and East Bengal, which would include North Bengal and Assam. This would weaken the burgeoning national movement by curbing the political influence of the Bengali political leaders of Calcutta and alienate the Muslim majority in East Bengal and Assam, who would now welcome the opportunity to have a Muslim majority province. Curzon's bait of a huge loan at a low rate of interest to Nawab Salimullah of Dhaka was intended to further his divide and rule policy.[71] To the Secretary of State John Brodrick, Curzon wrote that he would dig the grave of the Indian National Congress before laying down his office. As news of an impending partition sparked off massive protests, Curzon stood firm, overruling the hesitation of the home government. He

declared bluntly, 'The Bengalees consider themselves as a separate
nation and indulge in dreams of driving away the British and
putting a Bengalee *babu* in the Government house as governor-
general. The partition of Bengal would undermine their sense of
superiority and destroy their dreams.'[72]

The key thrust of Nivedita's message at this time was 'nationalism' or
the forging of a pan-Indian identity. This cry grew more intense as
the movement against the proposal of partition gained momentum.
Her inspiring call was:

> Our watchword then, is no longer 'reform!' In its place, we have
> taken the word 'construct!' We have to re-create the *Dharma*.
> We have to build again the *Maha Bharata*. The Church and
> its Protestants, Society and the Reformer are now to exchange
> achievements and become fused once more, for after all,
> Humanity is greater than any Church. Society was made for
> Man, not Man for Society.[73]

Acknowledging fully the significant roles played by social reformers,
political activists, religious teachers and economists who focused on
the many ills plaguing the country, Nivedita wished to stress that
these aspects had to be judged in the context of the encompassing
idea of Indian nationhood. As she put it,

> We are working comrades *because we are Indians*, children of a
> single-roof tree, dwellers around one bamboo clump. Our task
> is one, the rebuilding of Heroic India. To this every nerve and
> muscle of us tingle[s] with response. Who is so foolish as to
> imagine that a little political petting and pampering can make

half a nation forget its kinship with the other half? Nonsense! We *are* one! We have not to become one. We are one. Our sole need is *to learn to demonstrate our unity*.[74]

Nivedita's prescription was constructive work through an aggressive Hinduism. At Calcutta's Town Hall on 26 February 1904, Nivedita addressed a large audience and spoke about a Hinduism that lay in the minds of the people who were wedded to the soil. Explaining that many kinds of religious revival had taken place in India, which pointed to the fact that religion had an important place in its history, she hastened to add that 'there will never be a solution unless the truth is grasped that the goal to be sought is in the great word *nationality*. Religion has never dwelt in a creed that divides man from man; it is in a religion that becomes a nation-force that is the crying necessity for unity.'[75] Nivedita explained that 'when a Western child steps out of the nursery, it is not quietness, docility, resignation and obedience that his teachers and guardians strive to foster in him, as much as strength, initiative, sense of responsibility and power of rebellion'. For character-building among Indians, Nivedita spoke of the need to focus on being active, rather than passive. Drawing from mythology and history, she spoke of the combative aspects of the ten avatars of Vishnu and of the Kshatriya background of the Buddha and exhorted the youth to embrace aggressive Hinduism and become soldiers for the cause of their country's freedom.[76]

Nivedita's thoughts on aggressive Hinduism voiced in many lectures and articles were eventually compiled by her into a booklet in March 1905. Encouraged that Josephine had enjoyed her work, she wrote of the circumstances in which she had completed writing *Aggressive Hinduism*:

I love to look back on the writing of it. I sat down one evening, thinking, 'If this were my last word to the Indian people, let me try to write Swami's whole ideal for them in one message.' I

finished it in three evenings, and had copied it out and perhaps
sent it off by the Friday that week. Two days later, I was down
with brain fever, and no one knew whether I would live or die! So
it might really have been my last will and testament.[77]

In keeping with her belief in religious eclecticism, Nivedita
followed up her lecture on Hinduism in February 1904 with a series
of lectures on 'Islam in Asia' in March at the Corinthian Theatre,
which was organized by the Calcutta Madrasa. She ended with a
strong appeal to Indian Muslims.

What then was the duty of the Indian Mussalman today? It was
not to relate himself to Arabia. He had no need of that; his relation
to Arabia was of his very life-blood; it had been accomplished for
him by the faith and patient labour of his forefathers. No, his duty
was to relate himself to India, to throw into the national idea of
India—his home by blood or by adoption and hospitality—the
mighty force that was theirs by reason of the heritage into which
they had been born.[78]

Elsewhere she had exhorted, 'If you want to know the real India,
dream the dreams of Akbar and Ashoka. Patriotism is not learned
in books. It is a feeling which seizes the whole being. It is at once
the blood and the marrow; it is in the air one breathes and the
sound one hears.'[79]

Explaining her concept of syncretic nationalism, Nivedita
wrote in *Aggressive Hinduism*,

From the year 1858 onwards, there has been no possible goal
for the Indian people but a complete assimilation of the modern
consciousness. At that point, the medieval order was at an end.
Prithvi Rai and Shah Jehan, Ashoka and Akbar were mingled in
a common oblivion. Only the soil they had loved, only the people

they had led, remained to address themselves to a new task, to stand or fall by their power to cope with a new condition.[80]

On 1 April 1904, Nivedita gave a series of lectures on Bodh Gaya. The life and teachings of the Buddha had strongly influenced Nivedita's mind even before she had met Vivekananda. She had been thrilled to discover that her guru shared the same reverence for the Buddha. Indeed, she never forgot how on the day of her consecration she had been led by her Master to offer floral offerings at the feet of the Buddha statue. While in Patna in 1904, Nivedita decided to visit for the first time Rajgir, Nalanda and Bodh Gaya. Overwhelmed, she asked her dear Josephine why she had not been alerted before to the magic of the place, which was without doubt 'politically the most important spot in India—the heart of the future'.[81]

This was the time when Bodh Gaya was embroiled in a controversy started by Anagarika Dharmapala, leader of a Buddhist sect. He was a fellow delegate with Vivekananda to the Chicago Conference and became a later day critic. The Buddhists began an agitation, much reported in the newspapers that the temple at Bodh Gaya belonged to them. Nivedita had long discussions with the mahant of the temple in which he claimed that it was Shankaracharya who had placed his Order of monks in charge of the temple. He said that over the centuries, these monks had not only looked after the place but helped archaeologists to excavate the region and collect valuable historical artefacts. Nivedita's view, which echoed that of Vivekananda, was that Buddhism was not a religion separate from Hinduism but grew out of the mother religion. In her lecture 'Bodh Gaya: Its Place in Hinduism,' she emphasized that 'Hinduism is a synthesis, not a sect; a spiritual university, not a spiritual church and of this synthesis Buddhism is an alienable part.'[82] In October 1904, Nivedita returned to Bodh Gaya with a large group that included Jagadish Chandra and Abala Bose, Rabindranath Tagore, his son Rathindranath,

Jadunath Sarkar, Swami Sankarananda and others who were all guests of the mahant. This proved to be a memorable visit spent in regular discussions of the Buddha's life and work, readings from books, recitations and rendering of songs by the Poet, and time spent in silent meditation under the Bodhi tree. There were also group tours to neighbouring villages. Of special significance was the visit to Urbel. According to Buddhist legend, Sujata, the village girl who had given food to the Buddha just before he went into nirvana, used to live there. Nivedita took with her some soil from Urbel as a souvenir.

When the dispute about control of the temple precincts was decided soon after in the mahant's favour, he sent Nivedita as his appreciation, a token in the form of the Vajra, the emblem of the Buddhist thunderbolt, accompanied with a prayer for her to become a channel for divine energies. Nivedita saw this as the auspicious beginning of a new idea she had been nurturing—of creating an awareness of the richness of indigenous art forms, which in turn could strengthen the feeling of nationhood. Already during her recent visit to Bodh Gaya, Nivedita was fascinated at the archaeological finds and felt the old stones spoke of a lived past. She detected a continuity in the art traditions that had been laid then. At Rajagriha, she was excited at the sight of a huge Buddha in black stone that had emerged from the sand where it had lain buried for centuries. She went around huts in the villages to see whether unknowingly the villagers were using historic stone pieces for their daily grinding of spices, examining the stones for their texture and possible carvings. She visited small artisan sculptors and wood engravers to find that they had continued over centuries to produce the same kinds of figures. Nivedita exulted that in India's artistic heritage, the past, present and the future were knit in one continuous historical journey. She saw the need to preach the message of unity or 'yoga' through art, which could become the language of nationalism.[83]

In 1902, Nivedita had met E.B. Havell, head of the Calcutta School of Art, and shared with him her passion for India, which could bring about a tide in art. The conventional reliance on European examples of art for inspiration and the rigours on students to copy from Greek plaster models, Nivedita felt, kept them in the dark about their own rich art heritage, which they had to appreciate first in order to feel pride in their being Indian. Introduced to Havell's students, Nivedita built a meaningful relationship with them, inspiring them with nationalist ideas and attempting to wean them from their dependence on European art styles. Abanindranath Tagore was her greatest find and it was to him that she gave the responsibility of stylistically depicting the Vajra motif. He sent her a huge outline sketch from which the students in her school could embroider a banner. Nivedita dreamt that this would one day become India's national flag.

The boldness with which Nivedita asserted her convictions linking aggressive Hinduism to the larger issue of nationality troubled many questioning intellectuals like Rabindranath Tagore. Tagore had his own misgivings about the concept of nationalism. He defined it as an artificial method employed by the colonial administration to bind a diverse and pluralistic society into a structure where laws were laid down mechanically. He argued that 'India was a world in miniature' where 'the looseness of its diversity and the feebleness of its unity' made it impossible to fit into the straitjacket of a nation.[84] Tagore, however, did make a distinction between the 'Nation of the West', which he considered a mechanical and soulless entity, and the 'Spirit of the West' which he felt represented some of the Enlightenment values of equality, reason and scientific progress. He pleaded for this 'Spirit of the West', which could be invoked for reforming certain inherent social weaknesses in India such as caste inequity. Tagore was perplexed by Nivedita's advocacy of aggressive Hinduism and the attendant denunciation of Western influences. He realized that with his universalist view of interdependence of the East and the West, which was to become a key theme for his world university or Visva-Bharati, he could not possibly tread her path. Her combativeness and inability to accept a contrary opinion also deeply concerned him.[85]

Tagore could not conform to Nivedita's ideas on art either. For Tagore, Art was the expression of an innate creativity and its form could be the result of many experiences—some that were part of one's lived culture and some that were acquired through exposure to world influences. Art gripped Tagore's creative mind in the autumn of his life with a fervour that was to produce over 3000 paintings. He, however, never borrowed from any artistic tradition. Not formally trained, Tagore's paintings show how multiple influences ranging from abstraction and German expressionism to primitive aboriginal art might have influenced his style. Nivedita's unconditional condemnation of 'the miserable travesty of would-be Europeanism that we at present know' as art in India took him by surprise. According to Nivedita, 'An Indian painting, if it is to be really great, must appeal to the Indian heart in an Indian way, must convey some feeling or idea that is either familiar or immediately comprehensible.'[86] Elsewhere, she eulogized, 'Oh, for a pencil that would interpret the beauty of the Indian Sari; the gentle life of village and temple; the coming and going at the Ganges sides; the play of the children; the faces and labours of the cows!'[87] It was principally Nivedita who inspired Abanindranath Tagore, Nandalal Bose and others to visit the Ajanta caves. They began the traditional realism and revivalism of the Bengal School with its depiction of mythological figures and portrayal of women with the dreamy slanting eyes of the murals. Tagore, on the other hand, sought spontaneity and originality in any creative expression. He would constantly exhort his artist nephews, Abanindra and Gaganendra, to leave the comfortable environs of the southern veranda of their red house adjacent to his Jorasanko home and see the world outside for creative inspiration.[88]

Even as she encouraged the Moderates, Nivedita was becoming increasingly disillusioned with the government; she declared that the British Empire was 'rotten to the core—corrupt in every direction and tyrannical and mean. The English language may have a mission, but the Empire has only a doom.'[89]

Among the Anglo-Indian community of Calcutta, Nivedita had earned the reputation of being 'a gifted crank' who preferred an ascetic life in north Calcutta to the comforts of a Western home. For them, her fanatical anti-British ideas reflected the sentimental fervour of her Scottish and Irish blood.[90]

Her aggressive support of the Indian point of view often caused amazement and even a little amusement. A tribute to her mentioned an incident when at a crowded Ramlila in Lahore, she screamed at a policeman for pushing people in the crowd. 'You ought to be run in for assault,' she screamed, stunning the offending policeman into silence. The irony of the situation was not lost on the commentator as the common sight of the highhandedness of the police with the local people was being protested against by a white woman.[91] Her close friend Ratcliffe, remarking on the first time he saw Nivedita addressing Brahmo ladies in an Indo-European tea party on Loudon Street, Calcutta, in July 1902, commented, 'The whole affair was strange—the afternoon gathering, the meeting of the West and East and this Western voice speaking to Europeanized Indians of the greatness and enduring beauty of the customs and ideals from which they had cut themselves adrift.'[92]

The villain of the piece in Nivedita's eyes was Lord Curzon, 'the incarnation of insolence and evil'[93], who had initiated the Universities Commission, which in effect had killed all education, and especially all science education. In her eyes, 'Lord Curzon will stand in history as the most anti-British influence that India ever saw.'[94] With deep indignation, Nivedita spoke of the wrongs suffered by India and felt the need to emphasize the essential rights for which Indians had to agitate, namely, 'The right of India to be India; The right of India to think for herself; The right of India to Knowledge.' In deep anguish she asked, 'When will the Motherland rise again—the Gita in one hand and the Sword in the other?'[95] The period of pleading and petitioning seemed to be over. Desperate times seemed to require desperate measures.

Nivedita's acerbic comments on Lord Curzon were well known among her circle of friends. When William Stead of the *Review of Reviews* decided to write a piece on the pomp and pageantry of the Delhi Durbar of 1902, he cast Nivedita in his story as an irate spectator in 'Hindu costume with flashing eyes'. When Nivedita read the story sent to her by post she panicked, feeling it would be a 'fatal blunder' as she would be recognized. She feared stringent police surveillance, which would restrict her movements. She persuaded Stead to change her name and in the altered story, the protagonist was simply named Rose. Published in the *Review of Reviews* in January 1903, the story was titled 'The Star and the Strain at Delhi'.[96] It spoke of the Imperial festival being a veritable circus conducted by Daisy Leiter, Curzon's American wife, in the pattern of Barnum and Bailey's. In the story, a newspaper correspondent searches for a keyword to describe the decadent opulence and 'a singularly musical voice answered with a slight Irish accent "Byzantium"'. The story continued with the newspaper man seizing the word as a 'splendid peg' and rushing out to amend his telegram. In a letter, William Stead explained to Nivedita, 'You cannot complain of my putting the character in the story whose salient features resemble you. In fact, I think it ought to give an added interest to the tale.'[97]

Lord Curzon's disparaging comments about the integrity of Indians voiced at the Calcutta University Convocation on 11 February 1905 also drew a sharp response from Nivedita. Curzon had hinted that the highest ideals of truth, valued among the moral codes in the West, were not similarly honoured in the East where instead flattery prevailed; this could be seen either as a lie or as simply vile. Nivedita recalled having read Curzon's boastful comments in his book *Problems of the Far East* in which he wrote how he had lied about his age in an interview with the president of the Korean foreign office. Aware that in Korean culture respect was associated

with age, he felt it necessary to give his age as forty when he was then
only thirty two. Having leaked this information, the popular daily
newspaper, *Amrita Bazar Patrika*, in its report, juxtaposed Curzon's
convocation speech with comments from his book to highlight the
contradiction in his own position under the title 'Lord Curzon in
Various Capacities'. *Statesman* mentioned that 'the delicious little
comedy' would provide 'pure delight' in India and before long, in
England. Not one to give up, Nivedita continued the attack with
an open letter titled 'The Highest Ideal of Truth' in *Statesman*. In
it, she cited Max Müller's book *What India Has to Teach Us*, where
he had written on 'The Truthful Character of the Hindus'. Nivedita
also berated the audience squarely for not protesting against the
Viceroy's insinuations and defending their national character.[98]

In the years leading up to the Partition, Nivedita kept herself
occupied with a formidable schedule of lectures in cities around
the country. She also went to district areas like Midnapore where
in May 1903, she spoke thirteen times in five days in the samitis.
However, she realized soon enough that the boys found it hard to
understand her lectures, which often went over their heads. This
led her to explore other channels to communicate. The journalist
in her now used connections with newspapers and journals such
as Ratcliffe in *Statesman*, Motilal Ghose of *Amrita Bazar Patrika*
and Ramananda Chatterjee, editor of the *Prabashi*, then living in
Allahabad. She became a regular contributor in the latter's English
journal the *Modern Review*, and wrote on pressing issues of the day,
in the spirit of educational journalism. She was also requested to
contribute articles to *Bala Bharat*, a newspaper of Madras, of which
Subramania Bharati was the editor, to 'rouse the Sleeping South
from its lethargy'.[99] It was her grand idea to begin a great Indian
review with the help of William Stead, founder and editor of the
London *Review of Reviews*. In a letter she explained, 'The whole
task now is to give the word *nationality* to India in all its breadth
and meaning. The rest will do itself. India must be obsessed by this

great conception. Hindu and Mohammedan must become one in it, with a passionate admiration of each other.'[100]

Clearly then, Nivedita's concept of nation and nationality was very different from that of Tagore, whose critique was of nation according to a Western definition. Nivedita's nation was not a borrowed construct of a homogenous artificial unit bound by impersonal laws but the growth of a binding spirit among a disparate people built over centuries by shared history, thoughts, mythologies, artistic skills, and cultural practices. Defining her own mission of national awakening, Nivedita wrote, 'Let me plough my furrow across India just as deep, deep, deep to the very centre of things, as it will go. Let it be either as a hidden voice sending out noiseless things from a cell or as a personality, romping and raging through all the big cities—I don't care! But God and my own strong right hand grant that I do not have to waste my effervescence in Western futilities.'[101] Impressed by her self-effacing dedication, Henry W. Nevinson, special representative of the *Daily News* of London was to write, 'I do not know whether on the religious side it could be said of Nivedita, as of the philosopher, that she was drunk with God; but on the side of daily life and political thought it might certainly be said that she was drunk with India.'[102]

The hectic pace at which she worked proved a strain on her health; she fell seriously ill in March 1905, just after she had finished penning her booklet *Aggressive Hinduism*. Doctors feared for her life, as she was diagnosed with meningitis. Surrounded by love and care, with nurses by her bedside, Christine supervising her treatment, Sarada Devi visiting her, Gokhale spending nights giving her ice packs and cold compresses and the Boses, who had removed her from her home to one proximate to theirs, Nivedita rallied around. For her convalescence, the Boses also took her to Darjeeling for a couple of months. Shortly after, the Partition of Bengal was officially declared in July 1905 and Nivedita cried out, 'I think Curzon has broken the British Empire!'[103] From Darjeeling,

Nivedita exclaimed in a speech, 'Shame on my country of origin! But we shall continue the struggle until the sacrifice and heroism of the children of India compel the English to remove the insulting barrier which divides Bengal, until they treat us with respect.'[104] So deep was her disgust of Curzon that when a year later she got the news of the untimely death of Lady Curzon, her comment offered in private was, 'What misery it must be to live with such a man! And posing still! So utterly worthless!'[105] A couple of years later, from America she was to write to Ratcliffe that she had heard a rumour regarding the real reason for Curzon's bloodied expedition to Tibet in 1903–04. It was said that a Jew Mining Syndicate put pressure on Curzon through his Jewish wife so that opportunities were opened up for their surveying and prospecting in that area. Nivedita added cryptically, 'For them the 750 lives were lost that spring afternoon in the mountains—in order that a few more Jews might exchange their power in Whitechapel for 72, Bruton Street. Think of it!'[106]

Nivedita returned to Calcutta in time to join in the various protest meetings held against the government's decision to partition Bengal. The Partition was clearly perceived as a national insult and the immediate reaction of the educated Bengali was one of indignation and humiliation. At the Town Hall, under nationalist leader Surendranath Banerjee, it was decided to raise a Federation Hall as a symbolic protest, a decision warmly supported by Nivedita. The Moderate methods of petitions, meetings and conferences stood discredited. British reverses in the Boer War at this time and the unexpected victory of Japan over Russia in 1905, created a thrill of pride and gave strength to the movements of protest. Soon, novel methods like the boycott of British goods and institutions and the adoption of swadeshi, or encouragement of the indigenous handloom and cottage industry, began to emerge. Nivedita wrote to Gokhale[107] that the boycott, in which women too were actively engaged, was to test the nation's potential. The power that was dormant had now been unleashed and become a sign of hope. She reminded him that it was grit, defiance and self-sacrifice that had led the Russian people to turn Napoleon's march on Moscow into a disaster and helped the American people to win freedom. Abandoning the use of foreign goods, Nivedita took to swadeshi commodities, introduced weaving in her school, which was taught to students by a woman who was called Charkha-Ma.

On 16 October, the Partition formally came into effect and was received on a solemn note. Leading a procession to the Ganga, Rabindranath Tagore started a mass ceremony where wristlets of coloured thread (rakhi) were exchanged (Rakhi-Bandhan) as a symbol of brotherhood and it was pledged that hearths would be kept unlit (*arandhan*) as a sign of mourning. The air was rent with the songs that Tagore had composed for the occasion such as *Banglar mati Banglar jal* (invoking divine blessing in the name of the earth and waters of Bengal), *Bidhir badhon katbe tumi emni shaktimaan* (Are you so powerful that you can cut asunder the God-made bond that binds us?) and *Jodi tore dak shune keyu na ashe taube ekla chalo re* (If no one responds to your call, then go your way alone).

The foundation stone of the Federation Hall was laid by Ananda Mohan Bose and Surendranath Banerjee. Nivedita noted the day in her diary as 'National Day' and was always to remember it as a special day. Bearing in mind the success of the annual Warwick Pageant, Nivedita thought that a commemoration of an 'All India Day' on 16 October could be a creative initiative. Acknowledging that it had to be much simpler, she felt that the festive spirit, so evident during marriage processions and puja festivals and which had contributed to the spectacular success of the Delhi Durbar, could be harnessed into promoting national feeling.

From a letter written to Ramananda Chatterjee, it appears that Nivedita addressed all those outside Bengal in a circulatory note dated 16 October, where she wrote,

This day then designed to be the date of our division, is henceforth yearly to be set aside by us, for the deeper realization of our national unity. Having been made by this threat of division, overwhelmingly conscious of the essential oneness of the whole Indian Nation, the heart of Bengal goes out to all parts of our common Motherland. Thus to you from us of Bengal, is sent today this thread of Rakhi-Bandhan, in token not merely of the union of Provinces and parts of Provinces but of bond that knits us all as children of one Motherland together. Bande Mataram.[108]

Jagadish Bose sent Mrs Bull a rakhi, explaining in a letter, 'They have divided us by law, but *we* all over India bind ourselves by this symbolic tie to stand by each other all time, and stand and face everything . . . We have turned back on relying on strangers. We for India and for ourselves.'[109]

Government crackdown on protesters, especially students, was swift and came through measures such as banning the public singing of Bande Mataram and the circular of Chief Secretary R.W. Carlyle, which threatened the withdrawal of grants, scholarships and affiliation to institutions dominated by nationalists. This precipitated the boycott of official educational institutions and the organization of national schools that received a boost with the spectacular donation of Rs 1 lakh by industrialist and philanthropist Subodh Mullick.

Three distinct phases can be distinguished in the Swadeshi Movement between 1905 and 1908. The first can be called 'constructive swadeshi'[110] when demeaning mendicancy was rejected in favour of self-help through swadeshi industries, national schools, and village improvement programmes. The entrepreneurial business activities of Prafulla Chandra Ray; the national education movement supported by the Dawn Society; enunciation of a detailed programme for village reform by Rabindranath Tagore in his 'Swadeshi Samaj' address in 1904; and the Swadesh Bandhav Samiti in Barisal of Ashwini Kumar Dutta, which claimed phenomenal success in arbitration of village disputes, were all expressions of this trend. These, interestingly, anticipated much of the Gandhian programmes along the same lines that were to follow more than a decade later.

New industries were created spontaneously with people trying their hands at the manufacture of soap, matches, paper, ink and also pottery and bricks. Unrefined rock salt substituted imported salt and molasses substituted sugar. Indigenous handloom cloth tried hard to compete with foreign textiles.

This self-strengthening movement or *atmashakti* as described by Rabindranath Tagore soon lost its appeal for the restless educated youth of Bengal who in the second phase of the swadeshi movement sought a more political extremism. Journals like Bipin Chandra Pal's *New India*, Aurobindo Ghosh's *Bande Mataram*, Brahmabandhab Upadhyay's *Sandhya* and Barindra Ghosh's *Jugantar* spoke in terms of leading the swadeshi campaign into a struggle for Swaraj or self-rule. However, this movement was never intended to be violent at this stage. As Bipin Chandra Pal wrote,

> No one outside a lunatic asylum will ever think of any violent or unlawful methods in India in the present helplessness of her civic freedom . . . If we may not oppose physical force by physical force we may yet make the administration in India absolutely impossible any day . . . Our method is passive resistance, which means an organized determination to refuse to render any voluntary and honorary service to the government.[111]

Aurobindo, who had left his service in the Baroda state to come to Calcutta to try and unite in a single organization the small and scattered groups of revolutionaries, also made clear in a series of articles in *Bande Mataram* in April 1907 that the doctrine of passive resistance that would be followed. He advocated a policy of organized and relentless boycott since he considered the ideal of peaceful ashrams and self-help swadeshi programmes quite inadequate on their own. As part of the educational boycott, he took up the position of the first principal of Bengal National College. An excited Nivedita wrote, 'Education by the people for the people, is now at last being born in India. How Swamiji would have rejoiced to see the day.'[112] Aurobindo also enunciated a programme of social boycott by which he sought to shame unpatriotic Indians by shunning them socially and sending them to Coventry. The *Sandhya* of 21 November 1906 spelt out a non-cooperation doctrine which, in many ways, anticipated the Gandhian call in 1919. It said, 'if the chowkidar, the constable, the deputy and the munsif and the clerk, not to speak of the sepoy, all resign their respective functions, *feringhee* rule in the country may come to an end in a moment.'[113]

The Boycott Movement did achieve some initial success. The Calcutta Collector of Customs in September 1906 noted a twenty-two per cent fall in the quantity of imported cotton piece goods; forty-four per cent in cotton twist and yarn; one per cent in salt; fifty-five per cent in cigarettes and sixty-eight per cent in boots and shoes in the previous month as compared to August 1905.[114] The swadeshi mood also brought about a significant revival in handloom, silk weaving and some other traditional artisan crafts, which instilled pride. However, the movement could not be sustained for long enough to seriously threaten British control over key sectors of Bengal's economy. National education, too, failed to attract the student community because of its negligible job prospects. What survived till the end was the Bengal National College, a Bengal Technical Institute and about a dozen national schools. The Hindu revivalist content in the swadeshi campaign, with mass pledges taken before Kali, invocation of the Mother, celebration of Shivaji *utsav* and proclamation of aggressive Hinduism put off many Muslims who had initially supported the movement. Also, the British propaganda of divide and rule ensured that the new province would translate into more jobs for Muslims and so succeeded in swaying upper and middle class Muslims against the Swadeshi Movement. These classes of Muslims eventually went on to support Dhaka Nawab Salimullah Khan's move to found the Muslim League in 1906. A series of communal riots erupted in east Bengal, where the targets were largely Hindu zamindars and money lenders or mahajans who had systematically failed to assuage Muslim anxieties.

An irate Rabindranath declared in his Presidential address to the Pabna Provincial Conference,[115] 'Satan cannot enter till he finds a flaw . . . a great ocean separates us educated few from millions in our country.' Tagore's alternative of an inclusive development in villages with constructive work initiated by zamindars in a paternalistic fashion, as he was to initiate later in his ancestral estates in east Bengal, found little favour. Nor was Tagore comfortable with the educational boycott, which he realized was driving students to the blind alley of despair. It was his experience of the swadeshi period that made Tagore decide not to join Gandhi's non-cooperation call in 1919, facing all-round criticism at the apparent volte-face. In a letter to Gandhi, he explained that 'the anarchy of emptiness never tempts me even when it is resorted to as a temporary measure.'[116] The change in the mood of the Poet is best seen from two of his finest novels set in this period—*Gora* (1907–09) which ends on a note of hope and *Ghare Baire* (1914) which ends on a note of despair.

By 1907–08, the third phase of the Swadeshi Movement had set in, when there was a shift to violent means by the restive youth after widespread government repression. The impressive chain of district organizations or samitis had been incipient militant organizations. Although in the earlier phases of the swadeshi movement, the Anushilan Samiti or the Dawn Society had taken a lead in implementing techniques of passive resistance, and engaged in social work during famines, epidemics or religious festivals, there was gradually a move in the direction of targeted terror attacks. Trained rigorously in physical fitness, and in the handling of weapons, motivated morally on the doctrines of Mazzini and the Gita, bands of young men in the various groups felt driven to target rich households for monetary gains to fuel their movement and to

eliminate certain repressive British officials. An inner circle of the
Calcutta Anushilan under Barindra Ghosh and Bhupendranath
Dutta, with the tacit knowledge and encouragement of Aurobindo
Ghosh, attempted a few abortive actions. In one such, in 1906,
their plan to kill the very unpopular East Bengal Governor J.B.
Fuller misfired. A bomb-making factory had also been set up at a
garden house at Muraripukur in the Maniktala suburb of Calcutta.

What was the role of Nivedita in the Swadeshi Movement
of Bengal? A legend has grown of Nivedita being a kind of
Jeanne d'Arc of the revolutionary movement.[117] Girijashankar
Roy Chowdhury has claimed that she was a virtual co-leader
with Aurobindo of his revolutionary party and was 'a dangerous
anarchist'.[118] Reymond has written that Nivedita 'did not remain
unimplicated in the manufacture of bombs in the Muraripukur
Road Laboratory.' She writes that Nivedita used to help amateur
chemists by smuggling them into the laboratories of Presidency
College as assistants to professors Jagadish Chandra Bose and
P.C. Roy, totally unknown to the scientists.[119] Debojyoti Burman
contends that Nivedita had actually asked Jagadish Bose to request
P.C. Roy to make his laboratory available to the students.[120] It
was also suggested that Nivedita's inside information made her
send warnings to Aurobindo that his arrest and deportation were
imminent, so that he could escape in time to Chandanagore and
then on to Pondicherry.[121] Bimanbihari Majumdar, too, painted
Nivedita as an active revolutionary,[122] and Sankari Prasad Basu in
his masterly collation of documents on her, gives her pride of place
as the *agnikanya* or the daughter of the fiery epoch.

There is no doubt that Nivedita had given her full support to the
swadeshi campaign when it began and wholeheartedly backed the
Boycott Movement. She felt the Swadeshi Movement had given the
Indian people an opportunity to earn the respect of the whole world.
There was no more begging for help or cringing for concessions.[123]
Nivedita's equation with the youth was formidable since she had

trained them as co-workers during the plague outbreaks in the city. Due to her earlier support of the Irish home rule agitation, she was familiar with revolutionary tactics and with her understanding of Kali, destruction and bloodshed for a just cause were not unacceptable for her. Being of a very impulsive nature, it is also not inconceivable that she might have sneaked in a few young revolutionaries into the laboratories of Presidency College a couple of times using the reference of professors Bose and Ray. But there are also reasons to support a different view. It is highly unlikely for her to have jeopardized the career of her dear protégé Jagadish Chandra Bose. This was also the time she was actively helping Bose with his book *Plant Response* and was preparing to join him in England where he was to go in early 1907. Most importantly, Nivedita left Calcutta in August 1907 and did not return until July 1909. So, in effect, for the crucial period of violent revolutionary activities, she was absent from India. Aurobindo, too, has recorded[124] that he had not proceeded to Chandernagore on the advice of Nivedita, although she did warn him about the British considering deportation. He decided to stay on to write about his dissociation from politics in his last will and testament, which made the government give up its plan to deport him. He acknowledged on her return from abroad that he had given her the charge of editing the final issues of his paper the *Karma Yogin*, in his absence. Nivedita continued the edition for three months until it was suspended in April 1910.

Before her departure from India in 1907, Nivedita had been drawn into the vortex of the nationalist movement. But, apart from supporting the boycott campaign and encouraging indigenous cottage industries, she also remained in constant touch with the developments of the Indian National Congress. She attended both

sessions of the Congress in 1905 and 1906. A few days before the
session, Nivedita wrote in the papers,

> What is the real function of the Congress? It must train its
> members in the new way of thinking which forms the basis of
> nationality. It must foster in them prompt and co-ordinated
> action. It must teach itself to emphasize the mutual sympathy
> which binds all the members of the vast family that stretches
> from the Himalayas to Cape Comorin, from Manipur to the
> Persian Gulf.[125]

The Congress session in December 1905 was held in Varanasi
with Gokhale as president-elect. The Extremist group in the
Congress led by stalwarts like Tilak and Lala Lajpat Rai sought
this opportunity of forcing the Congress to accept the boycott and
swadeshi movements of Bengal within its programme. Moderate
leaders like Gokhale were, however, wary that it would incur the
wrath of the British with whom, for better or worse, India's destinies
were linked. He was cautious to the extent that he hesitated to permit
Sarola Devi, who was present, to sing Bande Mataram on popular
request, since there was a government ban. The feisty Sarola Devi,
however, chose to sing the whole song undeterred. The Extremists
were able to carry the day with a unanimous acceptance of their
resolution. Nivedita, who had been invited by Gokhale to attend the
session, felt that an extraordinary consensus had been reached by all
members of the Congress, an optimism that was to be belied by later
schisms within the party. Nivedita had taken up lodgings in a house
in Tilbhandeswar, which became a meeting place for all shades of
politicians, where she lent a hand in editing and re-writing many of
their speeches. There are reasons to believe that although she was in
general agreement with the Extremist position, Nivedita's friendship
and loyalty lay with Gokhale. In September 1905, when Gokhale, as
an Indian member of the Viceroy's Council, visited London, Nivedita

sent introductory letters[126] to her friends such as William Stead and Mrs Hesty to welcome him and introduce him to their large circle of friends who were friends of India.

At the 1905 session, after the deliberations were over and vote of thanks given, several Indian speakers addressed the meeting. In her speech, Nivedita spoke of the need to see the evolution of the great national sentiment that was enveloping India against the broader perspective of Europe and the world. The birth of nationality in Europe, she reminded the audience, had occurred a hundred years ago against the threat of Napoleonic expansion. But England had obviously forgotten her great role of the past and it was therefore imperative to remind them. Nivedita called upon 'Indian people to stand by and redeem English tradition, re-make it, re-create it, to make England true to herself'. Ultimately she concluded, 'Our dream of Indian nationality is not a selfish dream for India, but it is a dream for humanity, in which India shall be the mother of a great cause, shall be the fosterer and the nurse of all that is noble, human and great.' Nivedita's speech received loud cheers and her resolution was carried unanimously.[127]

After the Congress session had ended, Nivedita spent a day with the monks of the Ramakrishna Mission who had founded a hospital for the poor. She was also able to visit the Shiva temple where, years ago, Vivekananda's mother had offered prayers in his name. Before she returned to Calcutta, she fulfilled her long cherished wish of visiting Rajasthan, which had come alive to her after reading James Tod's *Annals and Antiquities of Rajasthan*. From Varanasi, she first visited Sanchi, Bhopal and Ujjain before going off to see Chittor, Ajmer and Agra. The sight of the silhouette of the Chittor Fort against a moonlit midnight sky filled her with wonder, which found expression in her later writings. Nivedita returned on 22 January 1906 to Calcutta, which was tense following widespread government repression. Other preoccupations, too, kept her fully absorbed.

Gopaler-Ma, who had been an important influence in the life of Ramakrishna, had been brought by Nivedita in December 1903 to her own house when she fell ill at the age of ninety. She had been happy to give shelter to her 'dear little grandmother' and 'dearest treasure' for over two and a half years. An affectionate bond grew between the orthodox old woman and Nivedita, a European woman whom she had initially shunned. While a young Brahmin widow Kusum looked after Gopaler-Ma's immediate needs, Nivedita would always find the time to sit with her by her bedside and massage her feet. On 6 July 1906, Gopaler-Ma passed away peacefully and Nivedita arranged for a puja in her memory.

Disturbing news came in September 1906 that East Bengal, which had been in the grip of severe famine, was now battling uncontrolled floods. This spurred Nivedita to action. Just as the plague outbreak had seen her immersion in rehabilitation work, now too, she decided to join a group for a fact-finding visit to the flood-affected areas. Wading through knee-deep water or sailing in palm boats across rice fields, Nivedita realized how government inaction stemming from a refusal to accept the realities of famine had compounded the disaster. Just like the great Irish potato famine in the middle of the ninth century this, too, had turned into a man-made disaster. In her book, *Glimpses of Famine and Flood in East Bengal 1906*, Nivedita gave heart-rending vignettes of her experiences as well as an in depth assessment of the crisis. The strain of her visit took a heavy toll on her health. Already weakened by an attack of meningitis the previous year, she now had malaria and was confined to bed with Christine constantly looking after her. She admitted 'the famine has cost me very dear.'[128] Without the supervision of the sisters, the school was closed down and the sisters moved to a house in Dum Dum, where Nivedita recuperated and slowly got back to writing. Since Swarupananda had suddenly passed away, she took over the task of writing the editorials of *Prabuddha Bharata* under the caption *Occasional Notes*.

The Congress session in December 1906 in Calcutta saw a steady crystallization of the opposing camps of the Moderates and the Extremists. The former was dominated by the Bombay caucus led by Gokhale and Pherozeshah, among others, and the Extremist camp by Tilak, Lajpat Rai, Bipin Chandra Pal and Aurobindo. However, the move to elect Tilak or Lajpat Rai as president of the Calcutta session was thwarted by inviting a universally respected father figure Dadabhai Naoroji to assume the position. The Extremists, however, saw to it that key resolutions on boycott, swadeshi, national education and self-government were passed. Nivedita, who attended the Calcutta Congress in 1906, was pained to see the bickering within, which seemed 'a sort of mental and moral Armageddon. Two sides ranging for battle, not for cooperation'.[129] In a strongly worded article, she berated the 'mutual recrimination and mutual attack' correctly noting that 'those who are fighting on different parts of the self-same field are wasting time and ammunition by turning their weapons on each other, instead of on a common foe'.[130] As Ramananda Chatterjee commented later in the *Modern Review*, Nivedita was an avowed nationalist who believed in the efficacy of presenting a united front and was therefore unforgiving of faction fights.[131]

Nivedita had for some time been trying to weave a pattern of unity by designing the banner with the Vajra motif, which now took on added significance. Initially having asked Abanindranath to sketch it, she described the banner as a 'consecration and a rallying cry. It is as an altar, at whose foot, whether for assault or defence, men's lives are freely offered up. Generations come and go. New combinations arrive and vanish, but that for which the national symbol stands—that ineffable union of *jana-desha-dharma* for which every people fights—remains for ever, simple and steadfast as Eternity, mirrored in the fugitive minds of its myriad worshippers'.[132] The vajra or thunderbolt was hallowed in Buddhist tradition as representative of honour, purity, wisdom, sanctity and energy. It also occupied a pride of place among the symbols of

Hindu mythology as the weapon of the god Indra, the trident of Shiva, and a weapon in the hand of the goddess Durga, standing for strength and justice. Besides, Nivedita never forgot how Swamiji often used the word for himself.[133] Most importantly, it was not an *image* and would not hurt Muslim sensibilities. Nivedita visualized on the banner, two inspiring refrains, 'Bande Mataram' and '*Wahe Guru ki Fateh*', which Vivekananda was so fond of uttering,[134] and hoped it would one day be adopted as the national flag.

At first, Nivedita designed the flag in colours of black on red only to realize later that it represented the Chinese war flag. Recognizing that it would not appeal to Indian sensibilities, she redesigned the flag in colours of yellow on red.[135] She got her students to embroider a large banner in scarlet and yellow on Abanindranath's sketch and had it displayed in the exhibition organized by the National Congress in 1906. Saddened by divisive forces within the Congress, what Nivedita wished for the most at this time was to project an art symbol that would raise people's morale above petty differences. As she put it, 'Not for us to ask how. Not for us to plan methods. For us, it is only to lay ourselves down at the altar-foot. The gods do the rest. The divine carries us. It is not the thunderbolt that is invincible, but the hand that hurls it.' In fervent prayer, she exclaimed, 'Mother! Mother! Take away from us this self! Let not fame or gain or pleasure have dominion over us! Be Thou the sunlight, we the dew dissolving in its heat.'[136]

Pursuing her dream that art could be the ultimate unifier, she also prevailed upon Abanindranath Tagore to make a painting that would, in essence, represent the motherland. The iconic painting made in 1905 originally conceived as *Banga Mata* was elevated to *Bharat Mata* at Nivedita's bidding. The young and full-bodied four armed ascetic figure holding sheaf, cloth, palm leaf manuscript and prayer beads in her hands was seen as a nationalist mother goddess bestowing the blessings of food, clothing, learning and spiritual strength on her children. Since the major issues that fuelled the

Swadeshi Movement were the agrarian, manufacturing, educational and political policies of the colonial government as voiced by the landowners, traders, students and the intelligentsia, the iconography of the painting was obvious. Nivedita saw the painting as art in the service of shaping nationhood and an uplifting abstract idea, which had been given flesh through paint. One of Abanindranath's first wash paintings, inspired by Japanese artists Hishida and Taikan, *Bharat Mata* assumed iconic significance in the swadeshi period. An enlarged copy of the painting made by a Japanese artist was carried as a banner in processions during the 1906 Congress session. However, after the fervour of the swadeshi period had died down, the painting, famous principally for its propaganda value, lost its place of primacy. Critics discounted its artistic merit and did not consider it to be among Abanindranath's masterpieces.[137]

Nivedita's deep appreciation of Indian handicrafts continued unabated as she extolled their values to her Western friends. For the wedding of Alberta, Mrs Leggett's daughter, while selecting saris she explained that these 'beautiful webs have to be admired and taken as they are, like Turkey carpets or Persian tiles, or not at all'.[138] For her sister's Christmas present, she selected a handmade silver bracelet, which she explained was a Dacca or Cuttack work crafted by an artisan who could not read or write. And yet with its 'dream of lotus buds and leaves and dewdrops it was a living craft'. Acknowledging that her sister would perhaps never wear the piece of jewellery since in England silver filigree was considered vulgar, she hoped that 'as a work of art it may bring you and your guests a little of the joy I find in it'.[139] Even later, when she was out of India, Nivedita was constantly on the lookout for artistic ideas that could inspire Indian artists. From Dublin, she sent artist Priyanath Sinha pencil sketches from the illuminated manuscripts she had seen at the Trinity College Library. She felt these could provide inspiration for making cards with Indian mythological themes and texts and which could possibly get a market in America.[140]

By 1907, events went completely out of hand. First, the Barisal Conference broke up in 1906 with the special induction of Gurkha soldiers by the government. Next, there was a final showdown between the two camps of the Congress at the Surat session in 1907. The obdurate Moderates then deliberately excluded the Extremists from future sessions. Perhaps with the Liberals in power in England and the famous Liberal political thinker John Morley appointed as secretary of state, the Moderate leadership reposed hope in the possibility of constitutional reforms. Simultaneously, there was a spate of violent incidents organized by the revolutionaries, and tough police reprisals followed in their wake. Nivedita reflected 'the Government seems to have gone mad and is now trying to crush the National Movement by wholesale arrests, deportations, etc., all because it dreads a repetition of '57. But this is of course the way to bring it about'.[141] Aurobindo, who had joined hands with Bipin Pal in editing the *Bande Mataram*, became the virtual leader of the Extremists. However, the government prosecuted him soon after as the editor of the journal. Bhupendranath Datta, brother of Vivekananda, who along with Barindra Ghosh was editing the *Jugantar* was arrested in July for writing a seditious article. Nivedita's offer of a bail to secure his release provoked comments in the *Englishman* that she was a traitor to her race. On the eve of Bhupendranath's rigorous year-long imprisonment, Nivedita presented him Kropotkin's *Career of a Revolutionist* and *In Russian and French Prisons* and four volumes of Mazzini's writings. He left her with a request to look after his distraught mother in his absence.[142]

Nivedita was crestfallen. She wrote 'when I think of what Swamiji planned that my life should be and how different I have made it, I feel utterly broken-hearted'.[143] Her mission to rouse India's vastly scattered millions to an elevated realization of nationhood had not taken off. She wrote:

We have failed. The country has not been roused from its slumber; it has not come back to life. We have been able to do almost nothing. The true spirit of India—what once made India the glory of the world and the heart of Asia, has not been revived. When will the nation be conscious of its glorious heritage, and the distinct place it once occupied in the growth of human thought and human civilization? When will that life, that spirit return?[144]

She also analysed that the swadeshi campaign, which had begun with great enthusiasm, could not be sustained because of problems in the two main areas of production and distribution. Production was sporadic and insufficient and the distribution channels of the swadeshi products were not well organized.[145]

In the meantime, Nivedita's dependable friend S.K. Ratcliffe had returned to England after resigning from the *Statesman*. Recognising that he had done 'yeoman service to our cause, as Editor of the *Statesman*,'[146] Nivedita requested Josephine, then in England, to welcome him and his wife to her circle of friends. Amazed that the Ratcliffes still planned to return to India, Nivedita made a personal request to Gokhale to provide him an opportunity to work in the new paper that was being started in Bombay. Writing to her friends with 'a world of love and gratitude and approval', Nivedita referred to Walt Whitman's *Song of the Open Road*. She mentioned encouragingly 'such is the invincible nature of man that it is better—is it not?—to be miserable with the true and the good and the beautiful than to be happy with the opposite?'[147]

Soon after Partition was declared, Lord Curzon resigned in August 1905 over a tiff with General Kitchener and was replaced by Lord Minto. Nivedita remained unhappy at the turn of affairs. She did not have much faith in Minto whom she considered 'weak'.[148] She was taken by surprise by a sudden letter she received on 27 January 1907 from Marie Hamilton Coates, who introduced herself as having been a disciple of Vivekananda in America. Marie Coates was well known to the Mintos and had suggested Nivedita's name to Lady Minto as one who would be able to tell her more about the needs of the Hindu women than anybody else.[149] Nivedita's reaction was blunt. She wrote to her confidante Yum, 'I have no desire to see Ly. Minto.' She did weigh in her mind the advantage of the Swadeshi Movement needing friends in high places though she doubted whether Lady Minto had 'the requisite courage', but she remained quite determined in her decision. She went on to elaborate:

> Swamiji was never, I think, quite clear on these points. He would have used the Curzons or anyone, to get money for me. I would not. It may be that He was right and I am wrong. I quite see this possibility. Even if so, however, I see my own conclusion so clearly that I must be true to it, and leave others to realize His. To me it would appear confusing and disastrous even to be asked to see Ly. Minto. To be asked to co-operate with her I would think mischievous. I think that what is done by the People themselves for themselves is well done. What the Government unwillingly does, in the way of extending primary education, one may show them how to accept and use. But my whole world of appeal lies in the People. Morally, I am one of them. And to be identified even remotely with the rulers would be to lose not to gain in helpfulness.[150]

Three years later in March 1910, a surprise visit by Lady Minto to her Bosepara Lane home gave Nivedita an opportunity to meet the Vicereine. Her interest in getting to know India did much to allay Nivedita's earlier misgivings.

Even as she was busy attending Congress sessions, taking care of Gopaler-Ma, assisting flood victims and designing a banner, Nivedita had been spending considerable time with Jagadish Chandra Bose. She was helping with the writing of his research books either at her Bosepara Lane house or at his residence at 93 Circular Road. Describing her routine, Nivedita wrote:

> We work now 3 and sometimes 4 days a week from 8 am till 5/30 pm with an hour or two omitted for meals. And in the holidays

we do almost more than this, every day. You can imagine how
exhausted we both are—for this has been going on continuously
since the beginning of October, 1904. But then, on the other
hand, one's love and pride are more than satisfied for 20 years
hence, when they have had time to understand it all, they will
say that the Science of Botany was revolutionised by a Hindu![151]

Jagadish Bose's major works *Plant Response* and *Comparative Electro-
Physiology* had now been published and created a sensation among
academic circles in the West. Many foreign universities invited
him enthusiastically to prove his thesis. However, Bose's request
to the government for deputation to go abroad was turned down.
An irate Nivedita, signing off in her letter to Gokhale as 'Nivedita
the Furious', wrote, 'When I reflect that this country is INDIA,
and see how foreigners can batten on her bounty, while a child of
the soil may have to undergo privations in his service of her, that
amount to punishment, I am exasperated.'[152] Ultimately granted a
two years furlough under medical pressure, Bose now prepared to
go to Europe and insisted on Nivedita joining the Boses. It was
perhaps this compulsion, along with a sense of unease that the
police was closely watching her that made Nivedita decide to leave
India. Nivedita left Calcutta on 12 August for Bombay where she
boarded a steamer on 15 August 1907 for Genoa from where she
made her onward journey to England. She dreamt of primroses
in Devon and Ireland, for which she had been yearning since the
days of her grave illness.[153] In Aden, she was heartened to read in a
letter from Christine that her cherished school had reopened and
the children had streamed back to their familiar routine.

5

The Legacy

Away from Indian shores, Nivedita felt she was once again at the crossroads, where she needed to redefine her mission of life. Clearly the school, in the efficient hands of Christine, did not need her immediate presence. The project of nationalism, which had fired Nivedita with a sense of immediacy and purpose, had lost its urgency. And demoralization had set in after the massive arrests. Nivedita felt free to go back to her first love—writing. Realizing that 'the written word was so much more powerful than the spoken,' she was relieved to find herself at peace and 'not anxious because my work is done at my desk'.[1] It is in books, articles, essays, reviews, interviews, edited manuscripts, and travel writings that Nivedita left behind her most enduring legacy. She often felt restless about completing her work as she had a premonition that time was running out. She braced herself with the realization that 'work is one long patience under disappointment'.[2]

Nivedita had an inquisitive and analytical mind. Since her early days as a teacher in England, she had sought to contextualize world developments in a historical and geographical framework to understand the evolution of society, culture and religion. Women figured as a key subject in Nivedita's writings and with great poignancy, she captured the travails and strengths of rural and urban women across countries and cultures. By linking the nun with the wife in terms of dedication and commitment, she brought a unique perspective to her analysis. Equally important was her sociocultural study of the mother in a familial setting leading to a study of mother goddesses.

Before she met Swami Vivekananda, Nivedita was part of the prestigious Sesame Club. Some of her writings published in leading newspapers at the time show a maturity which belies her young age. Interestingly, she used different noms de plume such as Nealas, Margaret Nealas Underwood, An Old Old Woman, *Vox Ignota*, or simply N or MN.[3] The use of pseudonyms provides an important insight into Nivedita's character. *Vox Ignota*, or Unknown Voice, revealed that though she sought to give her voice to urgent issues of the day, she realized that she was yet an unknown name.

In the background of the women's suffrage movement in England, which was gathering momentum in the 1890s, Nivedita's series of six papers on women's rights assume considerable significance. Although there was no mention of voting rights, they spoke of the need for women to exercise their choice so that they could live sensible lives and have well-appointed homes maintaining good hygiene. The first of these papers on 'Their Right to be Beautiful' defined in a practical sense the idea of beauty, boldly challenging the stereotypes of the time. Ridiculing the 'dress absurdities of the Victorian era', which forced feet into ill-fitting boots, cramped hands into tiny gloves and 'tight laced' the body in considerable discomfort, Nivedita wrote that English girls had to be educated about how these 'frivolous time-serving' fashion trends could have disastrous consequences on their health. 'How many girls,' she asked in the article, 'are aware that tight lacing injures the liver' or realized the evils of bad circulation. Declaring that real beauty lay in harmony, Nivedita pleaded for an organized system of instruction where women were taught the principles of health. In 'Their Right to Serve', Nivedita focused on the need for women to have a proper understanding and knowledge of home requirements irrespective of whether they were drawn to clerkship or other branches of service once considered exclusively masculine. The 'queenly dignity' with which every woman took her place on the 'home throne' gave her the ability to hold the household reins in her own hands, often making dinners or mending and darning in private or superintending housework in person without thinking these were beneath her. She emphasized that it was not her intention to advocate enforced home life for women but felt they should have a basic knowledge of first aid, in administrating artificial respiration, preparing a balanced diet and supervising conditions of sanitation and hygiene. In 'Their Right to Choose Houses', she argued that only a sound knowledge of health conditions could guide the housewife to select a home that was well ventilated and with a good drainage system. While advocating 'right', she reminded her readers that it had to be accompanied with 'responsibility' so that 'she who claims must be prepared to act and that she who wishes to know must be ready to learn.' In 'Their Right to Advance', she traced the journey of women's advancement from Anglo-Saxon times when women learnt delicate embroidery and needlework, to Norman days when warlike situations made women adept in nursing and surgery, to the days of Queen Anne when women were caught in the daily grind of pastry-making and cider-brewing and remained illiterate and dull, to the days of the Georges when with the spread of newspapers, discovery of steam power and the use of gas the first steps had been taken towards widening knowledge. In 'Their Right to Know', she elaborated this further to write that there should be an escape from 'examinational steam and cram' to something wiser and gentler so that a sound pattern of education was set up, which advocated women's right to knowledge of science. She ended the series with 'Their Right to Rule' where she spoke of women's rule, where educated and conscientious women could take the lead in small town societies such as in mining areas and initiate moves out of the pitfalls of health hazards, intemperance and bad sanitation. To be taken seriously, the young Margaret Noble signed off these articles as 'An Old Old Woman' ending with the advice 'Let us walk with our eyes open, let us seize all opportunities of learning, above all, let us be doers of the word, and not hearers only.'[4]

It is no wonder then, that when Nivedita came to India, she studied at close quarters the functioning of the Indian household where the mother was in control. Nivedita was appreciative of the mother's dignity and strength of character, and felt that her lack of book learning did not diminish her traditional knowledge and wisdom. Nivedita was concerned that India may lose its hold on its rich past in the face of an onslaught of modern Western practices. Using allusive imagery, she wrote, 'Shall we, after centuries of an Indian womanhood, fashioned on the pattern of Sita, of Savitri, of Rani Ahalya Bai, descend to the creation of coquettes and divorcees? Shall the Indian Padmini be succeeded by the Greek Helen?' She admitted that 'change there must be or India goes down in the shipwreck of her past achievements. But new learning shall add to the old gravity and wisdom without taking from the ancient holiness'.[5]

Also Nivedita's long-standing concern with home hygiene and sanitation explains the commitment and fervour with which she tackled the repeated attacks of plague in Calcutta. The filth and squalor that Nivedita often faced in her work in the slums did not deter her for she had already seen similar dismal settings during a visit to Wrexham. In an article called 'A Page from Wrexham Life,' she described in graphic detail the life she saw, which was 'a perfect epitome of degradation and uncleanliness' where the only ventilation in the homes consisted of 'air well saturated with the refuge of a dustbin and the poison-germs of defective sanitation, going and coming, going and coming, through the open door up the crazy chimney, depositing here and there its load of parasites and vermin, its diseases and its poisons, till the hole these people call a home is little more than a hunting ground of vice and death'.[6]

In India, Nivedita found a rich diversity—of people, topography, sound and colour and she made quick entries into her diary. Her writings, henceforth, concentrated almost exclusively on the many aspects of Indian society, culture and history to which she was introduced by the many lectures of Swami Vivekananda. These were enriched over time by her countless travels on which she embarked and her deep study of Indian literature, philosophy, mythology and history. Her world view and historical sense helped situate her thoughts on India within a wider framework. 'How can we know of India,' she wrote, 'if we know nothing of the world outside India? How shall we recover the truth about ancient Pataliputra, if we know nothing of Persepolis, of Petra, of Babylon, of China and the international relations of all these? Or how are we to understand the growth and significance of Benares, if we have never studied Cologne, Chartres, Durham or Milan? What will the history of Hinduism mean to us, if we have never considered that of Christianity or of Islam?'[7]

Nivedita never failed to acknowledge that she was following her Master's bidding to put on paper with precision, his rambling thoughts on a variety of subjects. She had recognized early enough how Vivekananda 'was longing for someone to pour His own mind and thought into'.[8] She saw the staggering vastness of Swamiji's writings on Hinduism and felt that 'a short sharp view with a clear ringing word' was what India needed at the moment and perhaps her 'very ignorance and want of depth' equipped her best for penning his thoughts,[9] for vast knowledge on a subject could often make it difficult to put down succinct and focused thoughts. There were moments when she wondered whether by writing down all that she heard from her Master was not tantamount to plagiarism. But then she consoled herself saying, 'Shall a child not rejoice in speaking its father's message?'[10]

The first booklet that Nivedita was to pen was *Kali the Mother*,[11] which included her two lectures on the same topic and an exposition of the Kali phenomenon as explained to her by Vivekananda. This proved to be inspirational to a host of people during the first stirrings of nationalism. Next was her book on a carefully selected theme— *The Web of Indian Life*, which was written over a few years, from 1901 to 1903, and published by William Heinemann, London, in 1904. It carried her thoughts on nationalism, a theme that had gripped her attention in the uncertain political scenario of early twentieth century Bengal. The positive response it received delighted Nivedita, who wrote to her favourite Yum: 'I almost imagine the "Web" has made a hit! If so, are you proud of your child?'[12]

Ever since the death of Vivekananda in 1902, Nivedita had been approached by many to pen her thoughts on her Master. Initially she had been overawed by the project but gradually her thoughts settled down and she appealed to her friends, Mrs Bull and Josephine, for the letters of Vivekananda so that she could put forth a compelling book. Nivedita realized that while Swarupananda and others had heard Vivekananda speak principally on Advaita, she had been privileged to have seen the many facets of a person with 'both a great brain and a great heart . . . a rare combination' revealing himself 'in the child-like mood, in the playful mood, in the tender mood, in the inspired mood, in the mood when He showed His great heart, in the poetic mood, or in the mood when you saw the King of the Rishis'.[13]

Mrs Bull was anxious that Nivedita should first be restored to health and given the peace and space to pen this important work. Enclosing a bank draft for a hundred pounds for her personal use, she wrote, 'It used to be my dream that someday Swamiji would have quiet, books and the favourable conditions for writing. May I not ask you to let me try to secure them to you? And to feel that you earn these by the trained efficiency you bring to your work?'[14]

In *The Master as I Saw Him*, which was Nivedita's most significant work, she admitted to bringing out 'very strongly the element of struggle between myself and Him, and this by the advice of the Man of Science,'[15] that is, Jagadish Chandra Bose, which made her account sensitive and moving. She explained that *The Master* had to be personal because 'it had to include a certain recognition of my own mind, as a factor to it, in order to give full value, as I thought, to the account, which is really a record of the swing of Swamiji's thought between East and West'.[16] She felt secure in the knowledge that her Master had a freedom of mind, which would allow her to represent his conflicting ideas on a subject and also accept her strong opinions. 'He said once of his own master [Ramakrishna], "He could not imagine himself the *teacher* of anyone. He was like a man playing with balls of many colours, and leaving it to others to select which they would for themselves."' And I imagine he meant this.'[17] The *Prabuddha Bharata*, which was the publication of Ramakrishna Mission, published *The Master as I Saw Him* serially from 1906 to 1910. In book form, the first edition appeared on 1 February 1910. Nivedita paid her respects by taking the book as her personal offering to his room and placing it on his sofa.[18] She lived for his approbation and cried, 'If only one could ever hear from Him, or know in one's heart that He would say "Well done! Good and faithful servant!"'[19]

Soon after its publication, *The Master* received much acclaim as a definitive work in biographical writing. Professor of spiritual studies at Oxford University, T.K. Cheyne, in his review of the book in January 1911 in the *Hibbert Journal* wrote, 'It may be placed among the choicest religious classics, below the various Scriptures, but on the same shelf with the *Confessions of Saint Augustine* and Sabatier's *Life of Saint Francis*.'[20] Overwhelmed with the fulsome comments, Nivedita wrote to the professor, 'You have praised the book far above its merit, I fear! . . . What a wonderful place in literature you have accorded to my book! I pray that it may prove to have deserved it!'[21]

Nivedita felt she owed it to the success of the book to be selective about possible translators. She has serious misgivings for instance about Madame Wallerstein, Josephine's friend, who had offered to translate the book into French. She considered Madame Wallerstein to be 'such a frightfully unromantic person that I should be a little afraid of hardness and clearness and emotional misrepresentation'.[22]

In *The Master as I Saw Him*, Nivedita analysed 'the Swami's mission considered as a whole'[23] and concluded that in many ways parallels could be drawn with the Buddha. According to her, Buddhism not only democratized the prevailing culture of Hinduism in India laying the basis of a civilizational unity it also 'swept out from the home waters to warm and fertilize the shores of distant lands scattering its message over the Eastern world'.[24] Similarly, Vivekananda while exhorting India to awaken to the full potential of its strength by overcoming internal differences and weaknesses, spoke to Western nations as the first authoritative exponent of the ideas of the Vedas and the Upanishads. They both combined in themselves two roles—'one of world moving and another of nation-making'.[25]

The corpus of Vivekananda's speeches and lectures was so large, with his messages for Eastern and Western audiences being significantly different in tone and focus, that misunderstandings were bound to arise over apparent ambivalences and contradictions. Nivedita sought to address many of these by choosing to be his mouthpiece and placing for posterity Swamiji's thoughts on various subjects. She hoped she could collate these from scattered lectures and give them a focus, essential for an understanding of his views. She decided not to take cognizance of some of Swamiji's severest critics but instead present his thoughts in a manner that would be generally understood. She believed that 'it will be *the* work of my life . . . He will guide my hand line by line, that I might write down those aspects of Him that are Eternal, and be enabled to discard remorselessly all the rest'.

The feisty Nivedita reined in on her combative instincts and confessed,

> You do not know how much I learn, in doing this. All the people who hurt Him—in a kind of way I find that I have to forgive them. I find that to pillory them, as they so richly deserve, and as I now have the means of doing, would be perhaps only to flaw His beauty and to immortalize them by placing them at His side. And so I have to throw away many and many a stone that I have kept in my pocket this many and many a year![26]

Nivedita explained clearly that Vivekananda, while expounding the philosophy of the Vedas and the Upanishads, had no dogma of his own. He had proclaimed, 'I have never quoted anything but the Vedas and Upanishads and from them only the word *strength*.' Nivedita pointed out that Vivekananda preached mukti instead of heaven; enlightenment instead of salvation; the realization of the immanent unity, Brahman, instead of god and the truth of all faiths instead of the binding force of any one. It is important to bear in mind this clarification offered by Nivedita, since there is a tendency to view Vivekananda as a Hindu revivalist.[27] Vivekananda's hesitation to criticize some of the antiquated ancient Indian practices was not because he endorsed them. As he explained to Nivedita, in the face of relentless attacks of missionaries abroad, he sought to refrain from washing dirty linen in public. Often he skirted awkward questions with his customary humour. For instance, in missionary tracts on India, it was said that Hindu mothers threw their babies to crocodiles. On one occasion, when Vivekananda was asked whether this was true, he replied it was indeed so but he personally had been rejected by discriminating crocodiles because as an infant he was much too fat! His thoughts on national regeneration were unique. He did not place much faith in the reform agenda and instead insisted on proclaiming the equality of all religions as advocated in his guru Ramakrishna's well-known saying 'Jauto maut tauto pauth' (there are as many paths to truth as there are points of view). In his Chicago address, Vivekananda had declared that all religions were not to be merely tolerated but to be accepted as true. His uniqueness lay in his spiritual and metaphysical exposition of the Vedantic ideal, which would transcend all differences and show a path that anyone could follow for self-realization. This was a fourfold path adopted according to one's temperament and inclinations—karma, action without attachment; bhakti, the path of devotion; *jnana*, the path of knowledge; and raja yoga, following the techniques expounded in Patanjali's *Yogasutra*. Vivekananda had been initiated into raja yoga by Pavhari Baba, the famous saint of Ghazipur, whom he had met during his wanderings as a monk. Much of Vivekananda's lectures and classes in America were devoted to teaching the paths, both in theory and practice of jnana yoga and raja yoga, making them accessible to the modern Western mind, temperament and way of life. While his book *Raja Yoga*, largely a compilation of lectures, earned him much appreciation, Nivedita was able to put together from his scattered notes and drafts *Karma Yoga* and *Jnana Yoga*, editing the English and style for publication. She wrote excitedly, 'I think great things of myself as a writer, out of Swami's notes. I think I get His Voice—and don't flatten it, as others do. How I wish I could have done it all!'[28]

In his addresses to Western audiences, Vivekananda never spoke of Puranic ritualistic duties so integral to Hindu practices and beliefs; he did not speak of his guru Ramakrishna as the incarnation of divinity and nor did he raise the question of idol worship. Nivedita was surprised when she arrived in India to find her Master in full support of each of these. There was certainly an ambivalence in his celebration of the ritual worship of Kali, Durga and Shiva and in his firm belief that Ramakrishna was a divine incarnation. But he was careful not to impose this conviction on others and create another sect. In time, Nivedita realized the reason behind his reticence to discuss such subjects since they might confuse and bewilder uninitiated audiences. Born a practising Hindu, Vivekananda became a Brahmo for a while and then under the spell of Ramakrishna, he went back to Hindu beliefs realizing that truth was composite and could absorb all these varying trends of thought. The doctrines of duality (*dvaita*), qualified monism and monism (advaita) were three successive stages in man's spiritual progress. While Christianity and Islam were dualistic faiths, Buddhism for him represented non-duality or yogic consciousness. Hinduism, which was dualistic in its first stage, embraced the non-dual, monist version of Vedanta as the end product of Indian beliefs and practices. Once exposed to these thoughts, Nivedita realized it would be ungenerous to dismiss this 'message of a new mind and a strange culture'. Like great music that wakes within and grows and deepens with repetition, the philosophy of her Master slowly dawned on her.[29]

In his addresses in India, Vivekananda made no mention of his Vedanta lectures. His focus was completely different. His emphasis was on the deprived and the underprivileged people of the country, in serving whom one would serve god. Spirituality was not for the weak or possible on an empty stomach. He sought, therefore, to create mass consciousness through education, regenerate the people by creating a national character, and believed social reform measures would follow in due course since they could not be forced on a people not ready for them. Describing the Hindu orthodoxy of his days as a religion of 'don't touchism' where virtue was found in the purity of the cooking pot, he did not hesitate to debunk the puerile practices that still existed in popular Hinduism. He said,

> Whether the bell should be rung on the right side or the left, whether the sandal paste mark should be placed on the forehead

or some other part of the anatomy; people who spend their days and nights in such thoughts are truly wretched. And we are the wretched of the earth and are kicked around because our intelligence goes no further.

Aghast that millions of rupees were spent on temple rituals while the living god perished for want of food and education, Vivekananda lamented, 'A mortal sickness is abroad in our land. The entire country is one vast lunatic asylum.' Continuing his outburst, he cried, 'Throw away the bells and the rest of the rubbish into the river Ganges and worship the incarnate God in man, worship all that are born as human beings.' As Professor Tapan Raychaudhuri concluded, such a man could hardly be called a Hindu revivalist.[30]

At the same time, Vivekananda's plans for national reconstruction gave priority to Hinduism with an agenda to correct its institutions such as the caste system so that inequity could give way to mutual respect. He considered all Hindus to be brothers and believed that in the time to come the Sudras, or the working class, who were lowest in the caste ladder, would initiate a revolution for their own space in the hierarchy. Elaborating on her Master's ideas, Nivedita wrote,

All castes are equal in Dharma. It is by the fulfilment of swadharma, one's own duty, not by the dignity of the task to be performed, that a man's social virtue is measured. The integrity of a scavenger may be more essential to the commonwealth at a given moment, than that of an emperor. All tasks were equally honourable that serves the motherland.[31]

Vivekananda spoke of taking back into the fold of Hinduism all those who had been constrained to leave it for Islam and Christianity because of certain intolerant practices. Interviewing Vivekananda for *Prabuddha Bharata* in 1899, Nivedita had asked her Master whether those returning to the fold would choose their own form of religious belief out of the 'many-visaged Hinduism', and she was told categorically that, of course they would have to choose for themselves. 'For unless a man chooses for himself, the very spirit of Hinduism is destroyed. The essence of our Faith consists simply in the freedom of the *Ishtam*.'[32]

Repeatedly, Vivekananda proclaimed his belief in communal synthesis by stating, for instance, that he wanted future Indians to have strong Muslim bodies and Vedantic souls. To Nivedita, he mentioned his intense pride in the artistic inheritance of the Mughal era and his admiration for the Mughal policy of taking Hindu brides so that the rulers of India had Muslim fathers and Hindu mothers. As Nivedita wrote of her Master, 'He was the modern mind in its completeness,' who never made the mistake of thinking the reconciliation of the old and the new was an easy matter. 'How to nationalize the modern and modernize the old, so as to make the two one, was a puzzle that occupied much of his time and thought.'[33]

In her introduction to the *Complete Works of Swami Vivekananda*, Nivedita explained that Hinduism needed to organize and consolidate its own ideas. Quoting Swami, she wrote,

We Hindus do not merely tolerate, we unite ourselves with every religion, praying in the mosque of the Mohammedan, worshipping before the fire of the Zoroastrian, and kneeling to the cross of the Christian. We know that all religions alike, from the lowest fetishism to the highest absolutism are but so many attempts of the human soul to grasp and realize the Infinite. So we gather all these flowers, and binding them together with the cord of love, make them into a wonderful bouquet of worship.[34]

In the context of the raging Brahmo-Hindu debate of the day between reform and revivalism, Nivedita described her Master as being neither a reformer nor a revivalist since he sought to go further to address the needs of the people at large and create consciousness that god lay within. Nivedita characteristically drew on examples from world history to emphasize that reform did not mean a break from the past but an improvement of the present. 'The Pope went to Avignon as a Protestant!' she exclaimed. 'But he came back,' she added, 'and when he did return, it was as a good Catholic, glad to be at home, in familiar places, glad to be freed from the necessity of protesting against anything. So of reforms in general.'[35]

Vivekananda's hesitation to support the agitation for the Age of Consent Bill despite his deep personal anger against child marriage or his lukewarm response to the issue of widow remarriage, despite his compassion for their plight, largely emanated from his belief that social change had its own momentum. At best, a climate of change could be created through education, propaganda and awareness-building so that people could work out their own destiny. Nivedita explained that on the question of women too his advice was not to change institutions, but to give these agency to solve their own problems.[36] Nivedita's own views on the reasons for educating women reveal her remarkably progressive mind. She argued that the motive could not be merely to make them eligible brides, responsible mothers or companionate spouses. The development of woman was an end in itself and 'if woman is really as much a human being as man, then she has the same right to her fullest possible development as he has. If we should hesitate to emphasize the sex of man, then we ought also to hesitate at emphasizing that of woman. If we seek by every available means to ennoble the one, then we must surely seek equally to ennoble the other'.[37] It is this conviction that made her sceptical of the movement for women's suffrage and the motives of those fighting for it. She tried to dissuade Josephine from giving 'any of your precious strength to the weird cause of Woman's Suffrage'. She said, 'Of course, Women ought to have the vote and must have it . . . theoretically the end is of course desirable, but practically the results will be very mixed in character—and one can see a great many lines of good which are quite outside the ken of *these* workers!'[38]

In *Religion and Dharma*,[39] a compilation of *Occasional Notes* written by Nivedita in the editorial column of *Prabuddha Bharata* and other short notes and articles written for the *Modern Review*, Nivedita clarified many of the oft-misunderstood ideas of her Master on religion, delivered at various platforms. Writing a preface to the book, Ratcliffe explained that the title appears confusing since the English and Sanskrit words—religion and dharma—were often taken to be practically identical in meaning. However, dharma as the force or binding principle between different customs and understandings of people had a larger and more complex significance than that of 'religion' as commonly used. Identifying completely with India and her spirit, with the constant use of 'we' and 'ours', Nivedita explained in her writings that dharma had to reinterpret, in modern terms, the faith and practice of the past. She elaborated that every religion was centred on some particular idea—ancient Egypt on death; Persia on the mystery of good and evil; Christianity on the redeeming love of a divine incarnation. Only Hinduism aimed at the spiritual heights of *vairagyam* and mukti. Vivekananda often spoke of the importance of redefining mukti or freedom, which did not necessarily mean only a retreat from the real world to austerity and renunciation. Mukti could also be attained through devotion to whatever was one's duty or work in life. It was perhaps a weakness in Hinduism that it did not emphasize enough the ideal of the householder and the citizen. It was therefore of paramount importance to exalt work, look on the world as a school and 'set our shoulder to the wheel and struggle unceasingly to attain the end we have set before ourselves'.[40] This was the main philosophy behind Vivekananda's repeated exhortations to a man-making mission. Another problem in Hinduism, Nivedita pointed out, was the difficulty, especially for foreigners, to distinguish between the Hindu religion and the social system, which was bound up in a network of semi-religious sanctions. But it was forgotten that the 'real crown of Hinduism' lay in the fact that, alone among all formulated faiths, it had a section devoted to absolute and universal truths, which were independent of social practices or mythological beliefs. Thus, Giordano Bruno would never have been burnt nor Galileo Galilei tortured if India had been their home and birthplace.[41] No distinction was made between the sacredness of different forms of truth—thus mathematics was also god's and men of science were also rishis.

Nivedita explained what Vivekananda meant by aggressive Hinduism was that:

> We ought to make our faith aggressive, not only internationally, by sending out missionaries, but also socially, by self-improvement; not only doctrinally by accepting converts, but also spiritually by intensifying its activity. What we need is to supplement religion by public spirit—an enlightened self-sense, in which every member of the community has a part.[42]

Further, she elaborated that 'religion in this sense is not superstition, it is not fear, or mythology, or the practice of penances. It is living thought and belief, with their reaction in *character*'.[43] She concluded that the modern *vairagis, tyagis* or renunciates will wear no *gerua* (saffron).

> Seated in an office or ruling over a factory; enrolling his fellows in unions, or studying with every nerve and muscle the organisation of labour on a large scale; giving himself to education, or even, it may be, ruling faithfully and devotedly over a household of his own, not in the name of its limited interests, but on behalf of the Indian people, such will be the gerua-clad of the new order. 'He who knows neither fear nor desire,' says the Gita, 'is the true monk'. Not the Sannyasin-clad, but the Sannyasin-hearted.[44]

One of the themes that Nivedita dwelt on in *The Master* was the subject of death.[45] With her Western upbringing, she had held that there was no reason to imagine, despite one's dearest wishes, that there could be any survival of personality beyond the death of the body. On coming to India, her views were significantly altered. Swamiji pointed out, she wrote, that in Western thought man was considered a body, which also had a soul. In Eastern thought, man was considered to be a soul, which also had a body. Pondering over this profound observation, with 'the mind within, not the ear without', slowly over time Nivedita came to acknowledge that the mind was dominant and she could not imagine it being extinguished by the death of the body. Explaining the mystery of existence, Swamiji said that each individual can only see his own universe, which is also his bondage. It dissipates with his liberation while it remains for others who are still in bondage. To explain the sense of this momentary universe, Swamiji drew the analogy of a wave in an ocean, which is bound by its name and form, but when it subsides, it is the ocean and its name and form vanish. This name and form was maya and the water was Brahman.[46] In 1895, in a letter to a friend in America whose father had died, Swamiji wrote,

> The earth moves, causing the illusion of the movement of the sun; but the sun does not move. So Prakriti or Maya or Nature is moving, changing, unfolding veil after veil, turning over leaf after leaf of this grand book—while the witnessing soul drinks in knowledge, unmoved, unchanged. All souls that ever have been, are, or shall be, are all in the present tense.[47]

The theme of death had always intrigued Nivedita, who in her early days in England had penned a fictional story titled Hag-Ridden, which was on paranormal activity. In August 1905, she wrote a slim volume *An Indian Study of Love and Death*, which was published by Sonnenschein and Co. in London. It was reprinted in 1908 by Longmans, Green and Co., London, and included an additional segment on 'Some Hindu Rites for the Honoured Dead', which consisted of free translations from Sanskrit prayers, hymns and litanies offered in ceremonies after death. The book, probably an expression of love and sympathy on the death of Madame Wallerstein, a friend of Josephine MacLeod, had as a dedicatory note 'For a Little Sister' and was inscribed 'Because of Sorrow' and signed simply N. Later, three articles on 'The Beloved', 'Death' and 'Play', which were found among the papers of Nivedita after her death and were published by *Prabuddha Bharata* and the *Modern Review* in 1911, were added to this publication.[48]

The *Notes of Some Wanderings with Swami Vivekananda* was first published as *Pages from a Diary* in the *Brahmavadin* from 1906 to 1910. In book form, it was published by the *Udbodhan* office in 1913. Significantly, it contains the impressions of Nivedita as she settled down in an unknown land and captures candid reflections of her first travels with Vivekananda across the country, when she received valuable lessons from him on India's culture, history and mythology. It also speaks of the complexities of her interactions with the Master, her personal anxieties and her ultimate understanding of him. With her interest in geography, she traced in detail the travel route undertaken first by train and then by mountain roads to high altitudes. She reflected how through that summer of 1898, Vivekananda 'would sit for hours telling us stories, those cradle tales of Hinduism, whose function is not at all that of our nursery fictions, but much more, like the man-making myths of the old Hellenic world'.[49] This gave her the idea to pen short stories on Indian mythology giving it the same title 'Cradle Tales of Hinduism'. In lyrical style, she sought to capture memories of the time spent in idyllic settings by the river Jhelum, memories which she constantly invoked in her letters with deep nostalgia over the following years. She wrote,

> Fain, if I could, would I describe our journeys. Even as I write, I see the irises in bloom at Baramulla; the young rice beneath the poplars at Islamabad; starlight scenes in Himalayan forests; and the royal beauties of Delhi and the Taj. Not then, in word, but in the light of memory they are enshrined for ever.[50]

The Northern Tirtha: A Pilgrim's Diary (renamed in 1921 *Kedar Nath and Badri Narayan: A Pilgrim's Diary*) published serially in the *Modern Review* in 1910 and published in book form the following year by *Udbodhan*, was another significant book in the genre of travel writings, which described her visit to Kedarnath and Badrinarayan in the summer of 1910. While *The Notes of Some Wanderings* were based on diary jottings soon after her arrival in India when she was still trying to grasp the unfamiliar culture and history of the land, *The Northern Tirtha* is a mature work written after the death of Swamiji, where her knowledge of the religious and artistic traditions of the mountainous regions she visited is impressive and displays scholarship. Above all, it tabulates meticulously the distances between major destinations as well as lists resting spots or *chatties*, with remarks on available accommodation to be found, ranging from dharamshalas, inspection bungalows, dak bungalows to fairly primitive *chappars*. Nivedita felt it was important to provide readers such authentic and detailed information of travel in these remote areas, as it was almost impossible to find in those days.

One of Nivedita's insightful observations in *The Northern Tirtha* was that most of the great pujari-Brahmins and mahant in the places of pilgrimages in the north were from south India. Perhaps this happened in the wake of the visit by Shankaracharya, who was supposedly born in Kerala in the eight century CE and who had travelled widely throughout India with his doctrine of Advaita

Vedanta establishing centres of spiritual practice. She remarked that even the guides or pandas—'the semi ecclesiastical couriers'—on the Badrinarayan road were from the south. To Nivedita, this was a sure sign of the spiritual interrelatedness of the country. Another observation was that women figured prominently among the pilgrims with 'neither fear, nor exaggerated shyness in their demeanour'.[51] She was also struck by the fact that the pilgrims seemed to know one another and there was a mood of going on a holiday together.

Following the course of the river after Vyasa Ganga, Nivedita realized that she was treading the Mahabharata country. She was awestruck by the beauty of the river at Deva Prayag, to secure a good view of which the surrounding houses seemed to be standing 'tip-toe behind each other'. Nivedita felt her inability to visit the Niagara Falls had been compensated when she sighted the gorge from the bridge at Deva Prayag where the swirling waters of the Alakananda and Bhagirathi met. She wrote: 'Wind and whirlpool and torrent overwhelm us with their fierceness of voice and movement. The waters roar, and a perpetual tempest wails and rages.'[52] Observing the temple architecture on the way, Nivedita detected a slow transformation from the *chaitya* form of Buddhist days to Vaishnava forms, commenting that the whole region had been the theatre of much religious monastic activity. The ascent to Kedarnath was arduous; it was supposedly the dolorous stairway to vaikunth (heaven), which the Pandavas had climbed in their *mahaprasthana* or Great Release. Nivedita noted that while Shiva was the principal deity at Kedarnath, there were remnants of the temples of Satya-Narayan and the mother goddess or Devi from the Shankaracharya period.

Describing the trek to Badrinarayan, Nivedita mentioned the many resting places on the way, the various temples passed en route and how the Shaivite character of the temples slowly transformed by the Vaishnava influences of Ramanuja. Badrinarayan, said to have been established by Shankaracharya, symbolized a medieval form of Vaishnavism. Standing as guard of the temple, was the statue of *Ghanta Karna*, the bell-eared, in the best tradition of *Hari-Hara*, the synthesis of Vishnu and Shiva. Although Nivedita found the architecture of the temple 'painfully modern' since it 'had undergone repair, without regard to history,' and found the conduct of the pandas 'irritating in the extreme,' she was struck by the aura of the place. There was the sheer beauty of the flowered turf covered with wild thyme, briar roses and violet primula.[53] Nivedita returned from her northern pilgrimage to Kedarnath and Badrinarayan with a strong sense of having visited the 'cathedral cities of two remote northern dioceses, upon which had broken for the last 2000 years, the tidal wave of every spiritual movement in Indian history', making it 'a great palimpsest of the history of Hinduism'.[54]

Glimpses of Famine and Flood in East Bengal in 1906 was serially published in the *Modern Review* in 1907. This deeply moving narrative reveals Nivedita's keen interest in the geographical features of Bengal's delta region, compassion for the human agony she witnessed, indignation at the official indifference and admiration of the individual relief initiative of the Barisal schoolteacher Ashwini Kumar Dutta. Part of an inspection team, when Nivedita entered the wide stretching delta lands at the mouths of the Ganga and Brahmaputra rivers, she recalled the beauty of Holland and Venice. In a lyrical description, she wrote, 'Like a great net, then, made of cords of shining silver blue, the waterways—broad rivers, narrower canals or *khals* and the narrowest of all the little water-lanes—hold lovingly in their clasp this beautiful land, which throughout the historic period has been known as the "Granary of Bengal."'[55] It was indeed unfortunate to see the extent of devastation wrought first by famine and then by excessive monsoon rains. The sight of 'gibbering starvation, [people] clad in plaintain-leaves for want of clothing,' of women in Matibhanga, the worst-affected village, immersed neck-deep in water to cover their nakedness, of families weeping for the dead, stunned her sensibilities and she realized, 'If misery is apt to brutalize the sufferer, it is still more true that it deadens the witness.'[56] On her return to Calcutta, she was appalled to read in the newspapers that relief was being discontinued since the famine-stricken districts had supposedly become accustomed to it. The presence of a foreign bureaucracy, she realized, made it impossible to gauge with sensitivity the human misery that existed.

In her analysis of the famine conditions in Bengal, Nivedita followed the approach of Prof. Patrick Geddes to study the social significance of the various agricultural crops and industrial products in the region under survey. She wrote to him, 'The administration of a country solely from the revenue point of view leads to strange results.'[57] Widespread cultivation of jute for the sake of the commercial value of its fibre, she found, had steadily diminished the traditional paddy cultivation. Since jute tended to exhaust the soil, both the crops could not give good yields when grown in rotation. In this way, the 'Granary of Bengal' was being transformed into one vast jute plantation.[58] Government inaction followed Lieutenant Governor Joseph Bampfylde Fuller's declaration that the famine was non-existent. Mounting popular anger was stoked further in the heat of the protest movement against the Bengal Partition and by the repressive actions of the Gurkha regiment that had been summoned by Fuller to break up the Barisal Political Conference. These circumstances created a movement of determined cooperation led by Barisal schoolteacher Ashwini Kumar Dutta who galvanized the youth to open voluntary relief centres on a mass scale throughout the district. Though it remained unrecognized by the government, this initiative described by Nivedita as 'the greatest thing ever done in Bengal' gave succour to thousands of helpless people, who would otherwise have been 'swept out of the ranks of the living by the ruthless hand of famine'.[59]

Studies from an Eastern Home published in 1913 by Longmans, Green and Co., London, consists of articles she sent to S.K. Ratcliffe

from 1905 for publication in the *Statesman* as 'Indian Studies'.
These included fascinating vignettes of her life in India. Dispelling
concerns, especially among English compatriots, that she would
certainly succumb to cholera or typhoid when she chose to live in
the Hindu quarter of north Calcutta, Nivedita wrote reassuringly
that she lived in good health in a charming, rambling old house.
She was fascinated with the courtyard designed in the middle of the
house in 'tropical fashion' describing it as 'a great well of coolness
and shadow in the daytime, and a temple of eternity at night, a
playground of merry breezes and an open sundial'; 'Who would not
love a house with a courtyard?' she asked.[60] She also wrote about
the 'other architectural beauty' of her home—namely the roof—
where 'at dawn or sunset or in the moonlight one can feel alone
with the whole universe'. Nivedita noted how important the roof
was as a getaway for the Hindu woman who was cooped up the
whole day with domestic chores and could indulge in merry talk
with other women across the roofs on summer nights. She wrote
about the travelling mendicant singing exquisite ballad songs of the
eighteenth-century poet Ramprasad Sen, whom she described as
the Robert Burns of Bengal. Nivedita's interaction with her waiting
woman who was over seventy years old and yet addressed as daughter
or '*jhee*' amused her. She mentioned how surprised she had been to
be served hot water for her tea by her jhee who appeared dripping
wet after a purifying bath since Nivedita had touched her tea tray.
Nivedita went on to observe how affectionate ties could be between
old attendants and their employers, whom they felt privileged to
scold while indulging their children. The sari fascinated Nivedita.
A practical garment with all the freedom of a skirt, its elegance was
heightened when the breeze caught the veil giving the appearance
of the *Sistine Madonna*. The colours of the sari were a mystery to
Nivedita, who with her artistic sense remarked, 'Dark blue is never
blue, but purple. Green is like grass lying in sunlight or shot with
rose. Grey is not altogether silver; there is a suggestion of the blue

rock pigeon in it too. A check or a dazzling combination of black and white, is an outrage impossible to perpetuate.'[61] Her preference, however, remained with the radiant purity of the widow's plain white cloth, silk for worship and cotton for daily service.

The regularity with which religious festivals occurred in the Indian calendar impressed Nivedita who often cited a European equivalent, by way of comparison in her articles. Writing of *dol-jatra* or Holi celebrated with colour and abandon, Nivedita mentioned that it seemed like May Day frolic or the yearly feast of Eros. Saraswati, in white, seemed to Nivedita somewhat widow-like in her ascetic purity offering a contrast to her sister Lakshmi in resplendent red with whom it seemed she had a sibling rivalry. A favourite goddess of every home like Athene in pre-historic Athens, Saraswati was worshipped only for a couple of days after which she was immersed. Nivedita's moving description of the ceremony of bidding farewell to the goddess conducted by women, which ended with the sprinkling of the 'water of peace' brought in after immersion, was a touching account, revealing a rare sensibility. In describing Durga Puja, Nivedita dwelt not on her martial incarnation worshipped in north India but on the Bengal tradition of regarding Durga as the loving daughter visiting her parental home with her children.

Religious mythology fascinated Nivedita and she realized that her appreciation of European art had been enhanced by her knowledge of Greek mythology. On coming to India, she found there was a world of folklore and mythology waiting to be discovered. Her initial lessons came from Vivekananda and when her interest was heightened, she went to libraries and consulted those she found knowledgeable like Jogin-Ma. *The Cradle Tales of Hinduism* was first published in 1907 but work on it had begun earlier in America when she began collecting stories to narrate to the children of Betty Leggett. She meant to tell 'the little ones about the Christ child and then on to the Indian Christ child—Dhruva, Prahlad and Gopala'.[62] She felt encouraged when a certain Mr Waterman offered to publish the stories. Ultimately, he did not and on 16 July 1906, she wrote to Mrs Bull, '*The Cradle Tales of Hinduism* are nearly ready. I hope to send one copy to England by the end of July and one copy to you—to try to publish independently and simultaneously in America. We have decided that if I could for this book get a hundred pounds down and a small royalty, say 2 cents or 1 d. a copy it would be good.'[63]

Written in the manner of the old-time itinerant storyteller who would gather people under a tree at sunset or around a well, captivating them with mythological stories, Nivedita described her collection as 'genuine Indian nursery tales'. She persuaded Abanindranath Tagore to paint for her the thunderbolt of Durga for the cover of her book and included in the frontispiece, his painting captioned, 'The Indian Story-teller at Nightfall'. In the preface, she declared that her information had the authenticity of being collected from by both word of mouth as well as from published material.

Nivedita arranged her stories in sections around themes or religious mythological figures. The Cycle of Snake Stories was taken from the Mahabharata, which she called 'that mine of jewels' while the section on Sati was from the Bhagavata Purana and the story of Princess Uma gleaned from both the Ramayana and Kalidasa's *Kumara Sambhava* (Birth of the Warlord). The story of Savitri, which enthralled her as the Indian equivalent of Alcestis, and the 'incomparable story' of Nala and Damayanti were from the Mahabharata. In a section called the Krishna Cycle, there were stories from the Puranas as well as from the Mahabharata. Nivedita wrote how she thoroughly enjoyed writing about Krishna since it led her to 'explore wonderful new worlds myself'.[64] In the section she named 'Devotees', were included stories on Dhruva, Prahlada, Gopala and his brother the cowherd taken from popular versions of the Vishnu Purana and the village tale about the judgement seat of King Vikramaditya. The Cycle of the Ramayana containing stories of Sita were intended to be a brief epitome of the great epic, which to her mind was the 'most important influence in shaping the characters and personalities of Hindu women'.[65] Nivedita pronounced the two Indian epics Ramayana and Mahabharata as being 'the outstanding educational agencies of Indian life.'[66] Across the country through the ages, epic tales in various versions, recensions and languages were enacted in plays, sung or recounted in storytelling, depicted in sculptures and art work. Nivedita wondered whether stories of the Greek Herakles had not travelled to India with cultural contact in the third century CE, as evident in the writings of Megasthenes, who reported to Seleukos Nikator of Syria and Babylon that Herakles was worshipped at Mathura. She put forward an interesting thought that perhaps Herakles of Greece and Phoenicia and Krishna of India being in the same 'culture region' might have had a 'distant Central Asian progenitor, common to the two—a mythic half-man, half-god, strong, righteous, and full of heroic mercy'. She also wondered whether Krishna of the Puranic stories and the Krishna Partha Sarathi of the Mahabharata were the same. She then hastened to add that these interesting speculations had to be taken up by trained Indian scholars since no foreigner could have the linguistic competence or theological knowledge to do so.[67] Many of the mythological figures, Nivedita found, were spiritualized by the Indian mind so that they became heroes in the sky, about which she penned an interesting article titled *The Star Pictures*, which was published in three instalments in the *Modern Review* in 1911 and 1912. It is 'a wonderful subject,' she wrote, but 'would be wonderful still if I knew something in detail of Astronomy'.[68]

A firm believer in the theory of Pestalozzi that a people could be understood only in the light of their own history, Nivedita took pains to read Indian history, carefully studying published works, among which historian Vincent Smith was her constant reference point. The footprints of history left through ages on ancient scriptures, poems, temples fascinated her and she wrote in a poem, 'The Footfalls', which formed the frontispiece of her book 'Where lead they O Mother/ Thy footfalls/ O grant us to drink of their meaning!' She wrote several articles in the *Modern Review* and lectured repeatedly on themes of Buddhism, places of Buddhist importance, the accounts of travellers like Fa Hien, the relationship between Buddhism and Hinduism, the rise of Vaishnavism under the Guptas and old Brahmanical learning. Many of these were collected for a publication titled *Footfalls of Indian History* in 1915 after her death.

Although not trained in art, Nivedita, as an amateur, had an artistic sensibility. Since her days as a teacher in England and as a member of the Sesame Club, she had interacted extensively with her artist friend Ebenezer Cooke on the educational value of art. The concept of art as an expression of a national and civic identity appealed to her and she drew inspiration from the idealistic art and craft movement that began in Britain in 1880 to protect the traditional skills and livelihoods of ordinary people from the effects of industrialization on design. The two most influential figures in this movement were theorist and critic John Ruskin and designer, writer, poet and activist William Morris, who examined the relationship between art, society and labour. Nivedita was much taken by the pattern designs on fabrics, wallpapers, handmade paper, and book binding done by Morris (1834–96). Morris turned to nature, flora and fauna for inspiration for his designs as the spiritual antidote to the decline in social, moral and artistic standards during the Industrial Revolution.

Nivedita also found great interest in tracing the civic role of cities like Florence in creating a consciousness among people about their tradition and history through mural paintings and folk art open to public viewing in buildings and open forums. Certain art works like *Saint Genevieve Watching over Paris* by artist Pierre Puvis de Chavannes left an indelible impression on her mind. The mural painting adorning the Paris Pantheon depicted the robed figure of Saint Genevieve, patron saint of Paris, standing vigil over the Parisian landscape as a guardian spirit protecting its civic ideals while the city slept. Raphael's *Sistine Madonna* also captivated her with its expression of compassion and protection.

When Nivedita came to India, she was fascinated with the wide range of local handicrafts and cottage industries that had continued in artisan families through the ages and were now under threat in the mechanical age. She found in Vivekananda a mentor who explained to her the traditional crafts heritage of India, which she found invaluable when she had to make a speech on the subject during her visit to America in 1899. At the Parliament of Religions in Paris in 1900, she heard Vivekananda's impassioned defence of the indigenous sources of Indian art refuting the Western view articulated by Professor Grünwedel in *Buddhist Art in India* that the source of the Indian art tradition was Hellenic.

In 1902, Nivedita met E.B. Havell, the principal of the Government School of Arts and Crafts in Calcutta. He shared with her his deep conviction that the golden past of India's art tradition was evident in the exceptional murals of Ajanta caves or the colossal masterpiece of the rock cut temple at Ellora or the sculptures of the Indian trinity at Elephanta. These traditions were not sufficiently known, which had led to Western scholars making erroneous claims about Hellenic art being their source. Havell wrote that India had a living, traditional and national art intimately bound with the social and religious life of the people unlike the secularized, commercialized and denationalized art of Europe.[69] He explained that although Hellenic contact in the fourth century CE may have been a powerful factor in Indian evolution, it could not impose its very different aesthetic ideals on Indian art, which had its own unique trajectory. Thus anatomical and physiological perfection in Hellenic art, which was imitative and realistic, was accepted as the mark of excellence in the European conception and was being followed in India by modern-day artists like Raja Ravi Varma. The ideal in Indian sculpture, however, lay not in imitation but in a suggestive quality, which was finer and more subtle than ordinary physical beauty. Havell concluded that the Gandharan sculptures in the Calcutta Museum in the Greek style represented smart military figures 'who pose uncomfortably there in the attitudes of Indian asceticism' and were in marked contrast to the lofty calm simplicity of the Buddhas of Magadha or the Dhyani Buddha of Borobudur.[70]

The stirrings of nationalism in the early years of the twentieth century made Nivedita eager to elaborate on the idea of Indian art with its indigenous roots as the binding force with 'a great common speech' and felt its rebirth was essential for the reawakening of the motherland.[71] She wrote to Yum, 'I sometimes think that our greatest work in modernizing India might be done through Art, instead of through the Press or the Universities. But it is Art as the Minister of the Civic Spirit—of the National Sense—of History, Not art immoral and anarchic—that we need.'[72] She was excited about the innate artistic sense that she detected in people and wrote, '*Everyone* in India can draw. The country is full, full, full of artistic talent—but there is no Cookie to teach us how to express ourselves through this.' She lamented, 'Oh, if only I had been able to carry him. If only I had been able to carry Mr Geddes! How I feel my defects of mind and power!—and above all, of education.'[73]

She sought the support of Havell to send out a clear message to Indian art students to desist from the existing practice of aping Western art, with its photographic realism and making portraits of people seated in styles that were European rather than traditionally Indian. She wrote that in India, where there was a sense of decorum in women's postures, she found paintings, presumably of Ravi

Varma, of young women sprawled full length on the floor writing a letter on a lotus leaf, ill bred. With a sense of Victorian morality, Nivedita remarked, 'I do not know of any country in which a young lady may stretch herself on the floor in public.'[74] When Nivedita came in contact with Abanindranath Tagore, the vice principal of the Calcutta Art School, she exhorted him to look beyond Western sources of art to the beautiful art heritage of his own country.

Nivedita sought to set benchmarks of art for the students that were intrinsically Indian, explaining that the Indian depiction of art, like Indian philosophy, went beyond the external form to the ideals that lay within. Nivedita found considerable support in these ideas from Okakura Kakuzo of Japan, who had been sent abroad by his government in 1886 to study European art history but returned with a heightened understanding and respect for Japan's own art traditions. A firm believer that Japan shared with Asia a common cultural ethos far removed from Western art traditions, he set up an art guild, the Nippon Bijitsuin, or Hall of Fine Arts at Yanaka, in the suburbs of Tokyo, consisting of indigenous artists who could perfect and preserve Japan's unique heritage of lacquer and paper painting, the wash techniques and pottery making. Nivedita hailed Okakura as being 'in some sense the William Morris of his country'.[75] Another distinguished art connoisseur who lent encouragement to Nivedita was Ananda Coomaraswamy of Ceylon, who sought to preserve the syncretic art tradition of his country, which had inherited an Indian art legacy but perfected it along indigenous lines.

Nivedita's views on art were never penned in a book but in several articles that she contributed to the *Modern Review*. Her introductions to the seminal works of Havell, Okakura and Coomaraswamy on art were also carried in the *Modern Review*.[76] She felt that works such as these with 'an unassailable background of knowledge and culture may be added to the sentiment of *swadesh* and the doctrine of Nationality'.[77] In extolling the virtues of the

Indian art tradition, Nivedita did not deny the historic impact of Hellenic or Western art on the Indian art tradition but she sought to make clear that these influences had a focus that was very different from the homegrown Indian art style that had a longer and richer history. Through this, she challenged the Western theory that prior to the impact of Hellenic art, India had little to show for itself.

Realizing at the same time that students had much to learn from select masterpieces in Western art, Nivedita requested her friends, Mrs Bull and Josephine, to send her cheap reproductions of some of the Western masters, invariably on the theme of womanhood, so that along with her critical observations in every issue of the *Modern Review*, she could present one painting. The articles would also be translated into Bengali and included in Ramananda Chatterjee's *Prabashi* journal. Among the pictures she included was, of course, her favourite *Saint Genevieve* by Puvis de Chavannes, where her explanatory notes linked the expression of the saint to the protective sincerity in a woman of an Eastern household, the eternal vigil keeper for the sleeping world. J.F. Millet's *Angelus*, depicting the scene of annunciation when Mary was apprised by the Angel that she was to be the mother of Christ, was selected by her to demonstrate that a painting could at the same time present realism and idealism. Set against a rural backdrop, the artist seemed to capture the spirit of nature and as such she felt that it had a special message for the modern Indian artist. Madonna and Child was an oft-painted subject and instead of presenting the more famous artists on this theme, Nivedita selected a modern Madonna by a living painter Pascal Dagnan-Bouveret to demonstrate the blending of the ideal with the real. Charged with symbolism, the mother could be either an Italian peasant woman or a nun but with an expression of universal motherhood. The portrait of Queen Louise, the mother of Kaiser William of Germany, by Richter was selected to display that despite her difficult life experiences she could maintain a lofty pride, sporting no jewels except her crown and becoming a kind of patron saint of

the new German tradition. The *Peasant Girls* by Jules Breton was
selected to show the beauty of commonplace life, reminding her of
the 'queenly beauty' she often detected among ordinary women on
Indian streets, whether coolies or peasants. Finally Guido Reni's
The Picture of Beatrice Cenci was selected to show the mournful look
of despair on the face of Beatrice as she is led away to execution
for having murdered her evil father, a painting which Dickens felt
haunted him with the look of transcendent beauty on the face of
Beatrice.

   In donning the hat of an art teacher to the students of Mr Havell,
Nivedita was characteristically overzealous, given to generalizations
and even some contradictions. While she considered the nudes of
Puvis de Chavannes unattractive and pictures of ladies smoking
cigarettes indecent, she found classical nudes like *Venus of Milo* or
Donatello's medieval *Girl taking a thorn* with a certain 'grandeur of
reverence'. However, she felt that 'pictures of the nude and semi-
nude are always best avoided in India, since . . . mistakes in taste on
such a subject are dangerous to moral dignity'.[78] One wonders if she
had had occasion to visit some of the erotic sculptures in India. She
had remarked that the famous Gandhara sculpture of the emaciated
Buddha at the Lahore Museum or the skeletal Kali in Jaipur
were 'wrong' since the true function of art was the pursuit of the
beautiful—not necessarily the sensuously beautiful but always the
beautiful. This is difficult to reconcile with her ecstatic praise for
the fearful Kali in temples with a necklace of human heads around
her neck, which was imposing but not beautiful. Her advice to the
students was that 'an Indian painting, if it is to be really Indian and
really great, must appeal to the Indian heart in an Indian way, must
convey some feeling or idea that is either familiar or immediately
comprehensible'. She pictured such scenes for painting as 'the lamp
left lighted on the threshold that the housewife, returning from
the river before dawn, may know her own door; the bunch of grain
made fast with mud to the lintel; the light beneath the tulsi plant or

the wending of the cows to the village at sundown'.[79] Nivedita also encouraged her artist friends to undertake more mural paintings, which in days of antiquity had adorned the Chaitya halls of the Buddhist abbeys in Ajanta and which could now be done in large assembly halls for popular civic education.

With Abanindranath Tagore now taking the initiative to look to the traditional art of India for inspiration, a new art movement began with his students moving away from the imitative style of Western art. The new Calcutta School of Art, which included the illustrious students of Abanindranath such as Nandalal Bose, Surendranath Ganguly, Asit Haldar and Venkatappa, not only received the support of Havell and Nivedita but also the approval and backing of art luminaries like Coomaraswamy, Gaganendranath Tagore, O.C. Ganguly and Sir John Woodroffe. In 1907, the Indian Society of Oriental Art was formally established, although their pioneering work was received with some scepticism. Nivedita took great interest in the work of this young group of artists, encouraging them to exhibit and pointing out to them what she perceived to be their deficiencies.

In February 1910, Nivedita attended the exhibition organized by these young artists and wrote a detailed report that appeared in the *Modern Review*. She was delighted that in these modern paintings was found the thread that connected them with the traditional past, where artists had used traditional symbolism with a great liberty of expression raising them to the exalted position of national art. She was ecstatic about Abanindranath Tagore's *Bharat Mata*, which she declared was a masterpiece and hoped it would augur the beginning of a new age in Indian art. Going into the details of the painting, she remarked that the 'Asiatically conceived figure' with four arms conveying the spirit of motherland as the giver of faith and learning, clothing and food, was at the same time a pure virginal figure who could be identified with every mother and daughter in the Indian land. She lauded the representations of *Sita* by Asit Haldar and Abanindranath since she saluted Sita in the

Ramayana first as a great woman and then as a great wife claiming that she should enjoy a pre-eminence in Indian art like the Madonna in European art.

Of Abanindranath Tagore's *The Passing of Shah Jahan*, Nivedita wrote in agreement with the view of Coomaraswamy that it placed the artist among the first order in Europe. Nivedita's review of the painting was an expression of her romantic poetic soul. She exclaimed,

> The sad minor mingles with the music. To joyous courtship succeeds long widowhood. On brilliant empire supervenes the seven years' imprisonment . . . The sucking sound of the river below the bastions fills him with the sense of that other river beside which stands his soul . . . the Taj, *her* taj, her crown . . . truly a royal passing—this of Shah Jahan! King in nothing so truly as in his place in a woman's heart—crowned in this, the supreme moment, of her to whom he gave the Crown of all the world.[80]

Abanindranath explained that the painting had assumed such poignancy because into it he had poured all the anguish of a father after having recently lost his daughter to plague.[81]

Nandalal Bose's *Sati* caught her attention for conveying a woman's strength of character even as she struggled in the spire-like flames. Nivedita's praise was directed not at the controversial institution of sati but at the spirit of martyrdom that she had seen immortalized by European masters in their depiction of martyred Christian saints. Nandalal's *Dance of Shiva* was to her 'Samadhi become dynamic'.

Kaikeyi's struggle between nobility and ambition transforming her beauty to a stern masculinity reminded her of Lady Macbeth. One painting in the collection of the Calcutta Art Gallery, *The Coronation of Sita and Rama* of the Lucknow School dating roughly 1700, was in Nivedita's opinion a masterpiece in shades of yellow.

With perfect perspective it revealed, beyond the seated royal couple, the white walls of the city of Ayodhya and could well compare with pictures of the Court of Heaven in European art.

Nivedita's biographer Barbara Foxe was to write that Nivedita, as an art critic of the *Modern Review* from its foundation in 1907, took liberty with her candid views which were often 'didactic in the extreme, highly moral, very personal and dogmatic in their attitude and expressions.'[82] She often criticized artists for the treatment of their subjects such as when she pointed out to Nandalal that his painting of Kali was not in proper order since she was clothed instead of being sky-clad. She referred him to Vivekananda's poem on Kali.[83] Once, she discovered artists Surendranath and Nandalal seated on her sofa in her drawing room awaiting her and soon after she arrived she ordered them to be seated cross-legged on the floor while she herself sat on the sofa. Taken aback, the offended artist duo was pacified when she told them that they had to be seated like Buddha in humility. This scene was later captured in a marvellous sketch by Nandalal. On another occasion, Nivedita displayed how 'in matters of art she could be dictatorial'.[84] Deciding that it was imperative for the young artists to get a first-hand knowledge of the finest specimens of Indian art, she ordered Nandalal Bose and Asit Haldar to accompany Lady Herringham, an art connoisseur who had arrived from England, to copy fresh paintings at Ajanta. Without asking them, she bought the tickets, fixed the dates and sent them off. After they reached Ajanta, Nivedita arrived there with Jagadish Bose and Gonen Maharaj. After making arrangements for their stay, she returned. Although the artists doubtless found Nivedita's ways bothersome and imposing at times, in retrospect they acknowledged that in forcing the decision she had pushed them on the road to discovering their rich artistic heritage. After her death, Abanindranath felt he had lost a guiding angel. Asit Haldar recounted how Nivedita tried hard to persuade them to remain with art and not be tempted to join politics since the revival of national art would be their contribution to the movement of national awakening and freedom. Nivedita had declared, 'The Rebirth of the National art is my dearest dream. When India gets back her old art, she will be on the eve of becoming a strong nation.'[85]

In the Bengal art movement, Nivedita acted as a catalyst setting off brilliant minds to debate, discuss and discover their own vocabulary of artistic expression. The influence of swadeshi nationalism did not have a permanent impact on the style of Abanindranath. After swadeshi politics had died out and the mentors of its art—Havell and Nivedita—had departed from the scene, the much-extolled *Bharat Mata* lost its contextual relevance. Critics felt it was in fact an aberration in the oeuvre of Abanindranath, which now showed refreshing innovativeness. By reorienting and reinterpreting old forms and symbols, Abanindranath often divested them of their original gravity and even transformed their character like the *patuas* did in their paintings or *jatra* players in theatre. In some of his works, Abanindranath portrayed amusing transformations such as the buxom Rati, rustic Kama, obese Mahadeva, all of which were 'attempts to reduce the sublime to the commonplace or elevate the commonplace to the sublime'.[86] In the opinion of K.G. Subramanyan, there was a Baudelairean espousal of imagination in Abanindranath's paintings like Shah Jahan's *Dream of Taj* in which, rather than in *Bharat Mata,* can be seen his sensibility and his attitude to realism.[87]

Just as Nivedita's encouragement of art was conditioned by her desire to awaken a national feeling, her espousal of science and in particular the work of Jagadish Chandra Bose was kindled by her pride in his achievements as an Indian scientist. She wished to challenge prevailing ideas of Western superiority by publicizing and giving prominence to his achievements. She also wanted to shame the reluctance of a racially prejudiced British government to further his scientific interests. As an amateur but with boundless intellectual curiosity, Nivedita tried hard to understand the work of the great scientist, help him pen and edit his manuscripts and explain in lucid prose his major inventions in letters, articles and reviews for popular understanding. This in itself was no mean contribution.

It was in London in 1901 that Nivedita first got involved in helping Jagadish Chandra Bose write his major work, *The Response in the Living and Non-Living*. Convalescing after surgery at her mother's home, Jagadish turned to Nivedita to write down the chain of thought that he was afraid of losing, making a list of six new papers he had in mind.[88] Faced with bitter competitive rivalry, he recognized that writing books would be his best mode of expression.[89] What attracted Nivedita to Bose's thought process was the interdisciplinary nature of his research and vision. Having studied chemistry, physics and botany for the natural science tripos at Christ's College, Cambridge, Bose had joined Presidency College, Calcutta, as its first Indian professor of physics in 1885. From 1894 to 1900, Bose studied the optical properties of radio waves and the effect of these on inorganic matter by designing and developing a number of instruments for his research. In 1895, Bose gave his first public demonstration of electromagnetic waves in the Town Hall in Calcutta. Significantly, this was achieved before Italian scientist Marconi had demonstrated wireless communication at longer wavelengths for which he was later awarded the Nobel Prize in 1909. In recognition of the value of his research, the University of London conferred on Bose the degree of doctorate of science. Around 1900, Bose's interest in biological research developed based on his observation that electrical responses of both inorganic and living matter to electrical, mechanical and chemical stimuli were similar. His novel method of applying the principles of physics and chemistry and the methods of mathematical analysis to understand how biological systems work displayed an academic eclecticism that appealed to Nivedita. She wrote excitedly that this interdisciplinary approach was 'one of the greatest generalisations of the Century . . . actually verifying the Vedanta doctrine of Unity for many departments of Physical Science'.[90]

Nivedita's decision to leave London for India in early 1902 vexed Jagadish Chandra for he sensed his work would suffer. He avoided meeting her for a while after her return to India, causing her much heartburn. On her part, however, Nivedita proudly narrated the scientific achievements of Jagadish Chandra during her return journey in February 1902 in a lecture at Madras where the ship had docked.

In October 1902, Nivedita wrote a comprehensive review of Bose's book *The Response in the Living and Non-Living*, which was carried in the *Review of Reviews*. Mentioning how ever since the birth of modern science men had been fascinated by the mystery of life and perplexed by what constituted the difference between the organic and the inorganic since there were plants which moved visibly and animals that never moved at all, she explained that the one criterion of proving life was the response to stimulus. It was Jagadish Chandra Bose who had demonstrated conclusively that with a galvanometer, an electric pulsation or twitch could trigger off sensations of pain, thrill, shock, fatigue and death, recording the multiple effects of the waxing and waning of life not only on organic matter like plants but also surprisingly on inorganic matter such as metals. Through his experiments, metals were found to respond to electric twitches proving that in no sense could they be called 'dead'. The same metal when administered with poison slowly showed signs of feebleness and rigidity until a dose of some antidote revived it back to normalcy. Jagadish Chandra sent the following newspaper cutting describing his demonstration in London to Mrs Bull.[91]

Can Metals Feel?

Can Metals feel? Last night at the Royal Institution Professor Jagadish Chunder Bose proved that they can, in much the same way as animate beings. He struck a piece of copper, pinched a piece of zinc, gave it poison and administered antidote and threw light upon an artificial retina. In each case, the electrical emotion, as registered by the galvanometer, was painful to witness. There is an opening for a society for the prevention of cruelty to metals.

Nivedita was quick to correlate these sensational experiments with the time-honoured truth in Hindu philosophy that all matter, living and non-living, was part of a universal oneness, a truth to which 'Dr Bose appears to have come, without intention and working by the most modern methods'.[92] Setting aside 'that technical jargon in which the man of science feels that his ideas must be buried', Nivedita pointed towards the spiritual queries that were bound to arise in the human mind—

Who is He that sits within, striking the molecules this way and that? Or what is He, 'Pure, free, ever the witness', who interprets the records of strain, using the brain as His galvanometer, and discarding alike the laboratory and its instruments when these no longer please Him?

The answer was provided by Bose himself. While ending his lecture at the Royal Institution, he declared that as a mute witness he had observed the pervading unity among all things, whether in the mote that quivers in ripples of light or the teeming life upon the earth or the radiant sun that shines above. This made him understand for the first time the profound utterance of his ancestors on the banks of the Ganga thirty centuries ago when they chanted, 'They who see but One in all the changing manifoldness of this universe, unto them belongs Eternal Truth, unto none else, unto none else!'[93]

Reporting in a letter to Rabindranath Tagore[94] about how the book *The Response in the Living and Non-Living* was 'now triumphant,' Nivedita went on, at the Poet's request, to make detailed observations on the nature of Bose's work and the difficulties he was facing. Asking for confidentiality, Nivedita listed with brutal frankness how Bose had been subjected to 'a strong race feeling of jealousy,' 'scientific opposition,' deliberate manipulation of his college routine to make it too arduous for him to find time for scientific investigation and unfairly low remuneration in comparison to his European colleagues in college. She was amazed that a scientist of his calibre, who would have received full government support elsewhere, was being treated so poorly. With passion she remonstrated, 'Ah India! India! Can you not give enough freedom to one of the greatest of your sons to enable him . . . to go out and fight your battles where . . . the contest raging is thickest?'[95]

Nivedita mentioned that even before she had come to India, the name of Prof. Bose as the discoverer of Etheric waves that penetrated minerals was well known in Europe. While Rontgen rays were known to be deterred by bone and metal, Bose's rays had been proved to penetrate these substances. Bose directed his research findings to the construction of an artificial retina or eye that could respond to waves of invisible and visible light making it 'a marvel of compactness and simplicity'.

Nivedita recounted in her letter to Tagore that Prince Kropotkin had narrated to her how at the Royal Institution, a professor had exhibited an apparatus several yards long to act as polarizer of light, while Prof. Bose, in the following week simply took up a book, a Bradshaw at that, to prove how the rays could pass one way and not the other, which demonstrated 'the simplicity of the highest genius'. Nivedita recalled Bose's obsession with 'accuracy and dogged persistence' for he was 'like a man haunted by the fear that if he failed at any point, his people would be held to have no right to education'. In her letter, Nivedita expressed her cherished hope that Bose would find the time and strength to work on a new publication that would be held 'as epoch-making as Newton's Law of Gravitation—a tribute worthy of India's contribution to world knowledge'. It was her fervent prayer that 'this man of science', as she fondly called Jagadish, could demonstrate to 'the empirical, machine-worshipping, gold-seeking mind of the West' how 'that same great Indian mind that surveyed all human knowledge in the era of the Upanishads and pronounced it One shall again survey the vast accumulations of physical phenomena which the nineteenth century has observed and collected'.[96]

Nivedita continued to be excited about the success of Bose's publications abroad and explained to Mrs Bull, 'Do you realize what the Bairn's publication in *Philosophical Transactions* means? It means that he plunged into Botany in February and March 1901 and in 1904 has written what the English people are proud to record as their Vedas on the subject!'[97] It was in Mayavati with Nivedita that Jagadish Chandra began his second major book *Plant Response,* which was published in 1906. After painstaking work over several years, Nivedita hoped the book would end what she called 'the vegetable detour'.[98] In November–December 1906, Nivedita helped Bose write his book *Comparative Electro Physiology.*

Realizing how invaluable was the contribution of Nivedita to the work of Jagadish and how indispensable she was for him, Mrs Bull wrote to her 'dear son' to acknowledge the contribution of Nivedita as his secretary and co-worker on a professional basis since earnings for her laborious work would give her some satisfaction. Voicing concerns about keeping his records and scientific manuscripts safe for posterity since life was uncertain, Mrs Bull suggested that he could perhaps make a will empowering Nivedita to act as the literary executor of his notes and scientific papers in the event of his death.[99]

In the last years of her life when Nivedita returned to India in 1909 to find the situation in India very demoralizing with the Swadeshi Movement shattered, journalism crushed and poverty growing worse, what kept her from descending into despair was her work with Bose. 'How blessed and how salutary is work! Without it, I think I should have gone insane at this time' she confessed.[100] A 'down-hearted' Nivedita wrote to Ratcliffe that the work of the man of science 'goes on by leaps and bounds. Such miracles of automatically working instruments and accurate record were never dreamt of. God pours Himself down in a flood of vision'.[101] It gave her great satisfaction to see that though Bose was working like 'a galley-slave', science was growing![102] With palpable pleasure she remarked, 'We are working away at a new book on science and all sorts of highly technical and world-shaking chapters are passing through our hands.'[103]

Through the months of May and June 1911 at Mayavati, Nivedita helped Jagadish Bose write twelve chapters of his book *Irritability of Plants*. Nivedita did not merely offer secretarial assistance to Bose, she also comforted him and gave him confidence in his decision to write without quoting from other published works. She explained,

> You know we decided on that deliberately because it seemed better not to quote names, whom to quote would simply be to pillory for foolishness and error. It simply means, as I said to the B, that he was to turn his face away from the past and look to the future. The old, whom he has superseded will hate him, but the young will hear his voice and follow him. Leaders and prophets must need be solitary . . . he says he is just a single-handed worker and two foolish women against the world.[104]

In many ways, Nivedita had come to realize that in their vision, Vivekananda and Jagadish Chandra complemented each other. When she had first heard her Master speak of the absolute and of knowledge being within, Nivedita confessed she had accepted it as a working theory. Now, after all these years with Bose she felt she had received scientific proof of that vision.[105] She felt truly proud that both Vivekananda and Bose were not only great men who had provided their service to India but 'in Religion, Vivekananda and in Science, Bose had made [significant] offerings to the World'.[106]

6

The Last Years

The autumn of 1907 saw Nivedita back in England amidst friends and family. Delighted to meet her mother, sister and brother after an interval of five years, she lived at her mother's home, regaling them with stories of her Indian experiences. She had brought them simple gifts of strings of tulsi and rudraksha seeds, incense burners, spice boxes, little handloom items and made precious offerings to her mother of Gopaler-Ma's beads and the holy water of the Ganga.

She also found time to meet Prince Kropotkin whose seminal work called *Mutual Aid* she reviewed for *Prabuddha Bharata* in December 1907.[1] She hailed the book for carrying the doctrine of evolution forward in a novel manner. Nivedita endorsed the author's claim that community feeling, party spirit and a sense of cooperation and fraternity among humans had over the ages led to considerable development, a fact often forgotten as struggle, warfare and bloodshed captured public attention. In an interview with Kropotkin carried in the *Modern Review* as 'A Chat with a Russian about Russia', Nivedita wrote about the sorrows of Russia as the revolution of the landed classes clamouring for a constitution was pitted against the socialist revolt of the peasants who wanted communal lands. Kropotkin placed his hopes on village consciousness and peasant common sense, which could be galvanized to wrest freedom.[2]

In November, Nivedita went for a brief while to Europe where she had an emotional meeting in Paris with her dear friend Josephine MacLeod, the first since the passing away of Swami. In Germany, she met up with the Boses and returned to England with them. To meet Dr Cheyne, Nivedita went to Oxford where she had profound discussions on life and death. She followed up with letters in which she wrote, 'There is no death, you know, for *in fact* there is no life—the whole thing was and is a dream . . . there is only the Will of God expressing itself in Time and Space.'[3]

With the opening of a new Vedanta Society in London in December 1907, Nivedita kept a busy schedule giving weekly lectures on Vedantic literature at the Caxton Hall, Westminster.[4] At the Lyceum Club before a crowded audience, she spoke on the 'historic background of Indian literature', where she explained how the epics, Ramayana and Mahabharata, through the ages had carried forward a stream of thought that was the idea of India. These two epics had 'made India what she is still today; they were part of her life; were the food on which Indian childhood was nourished; they have made India into India from generation to generation'.[5]

Meanwhile, disturbing news came in from India about the split into opposing camps of the Congress at its session in Surat in 1907. In a balanced article titled 'The Recent Congress' published in the *Modern Review*, Nivedita pleaded for a change of mood from despair to hope. Without being an apologist for rowdyism and obstructionism, she said that occasional scrimmages would have to be accepted when young blood boils and fists are clenched. 'We dislike the terms "moderates and extremists",' she wrote, concluding that the two groups had merely differences of method and not of principles.[6] When Nivedita came to hear of the aborted attempt on the life of the Lt Governor of Bengal, the Muraripukur Bomb case and arrests of Aurobindo Ghosh, Bipin Pal and deportation of Ashwini Kumar Dutta and eight other prominent nationalists in April 1908, it became evident how the militant nature of the revolutionary youth movement was being ruthlessly suppressed with tough government action.

To take her mind off, Nivedita accompanied by the Boses spent the month of September 1908 visiting Ireland with her brother Richmond and his wife. Describing her 'wonderful visit,' Nivedita wrote that she had been enthralled by the 'old castles and abbeys and pillar-stones galore,' which made her realize that the pagan culture of Ireland like that in India or Greece, was hardly Christian at all.[7] Elsewhere she commented, 'The more I see of England, the wider does the difference between it and Ireland seem. You see Ireland was early Greek but escaped the Roman occupation.'[8] Nivedita now kept herself busy editing *Swami Vivekananda's Letters*, which Francis Leggett had taken the initiative to get published. Cutting out whole passages to make some of the letters more grammatical, she justified herself saying, 'Swami has a right to the help of his disciples in this matter, has he not?' Awaiting numerous letters from Mrs Bull, Josephine and Mary Hale for chronological insertion, which would add to the value of the book she hoped to be able to carry the complete copy to America which she was to visit in October[9].

Nivedita's visit to America was largely prompted by an urge to fulfil her pledge to Swami that she would complete her books so that they remained for posterity. Coursing the seas towards New York on the White Star Lines ship *Cymric*, Nivedita wrote to her beloved Yum that she was hoping to meet Bhupendranath, Vivekananda's younger brother, who on release had reached America. Without a trace of his illustrious brother's great intellect but with a smile that reminded one irresistibly of him, Bhupen had a wonderful character, according to Nivedita, as he had invited a prison sentence only to screen others. She hoped that he could be accommodated with a job in some business establishment like Mr

Leggett's. She confessed that she would hesitate to ask Mrs Bull for this favour. She ended her letter on a serious note, 'I am intending to be very very careful in America. I shall not attempt to see there a man who has been waiting to see me for years.'[10]

The man in question was Okakura who had assumed the office of the curator of Asian art at the Boston Museum of Art. In the years after Okakura left India for Japan, he had been in close touch with Mrs Bull who had visited him and received his hospitality and made acquaintance of his wife. When Okakura was invited by the Boston Museum to come and classify their Asian collection, Mrs Bull offered to host him but with some reservations. Knowing his bohemian style and fondness for smoking and drinking, she hoped his wife would accompany him. She confided in her friend Emma Thursby, 'I could not receive or present him *without* her.'[11] Eventually he did stay at Mrs Bull's house from March to November 1905 where Sara Bull, who had learnt to appreciate Japanese art, hosted exhibitions with Japanese artists and arranged lectures. Okakura, who returned to Japan, came back again to take up the position of curator of the Boston Museum where he served until his death in 1913. Nivedita was as good as her word and never met him again.

On the long sea voyage, Nivedita had time to dwell on her favourite subject—the education of Indian women on which she had spoken extensively and written many articles. But it was in a letter to Alberta, Josephine's niece, penned on the ship *Cymric* that she gave perhaps the most lucid account of her vision, which has a startling relevance even today. 'Modern education', she wrote:

. . . as has hitherto been offered to the Indian woman, has always been more or less destructive . . . the power to read, unenlightened by a training in Indian classical literature, is apt to lead to unrestrained indulgence in cheap sensationalism. The substitution of foreign ideals (unconscious and involuntary on the part of the educator, very likely!) for those that are familiar leads to confusion of aims . . . *The fact is, Education, like growth, must be always from within.* It follows that if foreign elements are to be assimilated intellectually, the representatives of those elements must first be assimilated socially.

She felt that some of the early English teachers, having earned the love and respect of Indian men because of their proven commitment to Indian culture, were successful in imparting Western learning. Women needed to be even more convinced that their teachers had assimilated indigenous culture before they would allow themselves to be lectured on Western ideas. This is where Nivedita felt confident that she could make a difference.

We have gone through a preparation that makes Indian people regard us as integral parts of their civic life. Being so accepted, we are able to put them in the way of attaining knowledge for themselves . . . At the same time, we have no criticism to offer of the institutions with which they are familiar. We are not helping widows to re-marry, or girls, out of deference to our European birth to contract habits that their unsophisticated grandmothers would have thought unrefined. On the contrary, holding that every country has a right to lay down its own etiquette and feeling all possible respect for that of India . . . to show refinement in the Indian way. We don't teach religion, believing that that is the sphere of the home, but we refer freely to the ideas and ideals that are familiar to our pupils and we avoid reference to or over-much explanation of the unfamiliar.

Her eventual aim was the creation of 'a girls' school as it might be conducted by an Indian woman for Indian women, to the aid and furtherance of Indian social life, and not to its disintegration and destruction'. Nivedita hoped to be able to develop it in many directions to bring it nearer in efficiency and standard to her own conception of what such a school should be. To garner adequate resources for this purpose was one of her aims in America.[12]

On 5 October 1908, Nivedita arrived in Boston with the Boses and stayed with Sara. Mrs Bull had over the last few years suffered acute personal problems on account of her daughter Olea, turning to psychic help, which often affected her sense of balance and equanimity. The tragic death of Olea's infant daughter, her divorce proceedings, her illicit liaison with a childhood friend Ralph Bartlett that made Mrs Bull forbid her to enter her house, the child that she bore in anonymity in August 1907 in Switzerland, all caused Mrs Bull much stress. Eventually it was the newborn Sylvea's innocent charm that melted her sense of hurt, bringing about a rapprochement with her daughter. Although Nivedita had earlier sensed some mistrust on the part of Sara, growing from a conviction that she was being taken for granted, she was now relieved to find her restored to her usual state of motherly affection. The baby, Nivedita acknowledged, had made all the difference— 'such a simple thing, to cure all heart aches!'[13]

In America, Nivedita realized that the press was largely hostile to the Indian nationalist movement. It was a supreme irony, Nivedita wrote, that America was conniving with its sister power, England.[14] After a brief stay at the Community of Greenacre in the state of Maine founded by Sarah Farmer, which was hallowed by memories of Swamiji's stay there several years ago, Nivedita went to her favourite Ridgely Mansion where she was able to spend some meaningful time with her beloved Yum and her sister, Mrs Leggett. To collect funds for her school, Nivedita embarked on a crowded lecture tour visiting Winslow, Concord, Hartford, Albany, Pittsburgh, Philadelphia, New York, Washington and Baltimore. F.J. Alexander, who met her in the course of her travels, commented that he had rarely met one with such 'cyclonic personal energy'.[15] She also spent some time meeting the recently released young revolutionaries from Bengal that included Bhupendranath Datta, and planning with Bose his further education in New York.

In the midst of this busy routine, Nivedita also found time to finish her magnum opus, *The Master as I Saw Him*, while supporting the work of Bose, who had received a scholarship with the help of Mrs Bull. She was elated that the 'Man of Science is receiving much warmth of welcome amongst the University men,' and that the Biological Club of Technological Institute on hearing his lectures was 'crazy about him' and with 'no jealousy'.[16] Nivedita continued to post updates on the 'wild success' of the lecture tour of the Boses covering Urbana Illinois, Madison, Chicago and Ann Arbor, adding that at Ann Arbor, the distinguished professors who had read his books and were waiting to see his fine instruments now felt convinced that botany had entered a new era. She added that Abala was also a great success with her wit and presence in lectures. As she was considered 'extraordinarily beautiful', an oil painting had been made of her.[17]

In November came the distressing news that Nivedita's mother was terminally ill with cancer. In tears, she composed a letter to her 'sweet mother' fearing the pain she must be enduring and comforting her with the prayer:

> This world is all a dream. God alone is real!
> Siva! Oh Siva! Carry my boat to the other shore![18]

Nivedita rushed back to England to be with her mother in time to spend the last few days together at Burley-in-Wharfdale, in Yorkshire. Mary Noble died on 26 January 1909 surrounded by her daughters. Freed from the torture of nausea following doses of morphine, her mother, Nivedita felt, had died an 'Indian death' with a request for cremation.[19] Admitting that she had sensed 'many touches of the world beyond the Veil,' Nivedita wrote, 'I just felt that Swamiji was there, opening the door from one life to the other.

And I whispered "Hari Om! Hari Om!" So that it was the last sound that Earth had for her.'[20] Curiously, Olea was to write that at the same time that Mary Noble had passed away she had awakened with the feeling that someone had been standing over her bed for a moment. Her child Sylvea's cry that she had seen someone seemed to confirm what she had felt.[21] Easter Eve saw the Noble children interring the ashes of their mother in the grave of their father in Great Torrington in Devonshire. Nivedita wrote, 'Mother rests at last, hand in hand with the lover of her youth, in her home of the past and the pines sing eternally about them in a circle.'[22] It seemed to Nivedita that there was no reason for anything anymore. She had to get back to India as quickly and quietly as possible.[23]

With the return of the Boses from America, it was decided that before returning to India, a short visit would be made to Wiesbaden in Germany where Bose could find some relief for his gout in the hot spa. With Josephine and Mrs Bull deciding to join them, this proved to be a memorable period for Nivedita, surrounded by people she loved most. Before proceeding to Marseilles from where she would catch the ship back to Bombay, Nivedita spent a few days visiting Geneva. In the letter to her sister, she wrote ecstatically about her experience of Mont Blanc: 'Oh the grandeur! The unspeakable solitude—and immensity, the electric air! For the half hour that we were crossing, we were in the Arctic Regions.' The castle of Chillon struck her as being perfect in architecture and as she recommended to her sister to read up its history and the story of Bonivard, she also commented that no reading could make one realize the songs of birds, the fragrance of flowers, the shade of trees and beauty of the lake surrounding the grim dungeons with its 'worship of cruelty and power'.[24]

As she took leave of Yum, she recalled how grand it had been to meet again. On the eve of her sailing, she wrote, 'Goodbye Beloved, whether we shall ever meet again or not I cannot tell' but she asked for 'the blessing of His truest and closest and faithfullest of friends'.[25] As the *S.S. Egypt* went past Brindisi on the Italian coast on 4 July, she wrote again to her beloved Yum remembering it was the seventh anniversary of the Great Sorrow—the passing of Swami. But she comforted herself saying, 'But we are not departed from Him—for He lost nothing, in putting off the garment of the body—it is we alone whose sight is baffled for a while.'[26] In secular dress, borrowed from Yum, with a blue serge cap to match and with her hair coiffed, Nivedita was satisfied that her 'disguise is complete'.[27] She instructed her sister and friends to be guarded in writing to her suggesting that her letters should be sent inside covering letters addressed to Bose for she wanted to avoid their being read and stolen or lost.[28]

Nivedita landed in Bombay on 16 July, thrilled to be back. She confessed, 'Every sight, sound and smell, however, critically one might have regarded it in the past, brought one a throb of delight. The dirt, the (far from fragrant) smells, the Mahratta women in the costumes I had always imagined so ungraceful—I assure you, there was NO discrimination in my joy that morning.'[29] Nivedita had truly adopted India as her home. She did not fail to notice how on landing Indian passengers were subjected to unnecessary harassment by customs officials while her clearing agents (Grindlays) had retrieved her luggage smoothly. Nivedita went on to observe,

> As I crossed the pavement, I saw two officers on their knees over a pitiful little steel trunk, of the usual type . . . containing a towel, soap and such trifles for the most part as you and I might put into a hand-bag. There was such a ferocity, in the kneeling examiners that I said, in the hope of shaming them, 'That's an innocent-looking box!' They looked up, in amusement, 'Yes! But you see IT'S A NATIVE'S!'[30]

She felt saddened to see the irresponsible powers conferred on the officers and the defencelessness of their victims.

Back at her desk in Calcutta, Nivedita felt the past two years had been like a dream. In her 'dear lane' cooled by the monsoon rains and resounding with the evening puja bells, Nivedita suddenly felt happy.[31] Preferring to remain incognito for a while, she cautioned Ratcliffe not to mention her in letters. She wrote to Yum how lovely her borrowed clothes looked, with Christine remarking on her 'smart skirt' and lace blouse.[32] Nivedita did not lose time to pay a visit to the Holy Mother, who had been ill with small pox and looked aged. She felt encouraged by the visits in great numbers of the released nationalists who came to take Sarada Devi's blessings. They had been inspired by the message of Vivekananda and Ramakrishna. Nivedita gently reminded her of Ramakrishna's prophecy that although Sarada Devi had no children of her own, the day would come when she would have too many of them.[33]

In the period between 1908 and May 1909 when Nivedita was abroad, the sensational Alipore bomb case, variously called Muraripukur conspiracy or the Manicktolla bomb conspiracy was tried out at the Alipore Sessions Court in Calcutta. A number of revolutionaries of the Anushilan Samiti were charged with conspiracy to take the life of the sadistic Presidency Magistrate Douglas Kingsford in Muzaffarpur. Although the attempt misfired, Aurobindo Ghosh, his brother Barin Ghosh as well as thirty-seven other Bengali nationalists of the Anushilan Samiti were arrested. Following the murder of a key witness in jail, barrister C.R. Das, who later became a leading political leader, put up a spirited defence of Aurobindo leading to his release. However, his brother Barin and a number of others were convicted of the charges and faced varying punishments from life imprisonments to shorter jail terms.

Nivedita could sense that with the release of the Alipore prisoners, the country was teeming with interest and gossip. In a series of letters, Nivedita shared with Ratcliffe her concern at the rapidly changing political scenario. As she was to say much later, 'I am by nature political—and my interest in social questions is wholly indirect'.[34] She feared that in view of the renewed national interest caused by the release of political prisoners the government before long would swing into action, their moral being 'catch the awakener, and put him into confinement'.[35] She had heard of the new papers of Aurobindo *Karma Yogin* and *Dharma*, which had taken the place of *Bande Mataram* and that Aurobindo was lecturing widely though she feared 'unwisely' as 'religious experience and strategy are by no means the same thing, and ought not to be confused'.[36] She wondered if it was prudent to believe, as Aurobindo did, that he was 'divinely impelled' and therefore would not be arrested. She wrote, '*Certainly* GOD gives no promise of indemnity! Joan of Arc is a perpetual witness to the contrary.'[37] Although she heard rumours that the police were planning to deport the 'Bengal Mazzini' by 7 August,[38] Aurobindo decided to ignore such threats and stayed on to write of his dissociation from politics in his last will and testament that appeared in the *Karma Yogin*, which Aurobindo believed made the government give up its plan to deport him.[39] Eventually tipped off by a highly placed police official of the impending raid of *Karma Yogin* office, Aurobindo followed his divine voice to go to Chandernagore from where he reached French Pondicherry on 4 April 1910, where the British law could not get him.[40] Aurobindo was a changed man. Shunning politics, he now looked for a spiritual release in a 'Life Divine' and spent the rest of his life in Pondicherry. He left a message for Nivedita to continue editing *Karma Yogin* in his absence. Nivedita who believed that *Karma Yogin* was a 'magnificent' work of Aurobindo and 'a triumph of style and thought',[41] carried on this responsibility until the paper was suspended in April 1910. In the issues that she edited, Nivedita introduced some of Vivekananda's ideas and added her own concept of national unity that had come to dominate her thinking. Government censorship exasperated Nivedita, who exclaimed, 'They want to leave no adverse voice. A paper must be broken up if it shows the slightest independence . . . the only possible reply for the people would be secret press.'[42]

To tackle the growing political unrest in the country, the British government had adopted a three-pronged approach—outright repression, concessions to rally the Moderates, and the policy of divide and rule by granting only selective legislative concessions. The major instruments of repression had been the banning of seditious meetings in specific areas, newspaper acts enabling seizure of presses and the Criminal Law Amendment Act of December 1908, which permitted a ban on the principal samitis in Bengal and the deportation of political leaders. Realizing the need to assuage the disappointment the Partition had caused among the educated public, the British government sought now to reach out to the Moderate opinion in the Congress. It acknowledged that more Indians should be allowed into the legislative and even the executive councils through some reforms. The Indian Councils Act of 1909 initiated after lengthy talks between the Liberal scholar and Secretary of State John Morley and the Tory Viceroy Minto formally introduced the principle of elections. But by making special provisions for representation of Muslims, European commerce and landholders through a system of separate electorate, the reforms did not bring tangible gains for educated Hindus. Nivedita's friend in Congress, Gokhale, who had expected big concessions from the reforms, found himself powerless. His conciliatory speeches diminished his credibility and as Nivedita was to write, 'The Mahratta Brahmin . . . seems to have been putting his foot into it, and a very big foot it has been.'[43] She realized that even those with a personal affection for him would find indefensible 'the foolishness of Mr Gokhale's two now famous speeches'.[44] She lamented 'The

M. Brahmin has alienated everyone. The Gentle Party seems to have withered away like a husk.'[45] Analysing the impasse, Nivedita wrote that with a blow aimed at 'Moderation . . . men of real independence are driven to silence. And the only movement that has room to grow is the secret propaganda of terrorism and revolution.'[46]

Nervous of the undercurrent of incipient restlessness, the government often went to extreme extents such as the incarceration of half a dozen Bengali workmen employed by an English firm in Goa, during the visit there of Viceroy Minto[47] or the arrest of a hundred weavers in the district of Midnapore for weaving a certain song considered seditious into the borders of dhotis. Nivedita felt it was 'excruciatingly grave and funny'[48] since the illiterate weavers had no clue about what they were weaving! The attack on the country's education worried Nivedita, who wrote how boys were being refused at the Presidency College by the scores, country colleges had shut down and scientific education was systematically discouraged. 'So goes the attempt,' she wrote 'to turn a people of intelligence and civilization into beasts of burden.'[49] Grateful for the regular correspondence with Ratcliffe, who Bose reminded Nivedita was a real friend, she encouraged him to write more articles from abroad highlighting the serious situation in India. She wrote, 'Only by writing as you have now begun to do, will you yourself be able to realize the value of your own experience and knowledge of India . . . No other Englishman has it, or any approach of it.'[50]

Nivedita herself was not free from the government's vigilant attention. She remarked with sarcasm that she was 'honoured' to be in the annals of the CID with the 'funny accusation' of being the inspirer of *Jugantar*.[51] She was aghast to discover that she had been 'put down in the accounts of the Unspoken Wisdom Department as absolutely responsible for dacoities!'[52] She feared that even Ramananda Chatterjee might be hauled up with trumped up charges of dacoity.[53] Realizing that her letters were being tampered with, she wrote with disdain to the Postmaster General:

> It is of course easy to understand the overwhelming curiosity of some members of your staff about the confidences of my sister in regard to her babies and her cooking. I should be grateful, however, if you would kindly instruct them to *close up again* the letters they have opened and read.[54]

Disheartened with poverty all around caused by an increase in essential prices and the outbreak of a disease called beriberi, which was rumoured to have been due to an American adulteration of the cooking oil,[55] Nivedita felt worried for the future of her school. The rented building at 16, Bosepara Lane had to be given up and the entire school was now crowded into her own small house at number 17. Nivedita still found time to take the girls for day visits to the museum, the zoo and to Dakshineswar. During Christmas, she had the story of the birth of Christ enacted with children dressed as shepherds while a Christ child lay on the straw surrounded by little animals and Mrs Bose gave a lantern lecture followed by distribution of sweets, almonds, raisins and oranges.[56] Nivedita felt a sense of pride when she realized that in spite of all difficulties, the quality of the school had become well-known and people visited her for advice. She was excited when she was able to acquire a small patch of land near her house where she could develop a garden as Vivekananda had once assured her. To Josephine, she excitedly asked for flower seeds in a long list that included sunflowers, nasturtiums, snapdragons, petunias, especially purple, portulaca, sweet peas, and hollyhocks.[57]

Nivedita was also happily engaged at this time editing the 'perfectly splendid' book in English on the history of the Bengali language by Dinesh Chunder Sen, a Reader in Bengali at the Calcutta University and a close associate of Tagore.[58] She was fascinated to read about the whole range of Vaishnava literature and rather amused to find Dinesh Sen hesitant in sharing with her the lurid lines from Chandi Das. Nivedita admired the work of this 'wonderful peasant', the 'Dante of the 11th Century' and his 'perfectly ideal passion for the beautiful Rami, a young washer woman'. The hesitation of Dinesh Sen, Nivedita discovered, stemmed from his belief that she would find the story 'very repulsive' since it was about the attraction of a Brahmin for a lowly washerwoman. Nivedita realized how the prejudices of forebears lay buried in the subconscious and was moved to pity observing such 'sincere confusion of mind'.[59]

Of great concern to Nivedita during this time was the deteriorating health of Sadananda, chosen by Vivekananda ever since her arrival in India to remain by her side offering protection and advice and who had valiantly battled plague alongside her. Nivedita found a small house in Bosepara Lane for him where his band of young followers who called themselves 'Sadananda's dogs' served him with devotion. Sadananda had been the first of Vivekananda's disciples whom he had chanced to come upon at the Hathras railway station during the India pilgrimage he had embarked upon after the death of Ramakrishna. Sharat Chandra Gupta, as he was then called, was the assistant station master who had been drawn to the monk with searing eyes who sat at the corner of the station looking lost. Offering him food, he took Vivekananda to his home and a friendship began that ended in his giving up his job and becoming Vivekananda's disciple as Sadananda.

Nivedita reported that Swampsie, as she affectionately called Sadananda, had 'diabetes, phthisis and malaria all together. It is a tangle of pain and weakness—that strong and fine body!'[60] Nivedita racked her brains trying to give him comfort with a little port wine, sometimes trying to make Irish stew or preparing stock after asking for specific instructions and finally confessing, 'Oh if I could cook, I would! I try a little, but it is erratic and rather useless.'[61] As she saw Sadananda's sufferings she could not but reflect with a sense of relief that Vivekananda had gone 'voluntarily, rather than by disease. How unsightly and terrible are these tortures from which he was saved!'[62]

In September 1909, came the news of the sudden death of Francis Leggett who had been a good friend to Nivedita and a benefactor with publishing her works. In a letter to his wife Lady Betty, Nivedita wrote that in the lovely home she kept, where she had been guest so many times, she had sensed the close bond between them with Betty's 'warm caressing tone of voice' being like 'sunshine and hearth in one' to him.[63] The thought that she had enjoyed a loving and complete life would leave her now with a sense of fulfilment unlike what Nivedita herself felt with her mother's death, which left her only with a deep sense of regret.[64]

A couple of months later on 30 November, R.C. Dutt, whom Nivedita affectionately called Godfather, died. In a letter to Ratcliffe, she said, 'I only ask that the India of the Future may be led by men as disinterested and noble-hearted'.[65] Aware of the criticism he had steadily faced from the younger school of nationalists, Nivedita now took the opportunity to write an exhaustive and spirited defence of him in the *Modern Review*.[66] In her article, she recounted how Dutt 'with mingled shame and amusement' had spoken of his Anglophile background, which was the result of the age in which he rose and how gradually he came to understand the 'immensity of the Indian world and atmosphere' and found himself in the 'opposite camp', his heart being 'too proud to be courtier or sycophant'. She remarked on the 'splendid pluck' of Dutt, who along with Surendranath Banerjee and B.L. Gupta had made off to England in their boyhood as runaways to study for competing in the Indian Civil Service examinations, then considered the 'heaven-born service'. In subsequent years, Dutt took to writing on ancient India and history in a spirit of discovery and self-education. Though his books were criticized as being outdated and lacking original scholarship, Nivedita hastened to add that they were never meant to be anything but books of reference with precision of detail. His Rig Veda in the vernacular and Indian history and social problems in the form of Bengali novels revealed the simple straightforwardness of a man who no more wrote for the English world. Nivedita concluded that 'unassuming, generous to a fault' Dutt deserved 'reverent salutation' when the 'voice of criticism should be hushed and cleverness stand silent'.[67] She was distressed to read the biography of R.C. Dutt by J.N. Gupta, which she confided in Ratcliffe was 'bad, bad! I've done my best by correcting, sub-editing and suggesting'(and though) 'the thing should be hatched over again and hatched different . . . it is going to press now'. She just hoped that Gupta had the sense to remove from his book sensitive information of an extremely confidential nature, including Dutt's correspondence with Morley, which, if included, would amount to breach of trust.[68]

With her fascination for the artistic heritage of India, Nivedita was thrilled to read E.B. Havell's work on Indian sculpture and painting of which she made favourable appraisals in the *Modern Review*. On her return journey by ship, she had found the time to read the work carefully and complimenting Havell, she wrote, 'This is exactly the book we wanted—a readable, authoritative account, well-illustrated, of the psychological attitude in which competent persons might approach Indian art. For that is what it amounts to— and yours is the first attempt of its kind.'[69] Nivedita also mentioned to Havell about the visit that Mrs Herringham was planning to make again to Ajanta in winter on a sketching expedition, which she planned to join.

Christmas 1909 saw Nivedita and Christine in the company of Mrs Herringham on the much-awaited visit to Ajanta and Ellora. Nivedita hoped to gather in the course of the visit enough material for a year of writing.[70] Describing in detail the journey across the plains on bullock carts—'like Mary and Joseph journeying to a cave'—she mentioned the thrill of coming across the 'snow-white tents of Mrs Herringham's Camp', wishing her merry Christmas, spending 'three delightful days of art and history and books and walks and caves', sharing the plum pudding and iced cake they had brought along with blazing brandy to celebrate Christmas dinner in that faraway place.[71]

Nivedita's visit resulted in a rich harvest of articles that appeared in a posthumous collection called *Footfalls of Indian History*. With a historical overview of the period spanning several centuries when a chronological succession of religious ideas had impacted the style of Indian sculpture in the caves and with a detailed description of the art work in the twenty-six caves, the articles show her amazing eye for detail. To Nivedita, the Ajanta caves in their crescent formation sometimes appeared like a horse-shoe ornament and sometimes with their curves and columns like a giant organ. Financed by rulers seeking merit through donations, executed by peasants and village labourers, supervised by the monks, the caves appeared to Nivedita as a perfect example of what she held very dear—namely 'a marvellous cosmopolitanism'. She wrote that 'Chinese, Gandharan, Persian and Ceylonese elements mingle with touches from every part of India itself in the complexity of this superb edifice'.[72] To Nivedita, Ajanta with its spirit of community art was reminiscent of the work of Fra Angelico in the Dominican monastery San Marco in the vicinity of Florence or the magnificent work of Giotto in various abbeys. In many ways it seemed to her a grey old abbey-university like 'some wondrous Oxford, of a strange type.'[73] The great 'sculpture-cloister' at Ellora seriously challenged Albert Grünwedel's opinion that there were no major Hindu sculptures predating the Buddhist period.[74] The Elephanta caves on an island off the coast of Bombay, were described by Nivedita as a true synthesis of Hinduism with the trinity—Brahma as creator, Shiva as destroyer, and Vishnu as preserver depicted together in one great image representing 'a perfect microcosm of the Indian thought and belief of a particular period'.[75]

Returning from Ajanta to the prevailing reality of repressive government control, Mrs Herringham on her journey back had to face much trouble with the authorities on account of the crop of Bengali artists accompanying her.[76] Nandalal Bose and another were forcibly detained until telegrams clearing them were received. During the Ajanta visit, the Bengali artists were removed to a camp five miles away surrounded by armed guards as there was to be a visit by British dignitaries. Even so the inadvertent release of a musket by a sepoy had the whole visiting party go into sheer panic—in narrating this incident, Nivedita confessed to Ratcliffe, 'We have laughed over this story till we have cried—but I can quite believe that the victims found it less funny.'[77] As the aggrieved Mrs Herringham on her return to Calcutta sought to voice her protest, Nivedita cautioned her friend Ratcliffe to dissuade her since with an artist's temperament she was prone to be injudicious and it might cause more problems. 'For heaven's sake, let her lips be sealed, on all subjects save her art,' she signalled.[78]

Back in her Calcutta home, Nivedita ruminated pensively, 'Life is neither happiness nor sorrow, but infinite significance, using both of these, as its instruments.'[79] Soon an event of infinite significance was to come knocking at her door.

On 2 March 1910, a wealthy American lady, Mrs Phillipson, from Boston paid a visit to Nivedita accompanied by another lady whom Nivedita did not recognize. Their impromptu visit was caused by a curiosity to meet the English lady running a school in the native quarters of the city. After the visit of the school was over and just before leaving, the woman disclosed that she was Lady Minto, the Vicereine, who had chosen to travel incognito knowing that in the prevailing political situation she would never be allowed to visit north Calcutta without special police protection.[80] It is quite possible that Lady Minto's interest in Nivedita was aroused by reports that Ramsay MacDonald, leader of the Labour party in the British parliament and later to be Prime Minister, had been greatly impressed by her. MacDonald had visited Nivedita in her Calcutta home in November 1909 on the introduction of Henry Nevinson. Captivated with Nivedita's 'charming face' and 'very intelligent expression', Lady Minto confided how much she had disliked the Kali temple in the city only to be invited to come back instead for a visit to Dakshineswar, on the banks of the river where Nivedita's master Vivekananda had worshipped and meditated. The visit that was arranged shortly after was, according to Nivedita, 'a great success', which she reported in great detail typing her letters for the first time having mastered the instrument.[81] Lady Minto enjoyed the serene surroundings of the temple on the river although she was not allowed within. She wrote that the place seemed to 'breathe peace and contentment' and 'it was scrupulously clean and a marked contrast to Kalighat'. However, the little bedroom of Ramakrishna considered so holy by Nivedita appeared to her 'a curious mixture of squalor and comfort' presenting 'the only jarring note in the otherwise beautiful surroundings'. Returning by boat, Nivedita and Christine offered tea to the Vicereine, taking the opportunity to explain that from the biscuits to tea, sugar, cups and saucers all were swadeshi. Lady Minto, however, suspected that the tea, which was excellent must have been the best Orange Pekoe available; she preferred to take it without milk as visions of typhoid passed through her mind. She was satisfied that she had escaped recognition although the boatmen were surprised to receive a baksheesh which was more than a month's pay.

Lady Minto was moved to see how Nivedita saw beauty in all her surroundings and left her with encouragement to continue with her writing.[82] For her own security, she was advised to meet the commissioner of police, which Nivedita did. An invitation to a private tea at Government House followed on 18 March. Lady Minto felt satisfied to see how 'grateful' Nivedita was for the

Morley-Minto Reforms. Nivedita had, of course, been maintaining a social politeness while secretly being very critical of the Reforms. She confided to Ratcliffe, 'Lady M. thinks her husband will go down in history as having given India a parliament, but poor thing it is a toy-parliament.'[83] She admitted that 'Minto with his habitual gentleness and courtesy has made the very best of an impossible situation . . . but the councils are a farce.'[84]

The upshot of the Vicereine's visit, Nivedita realized, was that for the next few months she was spared the constant harassment of the police. Bose, who had briefly been introduced to the Vicereine, was visibly relieved, too, since for a while he had wanted to cultivate some official friends to escape the troublesome interference of the authorities. He declared that only the 'audacity' of an American could have dreamt of such a visit.[85] However, the general mood in the country was one of a restive silence with the press gagged, all public meetings stopped and prisoners systematically oppressed to make them informers. Frustrated with 'the long, slow vindictiveness of the governing race and the legal system,'[86] Nivedita wrote 'everything seems quiet—but what a quiet! Do they think *thought* is stopped because sound cannot be heard?'[87] When Lord Hardinge came as the new Viceroy in 1910, she feared the worst and confided that with 'an iron-set, coach and four physiognomy,'[88] he would surely 'bring in an Orgy'.[89] Fearing that the English 'are steering for the rapids,' she analysed 'the clique who rule are actuated by mercantile idea of rapid exploitation, not by true imperialism of giving birth to a brood of daughter-nations, highly vitalized and frankly admiring, as America at this moment is'.[90] Nevertheless, despite her serious misgivings Nivedita thought it would be a prudent move to get an introduction to Lady Hardinge and wrote to Josephine exploring the possibility.[91] As it turned out, Hardinge had an eventful term as Viceroy, which saw the visit of Emperor George V and the Delhi Durbar of 1911, the overturning of the Partition of Bengal and announcement of the move of capital from Calcutta to Delhi.

June 1910 saw Nivedita on an arduous pilgrimage to visit
Kedarnath and Badrinarayan in the Himalayas in the company of
the Boses. She recorded lucid descriptions of the journey in the
remarkable *Northern Tirtha: A Pilgrim's Diary*, which first appeared
in the *Modern Review*. Writing to her sister, she recounted how
they had started at Haridwar and followed the pilgrim's route,

> Where there was no provision whatever for Europeans or people
> of their ideas. Night after night we spent at the caravan *serais*,
> like those of Bethlehem—and in our last such experience we
> were the guests of a great neighbouring monastery, and so, as a
> very distinguished attention, a horse was turned out of his stable,
> to make a bathroom for Mrs Bose and me! But when I came
> an hour or two later for some extra handwashing, the horse was
> comfortably back again, and I am afraid I nearly cried! So you see
> how easily Joseph and Mary might be put into the stables when
> they found no room in the inn! All this part of our journey was so
> unthinkably primitive!

She concluded reassuringly that things were to improve later[92].
However, she was much relieved when they returned to Calcutta
with the man of science alive and sound though his poor wife Bo
or Abala had been seriously ill after a total of forty-two marches in
forty-eight days![93] On balance, she felt that the visit had been well
worth it.

By September 1910, Nivedita felt despondent. She had a
premonition that she was about to enter 'a very dark period which
I dread more for his [Dr Bose's] sake than for anything else. I have
still two years left, but no more. And this will probably be two years

of decline, instead of ascent of fortune.'[94] She sensed that her dear Mrs Bull was going through emotional insecurity and a feeling of desolation, and wrote to reassure her, 'You know this school is really yours and my writings are really yours, and the science books are yours, the laboratory will be yours. Don't you feel that it is a goodly array of things that you have made possible by your support?'[95] Speaking of the close bond with which Mrs Bull had embraced both Bose and herself, Nivedita wrote,

> For years I felt that you and the B. and I all breathed with one breath almost, and believed that the union between us all was deep, organic, fundamental like that between mother and children . . . We are not separate persons really, but expressions of one infinite soul. We melt into one another at times and you could not be cut off from Swamiji's blessing, nor could I. You were born for your part, I for mine, the B. for his. But they are not really separate, we are indeed one.[96]

The news that came shortly after to Nivedita in Darjeeling, where she had travelled with the Boses, was that Mrs Bull was seriously ill. Rushing to join her in her last moments, Nivedita travelled incognito in Josephine's clothes as Mrs Theta Margot, carrying medicines from India which might do Sara good even when she was so low.[97] Anxious to know whether she was leaving India for the last time, she implored Yum to ask some psychic what her future was and whether she would be able to work side by side again with her bairn.[98]

Nivedita arrived in Cambridge on 15 November 1910 and stayed with Alice, daughter of the celebrated poet Henry Wadsworth Longfellow, engaged to Sara's brother, Joseph Thorp. Visiting Sara daily and often staying overnight, Nivedita realized how vulnerable the severely anaemic Sara, who was now confined to bed with neurological degeneration, had become. Suffering from paranoia about the presence of evil spirits, 'Saint Sara', as she was lovingly called, or Dhira Mata, the steady mother, as Vivekananda had named her, was losing her mental balance. The presence of her daughter Olea upset her so much that Thorp had to write to his niece that it would help if she tried not to see her mother. Sara too signalled that she could not see Olea alone and preferred the presence of Nivedita in case she came. With Nivedita's arrival, Sara seemed slowly to get her strength back. Her spirits revived when taken out for a drive and she could write to Josephine who replied how happy she was to see that 'the tonic of Margot's coming' was reviving her.[99] Nivedita could sense Olea's anguish. She was grateful that Olea had visited her dying mother in England and felt saddened that her presence was resented so deeply. Even the Ayurvedic tonic she gave Sara was viewed with suspicion. On 11 December, Nivedita went into a church to pray for Sara and was reminded strongly of Sarada Devi to whom she wrote asking that her mantle of peace should descend on poor Saint Sara. Nivedita spent precious moments by the bedside of Sara who recalled their happy days with the Master and also poured out her heartfelt woes. In moments of clarity, Sara advised Nivedita to escape to French Chandernagore when she returned, as she feared that she might get arrested. Christmas was celebrated quietly with Olea and Sylvea joining the family for a while. On her last day, Sara seemed to feel better and asked for the brass Buddha that Nivedita had brought from India and was assured it would be on her table the next day. Nivedita realized it was the last flicker before the end. On 18 January 1911, at five in the morning in the presence of Mr Thorp and Olea, who had been called in by Nivedita, Sara passed away with Nivedita chanting 'Hari Om Ramakrishna'. In a spirit of surrender, Nivedita had written on New Year's Day: 'I . . . feel only the Ganges of Swamiji's will and personality, carrying us all onwards, towards the Ocean. Life or death—what does either matter for any of us, in comparison with the Great Tide of the Infinite!'[100]

Immediately after Sara's death, her daughter Olea decided to contest her mother's will, where Mrs Bull had amply provided for Nivedita, her school, and for Bose's scientific work. With Ralph Bartlett, her lawyer and lover, Olea decided to lay claim on all her mother's money. In a court case, which caught the headlines of every major American newspaper, Olea claimed that her mother had been driven insane by a Hindu cult and therefore her will stood void. Aspersions were also cast on the breathing techniques taught by Vivekananda that might have driven Sara to insanity. Such allegations drew sharp retorts from many of Swami's disciples. Writer Ella Wheeler Wilcox, explained in the *New York Evening Journal* that the Vedanta philosophy as expounded by Swamiji was a great intellectual and spiritual opportunity and it was absurd to find anything 'weird' or 'uncanny' about it.[101] Nivedita remarked that in comparison to Olea, Nero would appear to have been merciful to his mother.[102] She was aghast at how Olea had paid off Sara's household servants to testify against her mother. The case dragged on for six months and ironically on the very day the case was won in her favour, Olea died of suspected suicide. Declaring how the whole experience had been 'a moral cataclysm', Nivedita quipped, 'Death the supreme dramatist! I never before suspected him of a sense of humour!'[103] In the changed circumstances, Thorp was able to restore some of his sister's promises for her cherished causes in India.

Nivedita had not stayed much longer in America after Sara's death. Taking a ship first to England in early February she went to France, where the heartbroken Nivedita found great solace in meeting her beloved Yum with whom she could share her recent unpleasant experiences that she had not written much about. They were never to meet again. On her journey back to India, again in Josephine's coat and skirt, which made her feel 'as well dressed at dinner as anyone on board' and with the comfort of the hot water bottle that she had taken from her, Nivedita wrote how 'warm and beautiful had been every moment with you!'[104] Admitting her 'terrible attachment', which made 'one's heart cling so', Nivedita confessed, 'I could break down and cry like a child, at being alone!'[105] A couple of years ago she had penned a poem on her Yum Yum:

> Thou that art Knowledge Itself.
> Pure, Free, ever the Witness,
> Beyond all thought.
> And beyond all qualities,
> To Thee, the Only True Guru,
> My Salutation.
> Shiva Guru! Shiva Guru! Shiva Guru![106]

Back in her beloved India, Nivedita felt disheartened when she saw around her 'all this shooting and starving in order that a few people can continue to have motors, and wear laces and jewels in the mornings, in the streets, and plunge deeper into this dreary wasteful motiveless life of the Stupid Rich! Oh I'd rather be the poorest Hindu that ever was born, and have my glimpses of a life beyond the senses, and trampling them into dust!'[107]

She also steeled herself to accept whatever the outcome of the court case might be but she realized it was imperative to clear the good name of Saint Sara. She wrote to Ratcliffe to place articles, bringing out the personality of Sara and her distinguished husband in every possible way. 'The good must if possible be exaggerated—ordinary human weakness must not even be admitted. Her name *must* MUST MUST be lifted, from the line through which it has been dragged. Bless her!'[108] Nivedita herself wrote a glowing tribute in the *Modern Review*[109] where she described Sara Bull as 'one of the noblest of American women', 'a lavish giver' who avoided publicity to the extent that few were even aware of the ramifications of her wide charity which remained hidden in her sattvic character 'for she knew how to bestow an intimate respect and encouragement with a benefit'.

Nivedita wrote that her gifts carried no conditions and never was a word uttered as to the mode of the work. It was her love of music that had drawn Sara, then a young girl of nineteen brought up in the Midwest of the United States, to the much older virtuoso violinist from Norway, Ole Bull, whom she had the privilege of accompanying on the piano when he visited their home. After their marriage, she travelled far with her husband often as his accompanist. Ole Bull became a national figure, founding the National Theatre in Bergen. Nivedita had travelled with Mrs Bull when a bronze statue of Ole Bull was unveiled there in his memory in 1901. In the glowing piece she had written for the occasion, Nivedita acclaimed his 'pure Norse genius' which had drawn on the music of the land and enriched it with world music. Ole Bull had imbibed influences from other countries, creating a musical language that reflected 'the fugitive beauty of a living saga.'[110] His centenary celebration in 1910 received an ovation from the King of Norway. Ever since his death, Sara had been drawn to the spiritual philosophy of the Gita and on meeting Vivekananda in 1894, she became his greatest benefactor marking a turning point in Vivekananda's American career. 'His cause had found a mother or more'. On being asked in a discussion his definition of a saint, he had pointed to Sara Bull. With 'motherly craft' she would offer 'the holiday, or the invitation, or the journey, or the gift that would serve to tide one or another over a crisis here, or an illness there, make him forget a heartbreak or conceive new hope.'[111]

Bosepara Lane seemed emptier still, especially without Sadananda, who had passed away earlier in the year. Nivedita was practical to realize that the work at the school had to be wound up; she decided in any case to reduce their establishment and close the school for six months and disband it altogether if the case went against her.[112] At the same time, she remained determined not to accept any government funding or even the financial help offered by Lady Minto.[113] Sister Christine's decision at this juncture to leave the school to train a class of teachers and head the lower school, at the Brahmo Girls' School, which would earn her some money came as a relief to Nivedita. She was, in fact, 'delighted'[114] about it, and it was hardly 'the greatest shock of all' that hastened her end, as her biographer contends.[115]

After a short visit to Sarada Devi, which happened to be her last, Nivedita decided to go up to Mayavati with the Boses where she helped her man of science with twelve chapters of his book, *Irritability of Plants*. She reported excitedly to Ratcliffe,

The Man of Science has been concocting the most wonderful and doubt-destroying instruments all Winter—and now we are beginning the three-volume romance of the same . . . He has arrived at a stage where he puts a plant in an instrument and leaves it to excite itself, record itself, rest itself and then begin all over again! Untouched the while!!

It reminded her 'how very short life might prove—how suddenly it might end—for any one of us—and my one anxiety is to get the facts recorded—I don't care how roughly'. She was leaving behind a corrected edition of Swamiji and materials for a memoir of the man of science and was beginning to 'think my responsibilities are ended'.[116]

Before leaving for Mayavati, she had mailed Josephine two packets of letters—one of Swamiji's and one of her own written during his life and now from Mayavati she sent another bundle of personal papers.[117] In the relaxed settings at Mayavati, she wrote to her dear Dr Cheyne how peaceful it was amidst pines and deodar cedars where there was scope for saintly meditation much in the way as his peaceful study in beautiful Oxford was the abode of aspiring meditating souls.[118]

On her return to Calcutta, she faced a series of deaths. Bhubaneswari Devi, Vivekananda's mother passed away on 25 July. Nivedita was by her side on the day she died and followed her body to the cremation grounds, which seemed to her like 'another of those milestones of solemnity in life'. She reflected, 'But I have a great love of the shadow of death, you know. It is so terrible to foresee. Yet so beautiful when one stands within it— so much more real than this fretfulness called Life!'[119] Two days later, Bhubaneswari's own mother died. In August came the news of the death of Swami Ramakrishnananda, much respected in the Order, who had befriended Nivedita on many occasions. Nivedita exclaimed, 'So Swamiji has gathered His own to Him once more— and now His very shrine is gone.' She herself was in a mood to give up on life. 'Oh Yum', she wrote, 'I would be glad to die . . . I dread outliving everyone I care for'.[120]

Meanwhile, anxieties about the case remained. Regular press clippings that she received made it obvious how she was being shown in a most unsavoury light. These brought on 'horrible spasms of nervousness, whenever anything new arrives'. What upset her most was 'the disgusting exposure of privacy', the 'moral nightmare' of seeing the honesty of persons compromised under greed of a little gold to make false depositions. To see such traitors where gratitude was due felt 'like church steeples in an earthquake'.[121] Eventually, the case ended in August bringing 'endless gratitude' although it did not leave her rich.[122] The school was reduced to a group of twelve to sixteen of the oldest girls, all wives and widows, who seemed to generate a great educational energy as she spent time lecturing these potential teachers twice a week on new educational methods.

To Alice Longfellow, Nivedita wrote at length in reply to her letter,[123] reflecting on 'the terrible story that we have seen played out'. Choosing to write at her favourite hour of evensong, when 'a wonderfully full and deep wave overwhelmed the soul at twilight', which Swamiji described as being 'beyond life and death', Nivedita wrote about Olea, 'the darkened soul, wilfully darkened, gone out with the infinite void. Saved!' But 'had she lived she would of course, have suffered—suffered terribly—eventually . . . the sinner has a *right* to his punishment—that scorching redeeming pain'. The hurt she gave her mother was infinite. Nivedita continued 'in the last weeks of dear S. Sara's life, I realized for the first time how she—far more deeply than Olea about whom we all knew it—had gone all her life seeking, seeking, to be realized as the mother.' 'What a bondage and what a darkness the body seems,' Nivedita lamented, 'how it binds as well as fetters us!'[124] Nivedita was especially thankful for Alice Longfellow's note on her which had appeared in the *Boston Evening Transcript* on 29 June 1911, putting in perspective the remarkable work and mission of Nivedita at a time when the press had been so critical and negative about her. Alice Longfellow had described Margaret Noble as an earnest, intelligent personality with 'the ardour and fire of a Celtic temperament' who saw everything from the Indian point of view, a country she had adopted; and yet, she never broke her connection with the English Church celebrating Christmas in the spirit of the early Franciscans.[125]

On 22 September, Nivedita left for Darjeeling in the company of the Boses but until her departure she had been busy corresponding with Josephine and her sister Betty Leggett about the details of the bas-relief that was planned for Vivekananda's 'Grave Chapel' at Belur. She also found time to visit the ailing theatre personality Girish Chandra Ghosh and meet at the Holy Mother's house Saradananda, Golup-Ma and Jogin-Ma. Sarada Devi was away in her village home.

In the spacious Ray Villa in Darjeeling, Nivedita was at peace and felt restful. Plans were made to visit the distant Sandakphu peak, a journey of two or three days on horseback. But destiny intervened and Nivedita suddenly had an attack of blood dysentery. She made light of it writing to her sister—her last letter—not to be alarmed since dysentery was 'the complaint characteristic of the Hills' and Bo (Abala) was being so kind though the whole expedition to the snows had to be abandoned.[126] Dr Nilratan Sarkar, the prominent physician of Calcutta who was then in Darjeeling was sent for and it was debated whether she could be brought down to Calcutta in an invalid carriage. As her condition worsened, Nivedita reconciled herself for the end about which she had pondered extensively. Already in 1904 she had shared with Yum predictions of her death. 'Do you remember how Chiro foretold that I would die between the 42nd and 49th years? I am now thirty-six. So I suppose I shall see *this* cycle through. I fancy I shall die in 1912.'[127] Death was to snatch her away a year earlier.

What is death? She had long wondered. Was it to change one's place? That would not be feasible since without matter there can be no place. In an article, she had argued that,

> Death . . . is to sink deeper and deeper into that condition of being more and more divested of the *imagination* of body . . . of just a withdrawal into meditation, the sinking of the stone into the well of its own being. There is the beginning before death, in the long hours of quiescence, when the mind hangs suspended in . . . that thought which is the residuum of all its thoughts and acts, and experiences. Already in these hours the soul is discarnating, and the new life has commenced.[128]

Writing to Mrs Wilson, Abala Bose who was with Nivedita in her last moments, recounted that Nivedita suffered silently, without a moan, refusing all nourishment, medication and oxygen towards the end since she did not want to prolong her life. At two-thirty at night, she told Abala that the boat was sinking but she would still see the sunrise. As morning dawned on 13 October, life ebbed out of her.

In the last fortnight of her life, Nivedita prepared a will leaving her all to India. She wondered if Christine would keep her work going in the school. Each day during her illness, she would greet Jagadish Bose with a smile and hear him reading out passages she loved. On her last day, when he omitted something because he felt emotionally overwhelmed, she coaxed him to continue and to give in to his feelings and not hold back. 'You do not know how it hurts me to write of her as one who is no more,' Abala wrote, 'she is with us in spirit I am sure, though God has cruelly removed her from our sight.'[129]

As news of her death spread in the small town of Darjeeling, many prominent persons of Calcutta who happened to be there, which included Dr P.C. Ray, Bhupendranath Bose and Rai Nishi Kanto Bahadur, came to see her for the last time. Gonen Maharaj of the Ramakrishna Mission lit her funeral pyre and performed her funeral rites according to Hindu tradition. In her memory, a cenotaph was raised on the cremation spot in Darjeeling that read, 'Here reposes Sister Nivedita who gave her all to India.'

Christine, who was then at Mayavati and had prepared to leave for Darjeeling on learning that Nivedita had taken ill, was shocked with the news of her death, which came soon after. As she wrote to Josephine, in their years together it was Nivedita who was the strong one while she was always collapsing in Calcutta. She felt convinced that 'the thing that killed her was the Will Case. There is no doubt whatever about that.'[130] Josephine wrote, 'I am glad to know she was surrounded by love and the best of care (the famous Dr Sircar). Precious child: she fought bravely and was killed literally, but not as she expected to be—the boomerangs we send out come back to us. When will we ever learn that love alone can heal and help!'[131] In a salutation to Nivedita, Josephine remarked to a friend, 'She stands at the head of women—just as Swamiji stands at the head of men—and you and I are indeed honoured in knowing them'.[132] Abala Bose reported to Nivedita's sister that 'her constitution was quite ruined by her last year's suffering, and the disease attacked her in all its strength'.[133] A distraught Alice Longfellow wrote to

Josephine, 'How can Olea bear to think or face, if this is *Karma*, all the misery she has caused, and for what ends?'[134]

The grief-stricken Jagadish Chandra wrote to Mrs Wilson, 'The book which she was helping me to write is staring me in the face. I have not at present the strength to do anything with it . . . why did you not have another sister?' But he soon recalled that Nivedita was not one who would give in to despondency or despair and let a single hour go by since 'she had not body, it was all mind'.[135] Jagadish made haste to plan his research institute in Calcutta, which was her dream for scientific research and education encouraging the growth of a national character. Nivedita did not live to see the day when the institute, which was 'not merely a laboratory but a temple' was opened in 1917. Without naming her, in his opening speech Dr Bose mentioned how in his struggling years he had never been alone since he was privileged to have the support of one, 'now in the City of Silence' who shared his hardships and while the world doubted him, never wavered in her trust in him.[136] The Bose Institute, which was the embodiment of Nivedita's prayers, was designed aesthetically to include a large stone lotus basin with water lilies, by the side of which would lie a receptacle with Nivedita's ashes. Overlooking it would be a bas-relief of a woman with prayer beads and a lamp in her hand. There would be two stone seats under a shefali[137] tree, a sapling grown from a seed she had brought from Ajanta, which in due time would shed a carpet of fragrant white flowers under it.[138]

Tributes poured in after her death from those whose lives she had touched. In a touching homage,[139] her friend S.K. Ratcliffe wrote,

> It would be true to say that no Englishwoman has ever made for herself a similar place in the affections of the Indian people, or has tried to do the work to which she put her hand . . . there were few Indians of distinction unknown to her; she identified

herself with their culture and thoughts and as a consequence her influence was incalculable . . . To many of us her death means the passing of a rare intelligence and of a dauntless and most beautiful soul.

As a good friend, Ratcliffe had often been critical of Nivedita's laboured oratory, which was often not understood. As he explained, 'Always rather at the mercy of a too difficult thesis, given to the use of socio-philosophic terms and a far too compressed method of exposition she sometimes soared far above the comprehension of her audience.'[140] But of her sincerity there was no doubt and Ratcliffe came down heavily on a cynical editorial observation in *The Statesman* that said: 'One can only surmise that a woman of her keen intellect and wide reading must have felt herself stifled after a time in the narrow little world in which she strove to play at Hinduism. *For it was play.*' In an angry rejoinder, Ratcliffe wrote, 'If this was play, then may grace be given us all to play the game.'[141]

Abanindranath Tagore wrote to E.B. Havell, 'It will be hard to find another like her again. How keenly we feel her loss.'[142] Girish Chandra Ghosh who was engaged in writing his drama *Tapobal* when she had visited him before going to Darjeeling, now dedicated it to her as a 'tearful gift'.[143] Ramananda Chatterjee, in whose *Modern Review*, Nivedita was a regular contributor, wrote that she was a born journalist with 'brilliance, vigour and originality' writing even on commonplace themes with 'inspired fervour'.[144] Surendranath Banerjee commented how she was 'an Indian through and through, an Indian to the very marrow of her bones. Her nationality was but an external incident—her soul was Indian.'[145] Gokhale commented on her 'marvellous intellect, her lyric powers of expression, her great industry, the intensity with which she held her beliefs and convictions, and last but not the least, that truly great gift—capacity to see the soul of things straightway.'[146] Lady Minto in a condolence letter to Christine wrote how she had been struck by the 'wonderful personality' of Nivedita and had admired her 'enthusiasm and single-minded desire to assist others'.[147]

Rabindranath Tagore who had recognized the exceptional versatility of Nivedita had initially been put off by her combativeness. He had realized early in the day that where it was not possible to agree with her, it was impossible to work with her.[148] And yet in a male-dominated, colonial Bengali society that Nivedita had entered as a foreign woman, acting on her own steam, she eventually succeeded in receiving an attentive audience in the most conservative male bastions of academic, political, spiritual and British bureaucratic circles and equally in traditional Hindu women households. This incredible accomplishment, partly realized by the initial endorsement of her work by Swami Vivekananda, was largely on account of her forceful personality and the undeniable sacrifice she made with her dedicated social work.

About her own argumentativeness, impulsiveness, passionate and personal attachment to causes and people instead of the detachment expected of her, Nivedita was well aware and would burst into rare confessions to her beloved Yum from time to time. She wrote, 'I think the sense of being disapproved of, or of deserving to be disapproved of is wrought so deep into every fibre with me, that I always act with a sense of protest even in the most private things, a feeling of justifying myself by force against some unseen judge.'[149] Elsewhere she said, 'In your freedom, you can afford to cultivate this social sweetness. But in *my* battle for life if I had looked at it your way, I should have been lost . . . You love everyone perhaps—but there are many whom I very frankly loathe and despise. Nor shall I ever think it a virtue to try to conceal this!'[150] She pronounced clearly that 'strangers may say and feel anything they like about me. I am absolutely indifferent.'[151] She recognized her own *weakness* in having two streaks in her. 'I am apt to be enemy or bond-slave. It is much better to be the former. Of course, I am talking here of questions of *principle*, not mere courtesy.'[152] Sometimes, her attachment in a personal way made her lose objectivity and she was reminded of Swamiji's admonishments, 'I don't know how to lay down the law at all—at all. I suppose this is what Swami always warned me against as "the overflow of the senses". He said it was poison and I was full of it! Well! I suppose I must struggle hard.'[153] These candid outbursts from Nivedita lay bare her very human qualities that point to a self-deprecative honesty, trying at times, but also endearing.

Tagore the humanist must also have slowly reflected on the merits of some of her arguments. When she came to Shelidah, they had debated the positions of the main protagonists in his novel-in-the-making, *Gora*. He admitted that these exchanges with Nivedita made him eventually change the dénouement. He also watched with admiration and gratitude, the tremendous support and affection that she extended to his dear friend Jagadish Chandra Bose often interpreting for Tagore the main nuances of Bose's scientific achievements in terms that he could comprehend. In his introduction to a later Indian reprint of Nivedita's *The Web of Indian Life* in November 1917, Tagore acknowledged wholeheartedly that at a time when national self-esteem was at an all-time low with disparaging comments constantly being passed by Europeans and missionaries on India's inefficiency and 'moral obliquity' it took a 'great-hearted Western woman' to rebut all criticism and give utterance to a supreme defence of Indian life and thought.[154] Shortly after her death, Tagore wrote a seminal article in Bengali in his *Parichaye* collection titled 'Bhogini Nibedita'. It is the most comprehensive, balanced and generous appraisal of her work.[155]

Tagore wrote that[156] despite his trepidations about Nivedita's forceful attacks (*baulobaan aakromon*) over the years he had come to acknowledge that she had perhaps bestowed on him a favour as no one else had. He had been privileged to see for himself how one could completely dedicate and surrender oneself to the cause of others. Her health, her European habits, nostalgia for family left behind, the weaknesses and inadequacies of those for whom she was making a sacrifice—none of these could deter her from her resolve. In life one failed to value those gifts which were obtained without a price. And so sitting at home when one experienced the benefits of such selfless sacrifice as hers, it was taken for granted and even credit claimed that she could make such sacrifices because she had adopted Hinduism. It was forgotten that the common definition of Hinduism was never accepted by her. She looked at Hinduism from a historical and scientific point of view; if one could accept her point of view challenging age-old stereotypes and superstitions, the foundations of the whole structure of popular Hinduism would be dealt a severe blow.

One had to respect her not because she was a Hindu but because she was an outstanding human being. One had to salute her not for being like the rest of us but being better than us. She could claim pride from all not because of her Hindutva but because of her humanism. She was outstanding because she was a thinker and a doer. Normally thinkers are negligent of work just as workers have little time for philosophy. Sister Nivedita was engaged in work which had a defined focus, choosing to live in an obscure lane, which was her workplace. She had an inherent integrity, which would not stomach exaggerated publicity, nor seek monetary support from others.

Nivedita had the qualities with which she could easily have established herself in her own country where the strength of her character was well acknowledged by those she had come in contact with. But she never ever looked back at the fame that she might have earned. In India, too, she worked selflessly without an eye to claiming a pride of place which other Europeans who had worked in India were known to desire. It was only with a sense of love that Nivedita surrendered herself to India without holding back anything. But she was by no means a soft-spoken, self-effacing person. As mentioned before, there was a tremendous force in her character that she did not direct against anyone in particular. Instead, when she decided on something, she would pursue it with full heart and mind brooking no opposition whatsoever. This western trait of aggressive pursuit did not always have harmless consequences but on balance her generosity outweighed her assertiveness. The victorious outcome of her resolves was never meant to be personal triumphs. She could well have established herself as a leader of people but she decided never to leave the place of truth and conviction within and descend to the thoroughfare outside. She left behind therefore her life and not a (political) party. This was not because she was lacking popular support. It had to be seen how completely she could dedicate herself to popular causes. While our sense of duty to people was largely derived from book learning, Nivedita approached 'people' with the sensibility of a mother directing all her love to this conglomerate as if it were a particular person. Had it been a child she would have drawn it to her lap and nursed it with her life.

In truth she was 'Lok Mata'—the People's Mother. Such motherly feeling extended to a whole country has never been seen before though there have been glimpses from time to time of men operating from a committed sense of duty. When she said 'our people' there was implicit in it a deep sense of familial belonging which can hardly be detected when we make the same address. Those who have seen how Nivedita loved this country would surely realize that while we might devote our time, money and even lives for our country we would not necessarily be dedicating our hearts to it. This was because our dedication came from our minds alone while Sister Nivedita entered people's lives by touching them, observing them with her eyes and not only with her mind. I have seen how she had addressed a simple

Muslim woman dwelling in a hut in the country's interior with an unqualified respect, which I do not feel it possible for others to follow. The reason is that it is an extraordinary gift to see the wider world reflected in a single individual. It is because Nivedita effortlessly had this vision that she could dwell for so long in India without losing sight of it. Nivedita's simplicity and generosity of heart did not allow her to bestow help from afar. She sought company so that she could get to know people thoroughly. She tried to learn and accept with compassion their religious practices, folktales, handicrafts and livelihood patterns eagerly discovering with a maternal affection whatever beauty and truth lay in them. It is not that she did not make mistakes but these pale into insignificance against the respectful sincerity with which she sought truth.

Any good teacher would know that in a child's nature lies the key to testing and teaching him—whether it is in his restlessness, endless curiosity or in his love for sports. In people, too, there is a childlike nature, which is why they take resort to various ways of learning or devising methods of finding consolation. Just as the childishness among children is not without meaning so too the various traditions and rituals of people are not necessarily dumb practices. They are the result of age-old efforts of people trying to educate themselves. Motherly Nivedita viewed these rituals and practices from this point of view. With considerable affection, she went beyond the rough externals to understand the age-old human quest for knowledge. Her motherly affection for people was on the one hand compassionate and kind and on the other fiercely protective like a tigress is of her cubs. She could never tolerate any undue criticism from outside or attempt by the government to unjustly hurt them. Without complaint, she herself put up with much meanness and treachery in order to protect her 'people' from injustice. It was not that she sought to conceal anything but she was aware how easy it was to hurt

people with a superficial view from the outside without delving
into the truth within. She did not spare those Indians either, who
were ashamed of their own poverty and appealed to foreigners
hailing them as their sole deliverers. To them she directed her
lightening shafts of anger.

We have heard of Europeans who have studied our texts,
discussed our Vedanta and attracted by India have come to live
here. But failing to find the truth beyond the poverty and weakness
they saw, they left disillusioned. They had lived under a spell
which was broken when faced with reality. But Sister Nivedita's
respect for India was based on truth and not a spell. She did
not seek to discover philosophical wisdom in the people but only
sought to touch their humanity. This is why acute poverty did
not discourage her. Our traditions, speech, dress, daily practices
could easily have offended a European just as in our own country
the diverse practices of castes and classes can. Therefore, we
have to understand how during Sister Nivedita's stay in a lane
in Calcutta's Bengali quarter, there were hidden pains she must
have suffered night and day. She was very sensitive and our sloth,
unhygienic ways, laziness, disorder, lack of enterprise must have
caused her endless agony but could not demoralize her. The most
daunting tests are those one faces every moment and from these
she emerged bold, undeterred.

The unalloyed love that Sati had for Shiva, made her survive
ordeals of hunger and fire after subjecting her delicate body
and soul to rigorous privations. Nivedita was this Sati who day
after day did penance, enduring hardships, often going hungry,
living in a house in a lane where there was no breeze, spending
sleepless nights in the summer heat, refusing to relocate despite
requests from doctors and friends yet spending days in perfect
harmony and happiness leaving her dedication unbroken. This
was possible because at heart lay the well-being of India as
her only truth—it was not just a fleeting attraction. This Sati

made her total surrender to the Shiva that lay latent within all. What could be a tougher test than accepting, through complete dedication, the eternal Kailash-Shiva latent within man, as the ultimate husband? One day Maheswar himself had appeared in disguise to Sati in deep meditation and asked whether her object of devotion, who was poor, old, ugly with strange manners, deserved the stringent penance of one so beautiful? The enraged Sati answered that whatever was said might well be true but only in him did her prayers remain steadfast. Sister Nivedita found God in the poor and cast her garland around the neck of those from whom others had fled repulsed by their lack of beauty. Seeing the *tapasya*, the meditation, of this Sati may the stranglehold of our own disbeliefs be swept away—may we be able to admit freely that Shiva dwells in all people—from the humble dwellings of the poor to the villages of the outcastes.

When Nivedita had set sail from America for the last time, she had sent as a farewell greeting this Indian daily prayer, greatly treasured by its recipient, Alice M. Longfellow:[157]

In the East, and in the West,
In the North, and in the South
Let all things that are
Without enemies, without obstacles,
Having no sorrow, and attaining cheerfulness,
Move forward freely
Each in his own path!

Notes

Introduction

1. Tagore, Rabindranath. 'Kalantar' in *Rabindra Rachanabali*, Government of West Bengal Special Centenary Edition, Kolkata, 1961, vol. 13, pp. 211–16.
2. Kopf, David. *British Orientalism and the Bengal Renaissance: The Dynamics of Indian Modernisation* 1773–1835, ed. K.L. Mukhopadhyaya, Calcutta, p. 250.
3. Ibid., op. cit., p. 249.
4. Banning widow immolation on the funeral pyres of husbands.
5. See Kopf, op. cit.
6. Blair, A.J.F. 'Nivedita: An Interpreter between West and East' in *Great Women of Modern India: Sister Nivedita*, ed. Verinder Grover (Deep & Deep Publications, New Delhi, 1993), vol. 2.
7. 'Notes of Some Wanderings with Swami Vivekananda' in *The Complete Works of Sister Nivedita*, 6 June 1898, vol.1, op. cit., p. 301.
8. Sankari Prasad Basu's volumes titled *Nibedita Lokmata*, (Ananda Publishers, Calcutta, 1968), for instance carry a wealth of information but are uncritically adulatory.
9. See Amiya P. Sen, *An Idealist in India: Selected Writings and Speeches of Sister Nivedita*, Primus Books, 2016.
10. *Rabindra Rachanabali*, op. cit., vol. 13, pp. 92–99.
11. Edward W. Said argued that 'Orientalism became a Western style for dominating, restructuring and having authority over the Orient' in his *Orientalism*, Routledge, 1978, p. 3.

The Saidian framework, which has been increasingly used by scholars across academic disciplines to critique assumptions of seamless cultural hegemony may be a simplified and overgeneralized construct. As Sumit Sarkar argues, 'The work of a generation of Indologists, from William Jones down to Max Muller and beyond—"Orientalist" in the original meaning of the word would be difficult to place in the broad category "Orientalism" which in Saidian critique has become a pejorative term.' See Sumit Sarkar, 'Orientalism Revisited: Saidian Framework in the writing of Modern Indian History' in *Mapping Subaltern Studies and the Post-Colonial*, ed. Vinayak Chaturvedi, Verso, 2000.

12. *Rabindra Rachanabali*, op. cit., vol. 13.

Chapter 1: Inspired by the 'King'

1. Mary was told by a missionary from India that one day Margaret would be called there for service. Her husband before his death had reminded her that a great call would come for Margaret and that she should stand by her. See Pravrajika Atmaprana, *Sister Nivedita of Ramakrishna-Vivekananda*, Nabapress Pvt Ltd, Kolkata, seventh edition, 2014, p. 215.

2. Sister Nivedita, *The Master as I Saw Him*, in *The Complete Works of Sister Nivedita*, Advaita Ashrama, Mayavati, 2006, vol. 1, p. 19.

3. *Life of Swami Vivekananda by His Eastern and Western Disciples*, Advaita Ashrama, Mayavati, Uttarakhand, April 2013, vol. 2, p. 50, henceforth *Life*.

4. *The Complete Works of Sister Nivedita*, henceforth *CWSN*, *The Master as I Saw Him*, henceforth *Master*, Advaita Ashram, Mayavati, Uttarakhand, April 2006, vol. 1, p. 21.

5. *Life*, op. cit., vol. 2, p. 147.

6. Ibid.

7. *CWSN, Master*, op. cit., vol. 1, p. 27.

8. *CWSN*, op. cit., April 2010, vol. 4, p. 400.

9. *CWSN*, op. cit., vol. 1, pp. vii–viii.

10. Ibid.

11. *CWSN, Master*, op. cit., vol. 1, p. 36.

12. 'A Page from Wrexham Life' in *CWSN*, op. cit., vol. 5, p. 420.

13. With MacDonald, a bank cashier, which failed after a year and a half—recounted in the memoirs of Mrs May Wilson. See Sankari Prasad Basu, *Nibedita Lokmata*, Ananda Publishers, Calcutta, 1968, vol. 1, part 2, p. 33.

14. Nivedita to Josephine, 26 July 1904, in *Letters of Sister Nivedita*, Nababharat Publishers, Calcutta, 1982, vol. 2, p. 661, henceforth *Letters*.

15. Sister Nivedita by Mrs J.C. Bose in *Great Women of Modern India: Sister Nivedita*, ed. Grover and Arora (Deep & Deep Publications, New Delhi, 1993) vol. 2, p. 374.

16. *The Life of Swami Vivekananda by His Eastern and Western Disciples*, henceforth *Life*, Advaita Ashrama, Mayavati, Uttarakhand, July 2011, vol. 1, p. 400.

17. Ibid., pp. 405–06.

18. Ibid., p. 416.

19. Quoted in *Life*, op. cit., vol. 1, p. 418.

20. Ibid., p. 474.

21. See Tapan Raychaudhuri, *Europe Reconsidered: Perceptions of the West in 19th century Bengal*, OUP, Delhi, 1988, p. 248.

22. *Life*, op. cit., vol. 1, pp. 515–16.

23. Ibid, p. 498.

24. Letter by Trailokya Nath Biswas, grandson of Rani Rashmoni and proprietor of Kali temple, reprinted under 'Vivekananda in Dakshineswar' in *Bangabashi* newspaper, 4 April 1897, *Vivekananda in Indian Newspapers:1893-1902*, ed. Sankari Prasad Basu & Sunil Bihari Ghosh, Modern Book Agency, Calcutta, 1969.

25. Eric Hammond's description quoted by Lakshmi Menon, 'Sister Nivedita' in *Women Pioneers: The Indian Renaissance*, National Book Trust, 2003.

26. Margaret to Mrs Hammond, 31 January 1898, *Letters*, ed. Sankari Prasad Basu, Nababharat Publishers, Calcutta, 1982, vol. 1, p. 4.

27. Nivedita to Yum, 1 May 1899, *Letters*, op. cit., vol. 1, p. 128.

28. Yum was the name of the chief of the three little maids in *The Mikado*, a Gilbert and Sullivan opera.

29. Vivekananda to Christine Greenstidel, 11 March 1898, *Life*, op. cit., vol. 2, p. 310.

30. Ibid., p. 310.

31. *CWSN, Master*, op. cit., vol. 1, p. 50.

32. *CWSN, Master*, op. cit., vol. 1, p. 53.

33. Ibid., p. 52.

34. Ibid., pp. 112–13.

35. *CWSN, Master*, op. cit., vol. 1, p. 117.

36. *Life*, op. cit., vol. 2, p. 318.

37. *Life*, op. cit., vol. 2, p. 319.

38. Margaret to Nell Hammond, 22 May 1898, *Letters,* Collected and edited by Sankari Prasad Basu, Nababharat Publishers, Calcutta, 1982, vol. 1, pp. 9–10.

39. Nivedita to Yum, 12 March 1899, *Letters,* op. cit., vol. 1, p. 81.

40. Nivedita to Nell Hammond, 8 March 1899, *Letters,* op. cit., vol. 1, p. 76, stress in original.

41. *Life*, op. cit., vol. 2, p. 320.

42. 'Calcutta Notes By An English Lady' in Appendix, 1898, *Letters*, op. cit., vol. 1, pp. 28–30.

43. *CWSN, Master*, op. cit., vol. 1, p. 77.

44. Nivedita to Nell Hammond, 7 August 1897, *Letters*, op. cit., vol. 1, p. 17.

45. *CWSN, Master*, op. cit., vol. 1, pp. 79–80.

46. From Miss MacLeod's notes and reminiscences in Romain Rolland, *The Life of Vivekananda and the Universal Gospel,* Advaita Ashrama, 1999, p. 114.

47. *CWSN, Master*, op. cit., vol. 1, p. 206.

48. Margaret to Nell Hammond, 22 May 1898, *Letters*, op. cit., vol. 1, p. 11.

49. Margaret to Nell Hammond, 5 June 1898, Ibid., p. 13.

50. Ibid.

51. *CWSN, Master*, vol. 1, p. 206.

52. Ibid., p. 222.

53. Ibid., p. 217.

54. Ibid., p. 215.

55. Ibid., p. 81.

56. Rolland, Romain. *The Life of Vivekananda and the Universal Gospel*, op. cit., p. 76.

57. Romain Rolland Journal, translated from French, quoted in *Tantine: The Life of Josephine MacLeod*, Sri Sarada math, Dakshineswar, Calcutta, 2008, p. 216.

58. *CWSN, Master*, vol. 1, p. 69.

59. *Life*, op. cit., vol. 2, p. 333.

60. Ibid., p. 335.

61. *Master*, pp. 287–88.

62. *Life*, vol. 2, p. 337.

63. *CWSN, Master*, op. cit., vol. 1, p. 73.

64. All these details are from *Life*, op. cit., vol. 2, pp. 365–67.

65. *Life*, op. cit., vol. 2, p. 364.

66. *CWSN, Master*, vol. 1, p. 91.

67. *Life*, op. cit., vol. 2, p. 373.

68. All the quotes here are from Nivedita to Nell Hammond, 7 August 1898, *Letters*, vol. 1, op. cit., p. 18.

69. Vivekananda to Nivedita, 1 October 1897, *Letters of Swami Vivekananda*, Advaita Ashrama, Mayavati, Almora, 1970, p. 363.

70. *Life*, op. cit., vol. 2, p. 379.

71. Nivedita to Nell Hammond, 13 October 1898, *Letters*, op. cit., vol. 1, p. 24.

72. Nivedita to unnamed (page missing) 13 October 1898, Ibid., p. 26.

73. 'Kali the Mother', *CWSN*, vol.1, p. 465.

74. Nivedita to Yum, 5 March 1899, *Letters*, op. cit., vol. 2, p. 1257.

75. 'Kali the Mother', *CWSN*, op. cit., vol. 1, p. 472.

76. *CWSN, Master*, vol. 1, p. 117.

77. *CWSN, Master*, vol. 1, p. 102.

78. Nivedita to Josephine MacLeod, 7 February 1898, *Letters of Sister Nivedita*, vol. 1, op. cit., p. 46.

79. Nivedita to Josephine MacLeod, 30 March 1898, Ibid., p. 95.

80. Nivedita to Josephine MacLeod, 26 March 1898 Ibid., p. 93.

81. *Life*, op. cit., vol. 2, pp. 449–50.

82. In *Kadambari*, Banabhatta's seventh century classic romantic novel, Mahesveta was the heavenly damsel dressed as an ascetic.

83. *Life*, op. cit., vol. 2, p. 82.

84. Dr Jadunath Sarkar in *Prabuddha Bharata*, 1943 January, quoted in *Nibedita Lokmata*, ed. Sankari Prasad Basu, Ananda Publishers, Kolkata, 1999, vol. 1, p. 302.

85. *Life*, op. cit., vol. 2, p. 440.

86. Lecture delivered on 13 February 1899 at Albert Hall, Calcutta, *CWSN*, October 2012, op. cit., vol. 2, pp. 426–27.

87. Ibid., p. 431.

88. 'An English Lady on Kali Worship', *The English Mirror*, 18 February quoted in *Nibedita Lokmata*, Sankari Prasad Basu, Ananda Publishers, Kolkata, 1999, vol. 1, p. 307.

89. Nivedita to Yum, 18 June 1899 in *Letters*, op. cit., vol. 1, p. 168.

90. Nivedita to Yum, 15 February 1899, Ibid., p. 52.

91. Conversation between Nivedita and Vivekananda sent in attachment with letter of Nivedita to Joy (Josephine), 28 May 1899, *Letters*, op. cit., vol. 1, p. 156–58.

92. Lecture on Kali worship at Kalighat Temple, Calcutta, 28 May 1899, *CWSN*, op. cit., October 2012, vol. 2, p. 435.

93. Nivedita to Sara Bull, 31 May 1899, *Letters*, op. cit., vol. 1, p. 159.

94. Nivedita to Nell Hammond, 9 March 1899, *Letters*, op. cit., vol. 1, p. 77.

95. Tagore, Abanindranath. *Jorasankor Dhare*, Visva Bharati Granthan Bibhag, Calcutta, 1971, p. 155–56.

96. Letter to the Editor, *Statesman* titled 'The Cleansing of Calcutta', 6 April 1899, *Vivekananda in Indian Newspapers*, op. cit., p. 660.

97. Nivedita to Sara Bull, 19 April 1899, *Letters*, vol. 1, p. 120.

98. Letter to the Editor of the *Indian Mirror*, 28 March 1899, *Vivekananda in Indian Newspapers*, op. cit., p. 210.

99. Lecture delivered on 22 April 1899 at the Classic Theatre, Beadon Street, Calcutta, *CWSN*, 2012, op. cit., vol. 5, pp. 217–220.

100. Nivedita to Joy (Josephine), 15 April 1899, *Letters*, op. cit., vol. 1, p. 101.

101. Nivedita to Yum, 8 April 1899 Ibid., p. 105.

102. Nivedita to Yum, 9 April 1899, Ibid., p. 111.

103. Nivedita to Yum, 25 April 1899, Ibid., p. 123.

104. Nivedita to Yum, on *Golconda*, nearing Sicily, 19 July 1898, Ibid., p. 185.

Chapter 2: Guided by the 'Master'

1. Nivedita to Joy, 1 January 1899, *Letters of Sister Nivedita*, ed. Sankari Prasad Basu, Nababharat Publishers, Calcutta, 1982, henceforth *Letters*, vol. 1, p. 31.

2. Ibid.

3. Nivedita to Yum, 30 January 1899, Ibid., p. 43.

4. Ibid.

5. *The Life of Swami Vivekananda by His Eastern and Western Disciples*, Advaita Ashrama, Mayavati, Uttarakhand, April 2013, vol. 2, p. 355, henceforth *Life*.

6. Nivedita to Yum, 12 March 1899, *Letters*, op. cit., vol. 1, p. 82.

7. Nivedita to Yum, 19 June 1899, Ibid., p. 183.

8. Recounted to Nivedita. See letter of Nivedita to Josephine, 21 May 1899, Ibid., p. 149.

9. Nivedita to Yum, 23 March 1899, *Letters*, op. cit., vol. 1, p. 92.

10. Nivedita to Rabindranath Tagore, 16 June 1899, *Letters*, op. cit., vol. 1, p. 165–66.

11. Nivedita to Yum, 15 October 1904, *Letters of Sister Nivedita*, Nababharat Publishers, Calcutta, 1982, vol. 2, p. 685–86.

12. See Appendix A 'Edward Thompson's notes written on 14 November 1913 as a private record for friends' in E.P. Thompson, *Alien Homage: Edward Thompson and Rabindranath Tagore*, OUP, Delhi, 1993, p. 110; also 'Sister Nivedita' in *Rabindranath Tagore: Poet and Dramatist*, Riddhi edu., Calcutta, 1979, p. 284.

13. 'Bhogini Nibedita' in *Rabindra Rachanabali*, centenary edition, West Bengal Government, 1961, vol. 13 pp. 192–93.

14. Tagore, Rabindranath. 'Introduction to *The Web of Indian Life*' in *English Writings of Rabindranath Tagore*, ed. Sisir Das, Sahitya Akademi, 1996, vol. 3, pp. 862–64.

15. Nivedita to Yum, 30 January 1899, *Letters*, op. cit., vol. 1, p. 45.

16. Reymond, Lizelle. *The Dedicated: A Biography of Nivedita*, Samata Books, Madras, 1985, p. 174.

17. See Debanjan Sengupta, *Nivedita O Rabindranath*, op. cit., p. 140; reference to Nivedita's tapasya as Sati in Rabindranath Tagore's essay 'Bhogini Nibedita', Ibid., p. 157.

18. See introduction by Meenakshi Mukherjee in *Rabindranath Tagore: Gora*. Translated by Sujit Mukherjee, Sahitya Akademi, Delhi,1998, pp. ix–xxiv.

19. Nandy, Ashis. *The Illegitimacy of Nationalism: Rabindranath Tagore and the Politics of Self*, Oxford Paperbacks, Delhi, 1994.

20. Mukherjee, Bimanbihari. *The Heroines of Tagore*, Calcutta, 1968.

21. See Krishna Datta & Andrew Robinson, *Rabindranath Tagore: The Myriad-minded Man*, Rupa & Co., Delhi, 2000, p. 154.

22. Tagore, Rabindranath. *Chithhi Potro*, Visva Bharati Granthanalay, Calcutta, 1957, vol. 6.

23. Nivedita to Yum, 15 February 1899, *Letters*, op. cit., vol. 1, p. 53.

24. *Pranam* is done by prostrating and touching the feet of the elder. Details recounted are from the letter of Nivedita to Mrs Bull, 23 February 1899, *Letters*, op. cit., vol. 1, pp. 64–65.

25. Nivedita to Josephine, 22 February 1899, *Letters*, op. cit., vol. 1, p. 62.

26. Details recounted are from the letter of Nivedita to Mrs Bull, 23 February 1899, *Letters*, op. cit., vol. 1, pp. 64-65.

27. Nivedita to Jo (Josephine), 21 February 1899, *Letters*, op. cit., vol. 1, p. 57.

28. Nivedita to Yum, 15 February 1899, *Letters*, op. cit., vol. 1, pp. 54–55.

29. Nivedita to Beloved Joy, 7 February 1899, *Letters*, op. cit., vol. 1 p. 48.

30. Nivedita to Yum, 15 February 1899, *Letters*, op. cit., vol. 1, p. 54.

31. Tagore, Abanindranath. *Jorasankor Dhare*, Visva Bharati Granthan Bibhag, Calcutta, 1971, p. 135.

32. Ibid., p. 136.

33. Nivedita to Joy, 28 February 1899, *Letters*, op. cit., vol. 1, pp. 66–67.

34. Ibid.

35. Reymond, Lizelle. *The Dedicated: A Biography of Sister Nivedita*, op. cit., p. 79.

36. Nivedita to Joy, 23 March 1899, *Letters*, op. cit., vol. 1, p. 90.

37. Ibid.

38. Chowdhurani, Sarola Devi. *Jibaner Jhaurapata*, Dey's Publishing, Calcutta, 2007, p. 152.

39. Nivedita to Yum, 5 March 1899, *Letters*, op. cit., vol. 2, pp. 1258–59.

40. Sarala Ray to Sister Nivedita, 4 May 1899, *Letters*, op. cit., vol. 1, pp. 285–86.

41. Nivedita to Joy, 1 January 1899, *Letters*, op. cit., vol. 1, p. 40.

42. Nivedita to Yum, 8 April 1899, *Letters*, op. cit., vol. 1, p. 108.

43. Chowdhurani, Sarola Devi. *Jibaner Jhaurapata*, op. cit., p. 152.

44. Ibid.

45. Nivedita to Yum, 1 May 1899, *Letters*, vol. 1, pp. 130–31.

46. Ibid.

47. Famous play of Henrik Ibsen.

48. Nivedita to Mrs Bull, 6 March 1899, *Letters*, op. cit., vol. 1, p. 75.

49. Raychaudhuri, Tapan. *Europe Reconsidered: Perceptions of the West in 19th century Bengal*, OUP, Delhi, 1988, p. 225.

50. Nivedita to Mrs Bull, 26 April 1899, *Letters*, op. cit., vol. 1, p. 126.

51. Nivedita to Grannie (Mrs Bull), 19 April 1899, *Letters*, op. cit., vol. 1, p. 119.

52. Scottish for child; Jagadish Chandra Bose (1858–1937).

53. Nivedita to Yum, 4 April 1899, *Letters*, vol. 1, p. 106.

54. Nivedita to Joy, 4 April 1899, *Letters*, op. cit., vol. 1, p. 102.

55. Ibid.

56. Nivedita to Grannie (Mrs Bull), 15 March 1899, *Letters*, op. cit., vol. 1, p. 85.

57. Nivedita to Joy (Josephine), 28 May 1899, *Letters*, op. cit., vol. 1, p. 153.

    Reference is to Gyanadasundari, wife of Taraknath Dutta, paternal granduncle of Vivekananda, who brought a law suit against Vivekananda's mother, Bhubaneswari Devi, claiming possession of part of the ancestral property, which Bhubaneswari Devi had bought in 1877. Although Gyanadasundari lost all the cases, the lawsuit continued till 28 June 1902, a week before Vivekananda's death, when Bhubaneswari devi got legal rights to her share of property. The long legal case left both sides in a state of penury. Ironically, Gyanadasundari had to turn finally to Vivekananda for help. For details see Sankar, *The Monk as Man*, Penguin Books, Delhi, 2011.

58. Nivedita to Yum, 8 April 1899, *Letters*, op. cit., vol. 1, p. 106.

59. Ibid.

60. Chowdhurani, Sarola Devi. *Jibaner Jhaurapata*, op. cit., p. 150.

61. Nivedita to Joy, 21 February 1899, *Letters*, op. cit., vol. 1, pp. 59–60.

62. Nivedita to Yum, 9 April 1899, *Letters*, op. cit., vol. 1, p. 116.

63. Nivedita to Joy, 5 April 1899, *Letters*, op. cit., vol. 1, p. 104.

64. Nivedita to Grannie (Mrs Bull), 15 March 1899, *Letters*, op. cit., vol. 1, p. 83.

65. Nivedita to Yum, 12 March 1899, *Letters*, op. cit., vol. 1, p. 79.

66. Nivedita to Joy, 5 April 1899, *Letters*, op. cit., vol. 1, p. 105.

67. *CWSN, Master*, op. cit., vol.1, p. 122.

68. Coasting Ceylon, Nivedita to Yum, 28 June 1899, *Letters,* op. cit., vol. 1, p. 172.
69. Ibid.
70. Nearing Sicily, Nivedita to Yum, 19 July 1899, *Letters,* op. cit., vol. 1, p. 186.
71. Nivedita to Yum, 15 July 1899, *Letters,* op. cit., p. 181.
72. Nivedita to Joy, 10 December 1899, *Letters,* op. cit., vol.1, p. 260.
73. Nivedita to Yum, 4 November 1899, *Letters,* op. cit., vol. 1, p. 225.
74. Nivedita to Yum, 15 July 1899, *Letters,* op. cit., vol. 1, p. 181.
75. Ibid.
76. Reymond, Lizelle. *The Dedicated: A Biography of Nivedita,* op. cit., p. 201.
77. Nivedita to Josephine, from SS Golconda, 21 July 1899, *Letters,* op. cit., vol. 1, p. 189.
78. Nivedita to Yum, 3 August 1899, *Letters,* op. cit., vol. 1, p. 193.
79. Nivedita to Yum, 7 September 1899, *Letters,* op. cit., vol. 1, p. 209.
80. Nivedita to Josephine, from SS Golconda, 21 July 1899, *Letters,* op. cit., vol. 1, p. 189.
81. Nivedita to Yum, 12 August 1899, Letters, op. cit., vol. 1, p. 197.
82. Nivedita to Yum, 17 August 1899, *Letters,* op. cit., vol. 1, p. 198.
83. Nivedita to Vivekananda, 23 August 1899, *Letters,* op. cit., vol.1, p. 202.
84. Nivedita to Yum, 16 November 1899, *Letters,* op. cit., vol. 1, p. 238.
85. Nivedita to Yum, 9 October 1899, *Letters,* op. cit., vol. 1, p. 211.
86. Quoted in Pravrajika Atmaprana, *Sister Nivedita of Ramakrishna-Vivekananda,* op. cit., pp. 97–98.
87. *Vivekananda in Indian Newspapers: 1893 –1902,* ed. Sankari Prasad Basu and Sunil Bihari Ghosh, Modern Book Agency, Calcutta, p. 555.
88. Nivedita to Yum, 11 November 1899, *Letters,* op. cit., vol. 1, p. 233.
89. Nivedita to Yum, 25 June 1899, *Letters,* op. cit., vol. 1, p. 169.
90. Nivedita to Yum, 11 November 1899, *Letters,* op. cit., vol. 1, pp. 233–34.
91. Ibid.
92. *Life,* op. cit., vol. 2, p. 497.
93. Ibid., p. 527.
94. Reymond, Lizelle. *The Dedicated: A Biography of Nivedita,* op. cit., p. 219.
95. Nivedita to Yum, 28 January 1900, *Letters,* op. cit., vol. 1, p. 313.

96. Nivedita to Yum, 16 November 1899, *Letters,* op. cit., vol. 1, p. 239.

97. Mormons, a religious and cultural group that became prominent in the US in mid-nineteenth century, believed in the example of Jesus Christ and had strict notions on marriage, sexuality and health practices.

98. Nivedita to Yum, 16 January 1900, Ibid., p. 301.

99. Nivedita to Mrs Bull, 26 December 1899 Ibid., p. 271.

100. Nivedita to Yum, 16 November 1899, Ibid, p. 239.

101. Nivedita to Yum, 4 June 1900, Ibid., p. 312.

102. Nivedita to Yum, 6 December 1899, *Letters,* op. cit., vol. 1, pp. 255–57.

103. Ibid.

104. There are a range of items of adoration in India, from amulets, plants, objects, apart from idols, and also a number of obsessions.

105. Pal, Bipin Chandra. *Markine Carimasa,* Yugayatri Publishers, Calcutta 1955, pp. 247-48; quoted in Pravrajika Prabuddhaprana, *Saint Sara: The Life of Sara Chapman Bull—The American Mother of Swami Vivekananda,* Sarada Math, Dakshineswar, Calcutta, 2002, pp. 362–68.

106. Nivedita to Yum, 18 May 1900, *Letters,* op. cit., vol. 1, p. 346.

107. Vivekananda to Nivedita, 6 December 1899, quoted in Pravrajika Atmaprana, *Sister Nivedita of Ramakrishna-Vivekananda,* op. cit., p. 103.

108. Nivedita to Yum, 4 June 1900, Ibid., p. 357.

109. Nivedita to Vivekananda, 13 March 1990, Ibid., pp. 321–25.

110. Nivedita to Yum, 23 January 1900, Ibid., p. 307.

111. Nivedita to Yum, 4 June 1900, Ibid., p. 360.

112. See *Life,* vol. 2, pp. 538–39 for details.

113. Ibid.

114. Reymond, Lizelle. *The Dedicated: A Biography of Nivedita,* op. cit., p. 224.

115. Nivedita to Yum, 1 August 1900, *Letters,* op. cit., vol.1, pp. 368–69.

116. Nivedita to Mrs Bull, 13 August 1900, Ibid., p. 378.

117. Nivedita to Geddes 11 September 1900 in *Prabuddha Bharata,* July 2015, vol. 120, no. 7 (from an unpublished collection of letters received from the archives of the University of Strathclyde and the National Library of Scotland).

118. Ibid.

119. Reymond, Lizelle. *The Dedicated: A Biography of Nivedita,* op. cit., p. 222.

120. Nivedita to Yum, 22 August 1900, *Letters,* op. cit., vol. 1, p. 384.

121. Nivedita to Yum, 29 August 1900, Ibid., p. 386.

122. Vivekananda's letter to Nivedita dated 25 August 1900 quoted in *Life*, op. cit., vol. 2, pp. 543–44.

123. Nivedita to Yum, 29 August 1900, in *Letters*, op. cit., vol. 1, p. 385.

124. Quoted in *Life*, op. cit., vol. 2, p. 547.

125. His prophecy came true two years later. See Pravrajika Prabuddhaprana, *Tantine: The Life of Josephine MacLeod*, Sarada Math, Dakshineswar, Calcutta, 2008, p. 114.

126. *Life*, op. cit., vol. 2, p. 554.

127. Nivedita to Yum, London, 15 November 1900, *Letters*, op. cit., vol. 1, p. 399.

Chapter 3: Blessed by the 'Father'

1.   Nivedita to Yum, 4 January 1901, *Letters*, vol. 1, p. 414.

2.   Nivedita to Yum, 11 January 1901, *Letters*, op. cit., vol. 1, p. 417.

3.   Nivedita to Yum, 10 June 1901, Ibid., p. 431.

4.   Ibid., p. 432.

5.   Nivedita to Yum, 15 March 1901, Ibid., p. 424.

6.   Nivedita to Yum, 15 November 1900, Ibid., p. 400.

7.   Nivedita to Yum, 11 January 1901, Ibid., p. 416.

8.   Nivedita to Yum, 19 July 1901, Ibid., p. 438; Tagore to Jagadish Bose, Kartik 1308 (Autumn 1901), *Chithi Potro*, Rabindranath Tagore, Visva Bharati Granthalay, Calcutta, 1957, vol. 6, p. 40.

9.   See Meenakshi Mukherjee, *An Indian for All Seasons: The Many Lives of R.C. Dutt*, Penguin, 2009.

10. Nivedita to Mrs Sara Bull, 23 July 1901, *Letters*, op. cit., vol. 1, p. 442.

11. Nivedita to Dr and Mrs Jagadish Chandra Bose, 5 November 1900, Ibid., p. 395–97.

12. Sister Nivedita's circular letter and response of William James appear in the Appendix 1901 in *Letters*, op. cit., vol. 1, pp. 450–51.

13. Tagore to Bose, 12 December 1900, *Nivedita O Rabindranath: Ek Bitorkito Samparker Unmochan*, Debanjan Sengupta, Gangchil Publications, Kolkata, 2006.

14. Nivedita to Mrs Bull, 29 November 1900, *Letters*, op. cit., vol. 2, p. 403. The reference is to a poignant moment in the story when the

itinerant peddler, Kabuliwallah, who has been away from home for a long time produces the inked hand impression of his little girl that he carries only to realise that she must be a young woman now and hastens back home to Kabul.

15. Footnote reference in *Chithi Potro*, Rabindranath Tagore, Visva Bharati Granthalay, Calcutta, 1957, vol. 6, p. 178.

16. Extract of letter from Nivedita with missing pages, dated 18 August 1900, op. cit., p. 381.

17. *Mutual Aid: A Factor of Evolution*, Heinemann, London, 1902.

18. Review of Mutual Aid, *Prabuddha Bharata*, December, 1907 in *CWSN*, published by Advaita Ashram, Mayavati, Uttarakhand, October 2012, vol. 5, pp. 291–301.

19. *Life* Mayavati Ashrama, Uttarakhand, April 2013, vol. 2, pp. 404–05.

20. Nivedita to Geddes, 19 March (year unknown), *Prabuddha Bharata*, July 2015, vol. 120, no. 7 (from an unpublished collection of letters received from the archives of the University of Strathclyde and the National Library of Scotland).

21. Nivedita to Geddes, 20 January 1903, Ibid., pp. 38–39.
   Geddes' work in improving slums in Edinburgh led to an invitation to advise on emerging urban-planning issues in India. He held faculty position in sociology and civics at Bombay University from 1919–25.

22. Ibid.

23. Nivedita to Anna Geddes, 13 June 1905, *Prabuddha Bharata*, August 2015, vol. 120, no. 8, p. 19 (from an unpublished collection of letters received from the archives of the University of Strathclyde and the National Library of Scotland).

24. 'Lambs among the Wolves', *The Westminister Review*, 1901; reprinted by R.B. Brimley Johnson, London, 1903, *CWSN*, op. cit., vol. 4, pp. 509–32.

25. Nivedita to Yum, 4 January 1901, *Letters*, op. cit., vol. 1, p. 414.

26. See letters dated 20 & 23 July 1901, *Letters*, op. cit., vol. 1, pp. 439, 441.

27. Nivedita to Yum, 10 June 1901, *Letters*, op. cit., vol. 1, p. 431.

28. Nivedita to Yum, 10 June 1901 Ibid., p. 430.

29. Nivedita to Yum, 4 January 1901, in *Letters*, op. cit., vol. 1, p. 415.

30. Nivedita to Yum, 19 July 1901, in *Letters*, op. cit., vol. 1, pp. 434–36.

31. Nivedita to Mrs Bull, 23 July 1901, *Letters*, op. cit., vol. 1, p. 441.

32. Nivedita to Yum, 22 March 1901, Ibid., p. 426.

33. Translation from Bengali by Nivedita herself of letter from Sarada Devi to her on 13 January 1901, Ibid., p. 412.

34. Quoted in Pravrajika Prabuddhaprana, *Saint Sara: the Life of Sara Chapman Bull—the American Mother of Swami Vivekananda*, op. cit., p. 396.

35. All references of Swami's communications from *Life of Swami Vivekananda by his Eastern and Western Disciples*, op. cit., vol. 2, pp. 588–9.

36. Vivekananda to Christine Greenstidel, quoted in Pravrajika Prabuddhaprana, *Saint Sara: the Life of Sara Chapman Bull—the American Mother of Swami Vivekananda*, op. cit., p. 609.

37. Gandhi autobiography, quoted Ibid., p. 615.

38. See Pravrajika Prabuddhaprana, *Tantine: The Life of Josephine MacLeod*, op. cit., p. 123.

39. Mukherjee, Meenakshi. *An Indian for All Seasons: The Many Lives of R.C.Dutt*, Penguin, 2009, p. 167.

40. Prabuddhaprana, Pravrajika. *Saint Sara: the Life of Sara Chapman Bull—the American Mother of Swami Vivekananda*, op. cit., p. 406.

41. *Life*, op. cit., vol. 2, p. 628.

42. Prabuddhaprana, Pravrajika. *Saint Sara: the Life of Sara Chapman Bull—the American Mother of Swami Vivekananda*, op. cit., p. 407.

43. *Young India*, 1927, p. 30.

44. See *Life of Swami Vivekananda by his Eastern and Western Disciples*, op. cit., vol. 2, p. 627.

45. Nivedita to Yum, 25 May 1902, *Letters*, op. cit., vol. 1, p. 469.

46. See Sankari Prasad Basu, *Nibedita Lokmata*, Ananda Publishers, Calcutta, 2012, vol. 2, p. 88.

47. Nivedita to Yum, 28 February 1902, *Letters*, op. cit., vol. 1, pp. 457–58.

48. Nivedita to Yum, Ibid.

49. Tagore, Surendranath. Okakura Kakuzo in *Visva Bharati Quarterly*, August 1936.

50. Ibid.

51. See Sankari Prasad Basu, *Nibedita Lokmata*, Ananda Publishers, Calcutta, 2012, vol. 2.

52. See letter of 3 March 1902 from Nivedita to Yum in *Letters*, op. cit., vol. 1, p. 458.

53. From Reminiscences of Josephine MacLeod in *Life of Swami Vivekananda by his Eastern and Western Disciples*, op. cit., vol. 2, p. 620.

54. Vivekananda to Sara Bull, 18 June 1902, parenthesis in original, *Saint Sara: The Life of Sara Chapman Bull*, Pravrajika Prabuddhaprana, op. cit., p. 416.

55. Nivedita to Yum, 21 April 1902, *Letters*, op. cit., vol. 1, p. 463.

56. Nivedita to Yum, 16 July 1902, Ibid., p. 480.

57. Ibid., p. 638.

58. Reference in Nivedita's letter to Yum 25 May 1902, *Letters*, op. cit., vol. 1, p. 470.

59. Nivedita to Yum, 5 May 1902, Ibid., p. 466.

60. Nivedita to Yum 21 April 1902, Ibid., pp. 460–62.

61. Ibid.

62. Nivedita to Yum, 15 June 1902, Ibid., p. 474.

63. Nivedita to Yum, 25 May 1902, Ibid., p. 469.

64. Quoted in *Life of Swami Vivekananda by his Eastern and Western Disciples*, op. cit., vol. 2, p. 642.

65. Nivedita to Yum, 25 May 1902, Ibid., pp. 468–470.

66. Nivedita to Yum, 15 June 1902, Ibid., pp. 474–75.

67. Ibid.

68. Nivedita to Yum, 7 August 1902, *Letters*, op. cit., vol. 1, p. 491.

69. Nivedita to Yum, 24 July 1902, Ibid., p. 483.

70. Nivedita to Yum, 27 August 1902, *Letters*, op. cit., vol. 1, p. 497.

71. Nivedita to Yum, 7 August 1902, *Letters*, op. cit., vol. 1, pp. 491–92.

72. Meditative mood.

73. A common superstition that the gecko's call endorses whatever has been spoken.

74. Details in letter of Nivedita to Mr and Mrs Hammond, 28 August 1902 in *Letters*, op. cit., vol. 1, p. 499; also see in *Life of Swami Vivekananda by his Eastern and Western Disciples*, op. cit., vol. 2, pp. 650–51.

75. Nivedita to Yum, 16 July 1902, *Letters*, op. cit., vol. 1, p. 481.

76. Nivedita to Yum, 7 August 1902, *Letters*, op. cit., vol. 1, p. 492.

77. Nivedita to Mr and Mrs Hammond, 28 August 1902, *Letters*, op. cit., vol. 1, p. 499.

78. Nivedita to Yum, 14 September 1902, Ibid., p. 505.

79. Nivedita to Christine, 7 July 1902, *Letters*, op. cit., vol. 2, p. 1271.

80. Nivedita to Yum, 16 July 1902, *Letters*, op. cit., vol. 1, p. 479.
81. Nivedita to the Editor, *Statesman*, 28 July 1902, Ibid., p. 530.
82. Nivedita to Yum, 16 July 1902, *Letters*, vol. 1, p. 479.
83. Nivedita to Yum, 6 November 1904, *Letters*, op. cit., vol. 2, p. 693.
84. Nivedita to Yum, 24 July 1902, *Letters*, vol. 1, pp. 482–83.
85. Ibid.
86. Nivedita to Mary Hale, 19 July 1902, Ibid., p. 478.
87. Nivedita to Yum, 16 July 1902, Ibid., pp. 450–51.
88. Nivedita to Yum, 24 July 1902, Ibid., p. 484.
89. Nivedita to Yum, 7 August 1902, Ibid., p. 490.
90. Nivedita to Yum, Ibid., p. 489.
91. Nivedita to Yum, 4 September 1902, Ibid., p. 500.
92. Nivedita to Yum, September 10, 1902 Ibid., pp. 502-03.
93. Nivedita to Yum, 21 December 1902, Ibid., p. 525.
94. Sarola Ghoshal to Nivedita, undated 1902, Ibid., pp. 533–34.
95. Nivedita to Yum, 28 July 1902, Ibid., p. 488.
96. Nivedita to Yum, 1 October 1902, Ibid., p. 511.
97. See John Rosenfield, 'Okakura and Margaret Noble (Sister Nivedita): A Brief Episode' in *Review of Japanese Culture and Society*, University of Hawaii Press, 2012, vol. 24, pp. 58–69.
98. Nivedita to Yum, 14 August 1902, *Letters*, op. cit., vol. 1, p. 494.
99. Nivedita to Yum, 10 & 14 September, 1 October 1902, Ibid., pp. 501–10.
100. Nivedita to Yum, 11 October 1902, Ibid., pp. 511–14.
101. Ibid.
102. Nivedita to Yum, 9 November 1902, Ibid., pp. 515–17.
103. Nivedita to Yum, 1 November 1902, Ibid., p. 509.
104. Nivedita to Yum, 9 November 1902, Ibid., pp. 515–17.
105. Nivedita to Yum, 8 September 1904, *Letters*, op. cit., vol. 2, p. 677.
106. Nivedita to Yum, 12 July 1905, *Letters*, op. cit., vol. 2, pp. 742–43.
107. Sen, Amiya P. *An Idealist in India: Selected Writings and Speeches of Sister Nivedita*, Primus Books, 2016, p. 2.
108. Nivedita to Yum, 19 November 1902, Ibid., p. 519.
109. Nivedita to Yum, 21 December 1902, Ibid., p. 526.
110. Nivedita to Yum, Ibid.
111. Nivedita to Yum, 1 October 1902, Ibid., p. 508.

112. *Prabuddha Bharata*, January 1953, p. 67.
113. Nivedita (written after 13 December 1902) from pages missing, *Letters*, op. cit., vol. 1, pp. 522–24.

Chapter 4: Nationalism

1. 'On the Influence of History in the Development of Modern India in Civic Ideal and Indian Nationality' in *CWSN*, op. cit., vol. 4, pp. 306–07.
2. Nivedita to Yum, 14 April 1903, *Letters*, op. cit., vol. 2, p. 552.
3. Nivedita to Yum, 20 January 1903, Ibid., p. 535.
4. Nivedita to Yum, 9 September 1903, Ibid., op. cit., p. 586.
5. Nivedita to Geddes, 19 January 1905, *Prabuddha Bharata*, July 2015, vol. 120, no. 7, p. 41, (from an unpublished collection of letters received from the archives of the University of Strathclyde and the National Library of Scotland).
6. Nivedita, *Studies from an Eastern Home*, 1913, p. xxxi.
7. Nivedita to Yum, 6 November 1904, *Letters*, op. cit., vol. 2, p. 694.
8. Rabindranath Tagore in Introduction, November 1917, to *The Web of Indian Life*, Advaita Ashrama, Mayavati, sixth impression, January 2010, henceforth *The Web*, pp. xi–xii.
9. Ibid.
10. *The Web*, op. cit., p. 2.
11. Ibid., p. 6.
12. Ibid., p. 14.
13. Ibid., p. 37.
14. Ibid., p. 83.
15. Nivedita to Mrs Bull, 12 December 1906, *Letters*, op. cit., vol. 2, p. 835
16. *The Web*, p. 85.
17. Rabindranath Tagore, *Shesher Kobita*, 1928, translated as *Farewell, My Friend* by Krishna Kripalani (1946).
18. Lecture, 'Has British Rule been beneficial to India or not?', *Amrita Bazar Patrika*, 15 November 1900 in *CWSN*, op. cit., vol. 5, p. 147.
19. *The Web*, op. cit., p. 79.
20. Nivedita to Yum, 12 July 1905, *Letters*, op. cit., vol. 2, pp. 742–43; italics in original.

21. *The Web*, op. cit., p. 74.
22. Ibid., p. 102.
23. Ibid., p. 100.
24. Ibid., p. 240.
25. Ibid., p. 235.
26. Ibid., p. 233.
27. Ibid., p. 132–34.
28. Ibid., p. 244.
29. Ibid., p. 187.
30. Nivedita to Mrs Bull, 17 March 1904, *Letters*, op. cit., vol. 2, p. 635.
31. Nivedita to Yum, 30 June 1904, Ibid., p. 652.
32. Nivedita to Yum, 21 September 1904, Ibid., p. 681.
33. Nivedita to Yum, 25 July 1904, Ibid., p. 660.
34. Nivedita to Mrs Bull, 28 July 1904, Ibid., p. 663.
35. Nivedita to Mrs Wilson, 11 August 1904, Ibid., p. 666.
36. Richmond Noble to Margot, 13 October 1904, Ibid., p. 708.
37. Gerald Nobel undated, 1904, Ibid., p. 709.
38. Nivedita to Mrs Bull, 28 July 1904, *Letters*, op. cit., vol. 2, p. 664.
39. Tagore's obituary on Bankim Chandra Chattopadhyay in collection *Adhunik Sahitya, Rabindra Rachanabali*, Government of West Bengal Centenary edition, Calcutta, 1961, vol. 13, p. 891.
40. Ibid., free translation.
41. Nabayuga was a term used at the beginning of the twentieth century by Shivanath Shastri, the first historian of what he called the 'New Bengal' (Navya Banga) in his historical work in Bengali titled *Ramtanu Lahiri and Bengali Society in His Time* (1903). Tagore too used the term nabayuga in his celebrated essay Kalantar or the 'Changing Times'. Perhaps the historical consciousness that a new age had dawned upon the country crystallized between 1894 and 1903. But the terms used to describe it remained indigenous until Roper Lethbridge translated Shivanath Shastri's work in 1907 with the significant subtitle, 'A History of the Renaissance in Bengal'.
42. Often such terms were coined in retrospect. The well-known coinage for this period by Marxist scholar Sushobhan Sarkar in the 1940s—the 'renaissance model'—might have been as an escape from the trying times in which he lived. Bengal had been shattered by the cumulative

impact of the Second World War, Famine and Partition. See reference to his *Notes on the Bengal Renaissance*, Calcutta, 1946, in *Writing Social History*, Sumit Sarkar, OUP, 1997, p. 161.

43. See Amales Tripathi, *The Extremist Challenge, India between 1890 and 1910*, Orient Longmans, 1967.

44. Free translation. Tagore, Rabindranath. '*Byadhi O Pratikar*' in *Parishishta, Rabindra Rachanabali*, Government of West Bengal Centenary edition, Calcutta, 1961, vol. 13, pp. 131–36.

45. Details here from Pravrajika Atmaprana, *Sister Nivedita*, op. cit.

46. Nivedita to Mrs Bull, 1 December 1904, *Letters*, op. cit., vol. 2, p. 701.

47. Sarkar, Sarabala. *Nivedita as I saw her*. Translated from Bengali (1912) by Probhati Mukherjee, Nivedita Girls' School, 1998.

48. Ibid., p. 29.

49. Ibid., p. 31.

50. Nivedita to Mrs Bull, 4 May 1905, Ibid., p. 732–33.

51. Nivedita to Mrs Leggett, 9 April 1903, *Letters*, op. cit., vol. 2, p. 551.

52. Nivedita to Yum, *Letters*, op. cit., vol. 2, p. 660.

53. Nivedita to Yum, 14 April 1904, Ibid., p. 644.

54. Quoted in Pravrajika Atmaprana, Sister Nivedita, op. cit., p. 164–65.

55. After Nivedita's death, the school was affiliated to the Ramakrishna Mission in 1918, and given the name Ramakrishna Mission Sister Nivedita Girls' School. On 9 August 1963, the school was handed over to the Ramakrishna Sarada Mission, an organization parallel to the Ramakrishna Mission, run by sannyasinis of Sri Sarada Math. Since then it has been known as the Ramakrishna Sarada Mission Sister Nivedita Girls' School.

56. Nivedita to Yum, 25 November 1903, *Letters*, op. cit., vol. 2, pp. 589–90.

57. Nivedita to Yum, 8 February 1905, Ibid., p. 719.

58. Nivedita to Yum, 4 November 1904, Ibid., p. 653.

59. Nivedita to Yum, 28 February 1905, Ibid., pp. 790–91.

60. Quoted in Sister Nivedita: The Rebel Child of a Great Master by Sanat Kumar Rai Chowdhury in *Great Women of Modern India: Sister Nivedita*, ed by Grover & Arora, Deep & Deep Publications, New Delhi, 1993, vol. 2.

61. Nivedita to Yum, 19 June 1903, Ibid., op. cit., p. 572.

62. Nivedita to Alberta and Hollister 28 January 1903, Ibid., p. 539.

63. Nivedita to Yum, 6 November 1904, Ibid., p. 693.

64. Reymond, Lizelle. *The Dedicated: A Biography of Nivedita*, op. cit., pp. 280–81.

65. Historical facts sourced mostly from *Modern India 1885-1947*, Sumit Sarkar, Macmillan, 1983, pp. 89–92.

66. Nivdita to G.K. Gokhale, 29 March 1903, Ibid., p. 548.

67. Nivedita to Gokhale, undated 1903, Ibid., p. 600.

68. Sarkar, Sumit. *Modern India 1885–1947*, op. cit., pp. 86–88.

69. Nivedita to G.K. Gokhale, 20 March 1903, Ibid., p. 547.

70. See Bimanbehari Mazumdar, *Militant Nationalism in India: And its Socio-Religious background 1897-1917*, General Printers & Publishing, Calcutta, 1966, p. 62.

71. See Nitish Sengupta, *History of the Bengali Speaking People*, UBS Publishers' Distributors Ltd, Delhi, 2001, p. 326.

72. Ibid., p. 309.

73. 'Revival or Reform' in *CWSN*, vol. 5, p. 85.

74. Ibid., p. 88.

75. See Lizelle Reymond, *The Dedicated*, op. cit., p. 301.

76. 'Aggressive Hinduism', *CWSN*, vol. 3, op. cit., pp. 494–95.

77. *CWSN*, vol. 3, op. cit., introduction by Pravrajika Atmaprana, p. xii.

78. Islam in Asia, *CWSN*, vol. 2, pp. 469–70.

79. See Lizelle Reymond, *The Dedicated*, op. cit., pp. 286–87.

80. 'Aggressive Hinduism', *CWSN*, vol. 3, p. 497.

81. Nivedita to Yum, 10 February 1904, *Letters*, op. cit., vol. 2, p. 626.

82. Quoted in *Sister Nivedita* by Pravrajika Atmaprana, op. cit., p. 174.

83. See Lizelle Reymond, *The Dedicated*, op. cit., p. 332.

84. 'Nationalism in India, Speech in America' in *The English Writings of Rabindranath Tagore*, ed. Sisir K. Das, Sahitya Akademi, 1996, vol. 2, pp. 453–65.

85. *Rabindra Rachanabali*, op. cit., vol. 13, 'Bhogini Nibedita', pp. 192–199.

86. 'Aggressive Hinduism', op. cit., p. 503.

87. Ibid.

88. See Reba Som, *Rabindranath Tagore: The Singer and his Song*, Penguin, 2009, p. 156.

89. Nivedita to Yum, 7 July 1903, *Letters*, op. cit., vol. 2, p. 574.

90. Sister Nivedita: An Interpreter between West and East by A.J.F. Blair in *Great Women of Modern India: Sister Nivedita*, ed. by Grover & Arora, Deep. & Deep. Publications, New Delhi, 1993, vol. 2.

91. A Tribute to Sister Nivedita by Novalis in *Great Women of Modern India: Sister Nivedita*, op. cit., vol. 2.

92. Sister Nivedita: A close friend by S.K. Ratcliffe in *Great Women of Modern India: Sister Nivedita*, ed. by Grover & Arora, Deep & Deep Publications, New Delhi, 1993, vol. 2.

93. Nivedita to Mrs Bull, 5 March 1905, *Letters*, op. cit., vol. 2, p. 726.

94. Nivedita to Yum, 4 July 1904, Ibid., p. 654.

95. Nivedita to Yum, 28 January 1903, Ibid., p. 540.

96. See Appendix—1903, Ibid., pp. 611–17.

97. William Stead to Nivedita, 1 January 1903, Ibid., p. 611.

98. See *Sister Nivedita* by Pravrajika Atmaprana, op. cit., pp. 186–89.

99. Tirumalacharya to Sister Nivedita, 16 April 1907, *Letters*, op. cit., vol. 2, pp. 890–91.

100. See Lizelle Reymond, *The Dedicated*, op. cit., p. 298.

101. See *Sister Nivedita* by Pravrajika Atmaprana, op. cit., p. 185.

102. See Lizelle Reymond, *The Dedicated*, op. cit., p. 282.

103. Nivedita to Yum, 13 September 1905, *Letters*, op. cit., vol. 2, p. 755.

104. Ibid., p. 321.

105. Nivedita to Yum, 25 July 1906, Ibid., p. 823.

106. Nivedita to Ratcliffe, 4 November 1908, Ibid., p. 925.

107. Nivedita to Gokhale, 20 September 1905, *Letters*, op. cit., vol. 2, pp. 757–58.

108. Nivedita to Ramananda Chatterjee, 16 October 1905, *Letters,* op. cit., vol. 2, p. 1274.

109. Jagadish Bose to Mrs Bull, 16 October 1905, Ibid., p. 778.

110. See Sumit Sarkar, *Modern India 1885-1947*, Macmillan India, Delhi, 1983; *The Swadeshi Movement in Bengal 1903–1908*, (New Delhi, 1973).

111. Bipin Chandra Pal in journal *Bande Mataram*, 18 September 1906.

112. Nivedita to Yum, 18 July 1906, *Letters*, op. cit., vol. 2, p. 821.

113. Quoted in Sumit Sarkar, *Modern India*, op. cit., p. 114.

114. Ibid., p. 116.

115. In February 1908.

116. Tagore to C.F. Andrews, *Modern Review*, May 1921, in *The Mahatma and the Poet, Letters and Debates between Gandhi and Tagore 1915–1941*, ed. Sabyasachi Bhattacharya, National Book Trust, 1997, p. 58.

117. See Sumit Sarkar, *The Swadeshi Movement in Bengal 1903–8*, op. cit., p. 475.

118. Roy Chowdhury, Girijashankar. *Sri Aurobindo O Banglay Swadeshi Yuga*, Calcutta, 1956.

119. Reymond, Lizelle. *Life Dedicated*, op. cit., pp. 336–37.

120. Debojyoti Burman, 'Sister Nivedita and the Indian Revolution' in *Nivedita Commemoration Volume*, ed. by Amiya Kumar Majumdar, Vivekananda Janmotsava Samiti, Calcutta, 1968, p. 199.

121. Reymond, Lizelle. *The Dedicated*, op. cit., pp. 336–37.

122. Majumdar, Bimanbihari. *Militant Nationalism in India and its socio-religious background (1897-1917)*, General Printers & Publishers, Calcutta, 1966, chapters 11, 111.

123. The Swadeshi Movement in *CWSN*, vol. 4, p. 276.

124. *Sri Aurobindo on Himself and Mother*, Sri Aurobindo International University Centre, Pondicherry, 1953.

125. Quoted in Lizelle Reymond, *The Dedicated*, op. cit., p. 321.

126. Nivedita to Mrs Hesty, 20 September 1905; Nivedita to William Stead, 20 September 1905, *Letters*, op. cit., vol. 2, pp. 756–57.

127. *Report of the Indian National Congress 1905*, pp. 95–96 from microfilm in Nehru Memorial Museum Library, Delhi.

128. Nivedita to Yum, 15 December 1906, Ibid., p. 832.

129. Nivedita to Ratcliffe, 8 June 1907, Ibid., p. 864.

130. *CWSN*, vol. 4, p. 271.

131. *The Modern Review*, November 1911, p. 517.

132. Ibid., p. 447.

133. Nivedita to Yum, 1 December 1904, *Letters*, op. cit., vol. 2, p. 699.

134. Nivedita to Yum, 25 July 1906, Ibid, p. 822.

135. Nivedita to Josephine, 8 February 1905, Ibid, p. 719.

136. *The Modern Review*, November 1911, p. 447.

137. See introduction by K.G. Subramanyan (Baroda, 5 October 2007) in R. Siva Kumar, *Paintings of Abanindranath Tagore*, Pratikshan, Kolkata, 2008.

138. Nivedita to Mrs Bull, 24 May 1905, *Letters*, op. cit., vol. 2, p. 735.

139. Nivedita to Mrs Wilson, 13 December 1905, Ibid., p. 768.
140. Nivedita to Priyanath Sinha, 4 April 1909, *Letters*, vol. 2, p. 962.
141. Nivedita to Yum, 27 May 1907, *Letters*, op. cit., vol. 2, p. 862.
142. Datta, Bhupendranath. *Swami Vivekananda Patriot: Prophet*, Nababharat Publishers, Calcutta, 1993, p. 68.
143. Nivedita to Mrs Bull, 12 December 1906, *Letters*, op. cit., vol. 2, p. 834.
144. Quoted in Pravrajika Atmaprana, *Sister Nivedita*, op. cit., p. 176.
145. The Swadeshi Movement in *CWSN*, vol 4, pp. 282–83.
146. Nivedita to Yum, 14 June 1906, *Letters*, op. cit., vol. 2, p. 813.
147. Nivedita to Mr & Mrs Ratcliffe, 11 October 1906, Ibid., p. 828.
148. Nivedita to Ratcliffe, 8 June 1907, Ibid., p. 864.
149. Marie Hamilton Coates to Sister Nivedita, 27 January 1907, Ottawa in *Letters*, op. cit., Appendix 1907, vol. 2, p. 888.
150. Nivedita to Yum, 14 March 1907, Ibid., pp. 850–51.
151. Nivedita to Yum, 22 November 1905, Ibid., p. 762.
152. Nivedita to Gokhale, 19 July 1907, Ibid., p. 867.
153. Nivedita to Mrs Bull, 25 June 1905, Ibid., p. 740.

Chapter 5: The Legacy

1. Nivedita to Yum, 24 January 1906, *Letters*, op. cit., vol. 2, p. 782.
2. Nivedita to Yum, 7 February 1906, Ibid., p. 786.
3. Nivedita's paternal grandmother was Margaret Elizabeth Nealus.
4. Papers on women's rights 1–6 in miscellaneous articles written before meeting Swami Vivekananda in *CWSN*, op. cit., vol. 5, pp. 386–411.
5. 'The function of art in shaping nationality' in *CWSN*, July 2000, vol. 3, p. 4.
6. 'A Page from Wrexham Life', miscellaneous articles written before meeting Swami Vivekananda in CWSN, op. cit., vol. 5, pp. 420–24.
7. 'On the Influence of History in the Development of Modern India' in *CWSN*, 2010, vol. 4, p. 309.
8. Nivedita to Yum, 26 July 1904, *Letters*, op. cit., vol. 2, p. 661.
9. Nivedita to Yum, 19 July 1901, *Letters*, op. cit., vol. 1, p. 434.
10. Nivedita to Yum, 18 January 1900, *Letters*, op. cit., vol. 1, p. 303.
11. 1898; first published in 1900 by Swan Sonnenschein & Co. of London.
12. Nivedita to Yum, 21 July 1905, *Letters*, op. cit., vol. 2, p. 745.

13. Nivedita in undated letter extract, *Letters,* op. cit., vol. 2, p. 1278.
14. Mrs Bull to Nivedita, 12 June 1905, *Letters,* op. cit., vol. 2, p. 773.
15. Nivedita to Yum, 8 March 1906, Ibid., p. 793.
16. Nivedita to unnamed, 10 January 1910, *Letters,* op. cit., vol. 2, p. 1051.
17. Nivedita to Dr Cheyne, 6 July 1910, Ibid., pp. 1109–10.
18. Nivedita to Mrs Bull, 2 February 1910 in *CWSN,* op. cit., vol. 1, p. xv; also in *Letters,* op. cit., vol. 2, p. 1063.
19. Nivedita to Yum, 26 December 1906, *Letters,* op. cit., vol. 2, p. 839.
20. Preface by Pravrajika Atmaprana in *CWSN,* op. cit., vol. 1, p. xv.
21. Nivedita to Prof. Cheyne, 16 January 1911, *Letters,* op. cit., vol. 2, p. 1181.
22. Nivedita to Yum, 4 August 1910, Ibid., p. 1125.
23. Title of Chapter XVIII, in *CWSN,* op. cit., vol. 1, pp. 156 et seq.
24. Ibid., p. 157.
25. Ibid.
26. Nivedita to Yum, 30 May 1906, *Letters,* op. cit., vol. 2, pp. 809–10.
27. Sen, A.P. *Hindu Revivalism in Bengal 1872–1905: Some Essays in Interpretation,* OUP, Delhi, 1993.
28. Nivedita to Yum, 28 April 1910, *Letters,* vol. 2, p. 1095.
29. *The Master as I Saw Him, CWSN,* op. cit., vol. 1, p. 21.
30. Tapan Raychaudhuri, Swami Vivekananda's construction of Hinduism in *Swami Vivekananda and the Modernisation of Hinduism,* ed. by William Radice, SOAS, 1996, London, pp. 1–16; Quotations from Vivekananda taken from this book.
31. 'Indian Nationality: A Mode of thought' in *Civic Ideal and Indian Nationality* in *CWSN,* op. cit., vol. 4, pp. 292–93.
32. Interview with Swami Vivekananda on the bounds of Hinduism, April 1899, reproduced from *Prabuddha Bharata* in *CWSN,* vol. 1, pp. 79–81.
33. *The Master as I Saw Him* in *CWSN,* vol. 1, op. cit., pp. 74, 211.
34. Introduction to the *Complete Works of Swami Vivekananda* written on July 1907 in *CWSN,* op. cit., vol. 1, p. 4.
35. 'Revival or Reform' in *CWSN,* op. cit., vol. 5, p. 82.
36. *The Master as I Saw Him* in *CWSN,* op. cit., vol. 1, p. 167.
37. 'Religion and Dharma', *CWSN,* vol. 3, pp. 482–83.
38. Nivedita to Yum, 4 July 1910, *Letters,* vol. 2, p. 1114.
39. Published by Longmans Green & Co., London in 1915.
40. 'Religion and Dharma', in *CWSN,* vol. 3, op. cit., p. 378.

41. Ibid., p. 386.
42. Ibid., pp. 390–91.
43. Ibid., p. 406.
44. Ibid., p. 412.
45. The Swami's Teaching about Death, chapter XXIV in *The Master* in *CWSN*, op. cit., vol. 1, pp. 235 et seq.
46. *The Master* in *CWSN*, op. cit., vol. 1, p. 244.
47. Ibid., p. 246.
48. *CWSN*, Advaita Ashrama, 2012, vol. 2.
49. CWSN, op. cit., vol. 2, p. 293.
50. Notes of Some Wanderings, in *CWSN*, op. cit., vol. 1, p. 276.
51. 'Kedar Nath and Badri Narayan: A Pilgrim's Diary' in *CWSN*, op. cit., vol. 1, p. 398.
52. Ibid., p. 406.
53. Ibid., pp. 435–36.
54. Ibid., pp. 448–50.
55. *Glimpses of Famine and Flood in East Bengal in 1906*, in *CWSN*, op. cit., vol. 4, p. 452.
56. Ibid., p. 456.
57. Nivedita to Geddes, 28 January 1903, in *Prabuddha Bharata*, July 2015, vol. 120, no. 7, pp. 39–40 (from an unpublished collection of letters received from the archives of the University of Strathclyde and the National Library of Scotland).
58. Ibid., p. 488.
59. Ibid., p. 491.
60. *Studies from an Eastern Home* in *CWSN*, op. cit., vol. 2, p. 288.
61. Ibid., p. 297.
62. Nivedita to Yum, 16 November 1899, *CWSN*, op. cit., vol. 3, p. x.
63. Nivedita to Mrs Bull, *CWSN*, op. cit., vol. 3, p. x.
64. Nivedita to Mrs Bull, 24 April 1907, *Letters*, op. cit., vol. 2, p. 860.
65. Preface to The *Cradle Tales of Hinduism* in *CWSN*, op. cit., vol. 3, pp. 141–43.
66. Ibid.
67. Ibid.
68. Nivedita to Dr. Cheyne in *Letters*, op. cit., vol. 2, p. 1217.
69. Havell, E.B. *Indian Sculpture and Painting*, London, John Murray, 1908.

70. Ibid.

71. 'The Function of Art in Shaping Nationality' in *CWSN*, op. cit., vol 3, p. 5.

72. Nivedita to Yum, 26 January 1905 in *Letters,* op. cit., vol. 2, pp. 714–15.

73. Nivedita to Yum, 4 February 1905, Ibid, p. 718.

74. Ibid., p. 16.

75. Ibid., p. 38.

76. Havell, E.B. *Indian Sculpture and Painting.* Okakura, Kakuzo. *The Ideals of the East.* Coomaraswamy, Ananda K. *Medieval Sinhalese Art.*

77. 'The Function of Art in Shaping Nationality' in *CWSN*, op. cit., vol. 3, p. 52.

78. Ibid., p. 17.

79. Ibid., p. 5.

80. Art Appreciation: Abanindranath Tagore in *CWSN*, op. cit., vol. 3, pp. 63–65.

81. Tagore, Abanindranath. *Jorasankor Dhare*, Visva Bharati Publications, Calcutta, 1971, p. 158.

82. Foxe, Barbara. *Long Journey Home: A Biography of Margaret Noble (Nivedita)*, Rider and Company, London, 1975, p. 199.

83. Atmaprana, Pravrajika. *Sister Nivedita of Ramakrishna-Vivekananda*, op. cit., p. 278.

84. Foxe, Barbara. *Long Journey Home*, op. cit., p. 198.

85. Nivedita to Mrs Bull, 16 July 1906, *Letters,* op. cit., vol. 2, p. 819.

86. Introduction by K.G. Subramanyan, (Baroda, 5 October 2007) in R. Siva Kumar, *Paintings of Abanindranath Tagore*, Pratikshan, Kolkata, 2008.

87. Ibid.

88. Nivedita to Mrs Bull, 3 October 1900, *Letters,* op. cit., vol. 2, p. 1267.

89. J.C. Bose to Mrs Bull, 13 April 1904, *Letters,* op. cit., vol. 2, p. 1285.

90. Ibid.

91. Bose to Mrs Bull, 16 October 1905, *Letters,* op. cit., vol. 2, p. 778.

92. Review by Nivedita of *Is Matter Alive?* by J.C. Bose in *Review of Reviews*, October 1902, in *CWSN*, op. cit., vol. 5, pp. 289–98.

93. Ibid., p. 298.

94. Nivedita to Rabindranath Tagore, 3 April 1903, *Letters,* op. cit., vol. 2, pp. 555–59.

95. Ibid.

96. Ibid., p. 558.

97. Nivedita to Mrs Bull, 28 July 1904, *Letters,* op. cit., vol. 2, p. 664.

98. Ibid.

99. Mrs Bull to J.C. Bose, 12 June 1905, *Letters,* op. cit., vol. 2, p. 724.

100. Nivedita to Mr and Mrs Ratcliffe, 12 June 1911, *Letters,* op. cit., vol. 2, p. 1205.

101. Nivedita to Mr and Mrs Ratcliffe, 14 September 1910, *Letters,* op. cit., vol. 2, pp. 1147–48.

102. Nivedita to Mr and Mrs Ratcliffe, 16 August 1911, *Letters,* op. cit., vol. 2, p. 1222.

103. Nivedita to unnamed, 29 September 1910, *Letters,* op. cit., vol. 2, p. 1159.

104. Nivedita, possibly to Mrs Bull (unnamed), 17 May 1906, *Letters,* op. cit., vol. 2, p. 808.

105. Nivedita to Yum, 6 December 1905, *Letters,* op. cit., vol. 2, p. 767.

106. Nivedita to Yum, 13 September 1911, *Letters*, op. cit., vol. 2, p. 1236.

Chapter 6: The Last Years

1. *CWSN,* vol. 5, pp. 299–301.

2. Ibid., pp. 361–64.

3. Nivedita to Dr T.K. Cheyne, 19, 27 December 1907, *Letters,* op. cit., vol. 2, pp. 884, 885.

4. *Prabuddha Bharata,* May 1908, in *CWSN,* vol. 5, pp. 365–66.

5. Ibid.

6. 'The Recent Congress' in the *Modern Review,* February 1908, in *CWSN,* vol. 5, pp. 160–62.

7. Nivedita to Mrs Wilson, 16 September 1908, *Letters,* op. cit., vol. 2, p. 910.

8. Nivedita to unnamed, 14 March 1909, Ibid., p. 958.

9. Nivedita to Francis Leggett, 13 July 1908, Ibid., p. 907.

10. Nivedita to Yum, 16 September 1908, Ibid., p. 911.

11. Quoted in *Saint Sara: the Life of Sara Chapman Bull* by Pravrajika Prabuddhaprana, Sarada Math, Calcutta, 2002, p. 444.

12. All relevant preceding quotes from Nivedita to Alberta Sturges (Lady Sandwitch) on board *S.S. Cymric*, 27 September 1908 in *Letters*, op. cit., vol. 2, pp. 913–16.

13. Nivedita to Yum, 8 October 1908, *Letters*, vol. 2, p. 917.

14. Nivedita to Ratcliffe, 15 October 1908, Ibid., p. 919.

15. See *Sister Nivedita* by Pravrajika Atmaprana, op. cit., p. 219.

16. Nivedita to Yum, 22 October 1908, *Letters*, vol. 2 p. 921.

17. Nivedita to Ratcliffe, 23 February 1909, Ibid., p. 954.

18. Nivedita to Mrs Richmond Noble, 17 November 1908, Ibid., p. 928.

19. Nivedita to Yum, 30 January 1909, Ibid, p. 948.

20. Nivedita to Mrs Bull, 4 February 1909 Ibid., p. 950.

21. Nivedita to Mrs Wilson, 15 May 1909, Ibid., p. 968.

22. Nivedita to Mrs Bull, Wednesday in Easter Week 1909, Ibid., p. 963.

23. Nivedita to Yum, 30 January 1909, Ibid., p. 948.

24. Nivedita to Mrs Wilson, 1 July 1909, Ibid., p. 977.

25. Nivedita to Yum, 1 July 1909, Ibid., p. 981.

26. Nivedita to Yum, 4 July 1909, P. & O *S.S. Egypt*, Ibid., pp. 981–82.

27. Nivedita to Yum, 4 June 1909, Ibid., p. 971. Pravrajika Atmaprana in her book *Sister Nivedita* (p. 222) has strongly denied that Nivedita was in disguise saying such claims were 'all fabrication'. She contests the theory that Nivedita was under any fear of arrest, but Nivedita's letters show that she had planned to don a secular dress for her journey to Wiesbaden and Geneva and onward to India by sea.

28. Nivedita to Mrs Wilson, 1 July 1909, Ibid, p. 977.

29. Nivedita to Ratcliffe, 21 July 1909, Ibid., p. 984.

30. Ibid.

31. Nivedita to unnamed, 27 July 1909, Ibid., p. 987.

32. Nivedita to Yum, 30 July 1909, Ibid., p. 988.

33. Nivedita to Yum, 5 August 1909, Ibid., p. 990.

34. Nivedita to Ratcliffe, 14 September 1911, Ibid., p. 1244.

35. Nivedita to Ratcliffe, 5 August 1909, Ibid., p. 994.

36. Nivedita to Ratcliffe, 21 July 1909, Ibid., p. 986.

37. Ibid.

38. Nivedita to Ratcliffe, 30 July 1909, Ibid., p. 988.

39. *Sri Aurobindo on Himself and Mother*, Sri Aurobindo International University Centre, Pondicherry, 1953, pp. 92–94.

40. Ibid.
41. Nivedita to Ratcliffe, 20 January 1910, *Letters*, vol. 2, p. 1057.
42. Nivedita to Ratcliffe, 7 April 1910, Ibid., p. 1087.
43. Nivedita to Ratcliffe, 20 October 1909, *Letters*, vol. 2, p. 1023.
44. Nivedita to Ratcliffe, 3 November 1909, Ibid., p. 1028.
45. Nivedita to Ratcliffe, 25 November 1909, Ibid., p. 1033.
46. Nivedita to Ratcliffe, 20 January 1910, Ibid., p. 1058.
47. Nivedita to Ratcliffe, 10 February 1910, Ibid., p. 1064.
48. Nivedita to Ratcliffe, 28 July 1910, Ibid., p. 1119.
49. Nivedita to Ratcliffe, 10 August 1910, Ibid., p. 1128.
50. Nivedita to Ratcliffe, 21 November 1909, Ibid., p. 1031.
51. Nivedita to Ratcliffe, 30 September 1909, Ibid., p. 1016.
52. Nivedita to Ratcliffe, 28 April 1910, Ibid., p. 1093.
53. Nivedita to Ratcliffe, 6 July 1910, Ibid., p. 1105.
54. Nivedita to the Postmaster General, 17 April 1910, Ibid., p. 1091.
55. Nivedita to Mrs Wilson, 15 September 1909, Ibid., p. 1006.
56. Nivedita to unnamed, 14 December 1909, Ibid., p. 1045.
57. Nivedita to Yum, 22 September 1910, Ibid., p. 1149–50.
58. Nivedita to Ratcliffe, 30 July 1909, Ibid., p. 989.
59. Ibid., p. 992.
60. Nivedita to Yum, 11 November 1909, *Letters*, vol. 2, p. 1031.
61. Nivedita to Yum, 24 February 1910, Ibid., p. 1071.
62. Nivedita to Yum, 17 March 1910, Ibid., p. 1080.
63. Nivedita to Lady Betty Leggett, 19 September 1909, p. 1009.
64. Ibid., p. 1010.
65. Nivedita to Ratcliffe, 1 December 1909, Ibid., p. 1038.
66. 'Romesh Chandra Dutt' by Nivedita in *Modern Review*, January 1910, reproduced in *CWSN*, vol. 5, pp. 261–65.
67. Ibid.
68. Nivedita to Ratcliffe, 7 July 1911, *Letters*, vol. 2, pp. 1249–50.
69. On the *S.S. Egypt* on 6 July 1909, Nivedita to Havell, Ibid., p. 982.
70. Nivedita to Yum, 14 December 1909, Ibid., p. 1043.
71. Nivedita to Mrs Wilson, 6 January 1910, Ibid., p. 1049.
72. The Ancient Abbey of Ajanta in *Footfalls of Indian History*, *CWSN*, vol. 4, pp. 45–103.
73. Nivedita to Ratcliffe, 31 March 1910, *Letters*, vol. 2, p. 1082.

74. Nivedita to Mr Havell, 7 April 1910, *Letters*, vol. 2, p. 1086.
75. Ibid., p. 115.
76. Nivedita to unnamed, 23 February 1910, *Letters*, vol. 2, p. 1070.
77. Nivedita to Ratcliffe, 23 February 1910, Ibid., p. 1069.
78. Nivedita to Ratcliffe, 10 March 1910, Ibid., p. 1077.
79. Nivedita to Mrs Wilson, 6 January 1910, Ibid., p. 1049.
80. All details of the visit of Lady Minto from Mary Countess of Minto, *India, Minto and Morley 1905–1910* quoted in Pravrajika Atmaprana, *Sister Nivedita*, op. cit., pp. 227–231.
81. Nivedita to Yum, 10 and 17 March 1910, Ibid., pp. 1078–80.
82. Nivedita to unnamed, 6 April 1910, Ibid., p. 1085.
83. Nivedita to Ratcliffe, 10 August 1910, *Letters*, vol. 2, p. 1127.
84. Nivedita to Ratcliffe, 31 March 1910, Ibid., p. 1082.
85. Nivedita to Mrs Wilson, 3 March 1910, Ibid., p. 1074.
86. Nivedita to Ratcliffe, 4 August 1910, Ibid., p. 1126.
87. Nivedita to Ratcliffe, 28 July 1910, Ibid., p. 1118.
88. Nivedita to Ratcliffe, 19 July 1910, Ibid., p. 1115.
89. Nivedita to Ratcliffe, 14 October 1910, Ibid., p. 1163.
90. Nivedita to Ratcliffe, 10 August 1910, Ibid., p. 1127.
91. Nivedita to Yum, 28 July 1910, Ibid., p. 1121.
92. Nivedita to Mrs Wilson, 12 June 1910, Ibid., p. 1101.
93. Nivedita to Mrs Wilson, 6 July 1910, Ibid., p. 1108.
94. Nivedita to unnamed, 29 September 1910, Ibid., p. 1158.
95. Nivedita to Mrs Bull, 11 August 1910, Ibid., p. 1131.
96. Ibid.
97. Nivedita to Yum, 14 October 1910, *Letters*, vol. 2, pp. 1160–61.
98. Ibid., Josephine's consultation with Dr. Coulter who predicted Nivedita's return to India greatly reassured her.
99. Details from Pravrajika Prabuddhaprana, *Saint Sara*, op. cit., p. 491 et seq
100. Nivedita to Yum, 1 January 1911, *Letters*, vol. 2, p. 1177.
101. *New York Evening Journal* dated 27 May 1911 quoted in *Nivedita Lokmata*, Sankari Prasad Basu, Ananda Publishers, Calcutta, 2013, vol. 1, part 2, p. 366.
102. Nivedita to Ratcliffe, 7 September 1911, Ibid., p. 1234.
103. Nivedita to Ratcliffe, 31 August 1911, Ibid., p. 1226.
104. Nivedita to Yum, 24 March 1911, Ibid., p. 1187.

105. Nivedita to Yum, 3 March 1911, Ibid., p. 1188.

106. To Yum Yum, 21 October 1908, *Letters*, vol. 2, p. 920.

107. Nivedita to Ratcliffe, 14 September 1911, Ibid., p. 1242.

108. Nivedita to Ratcliffe, 31 August 1911, Ibid., p. 1226.

109. 'In Memoriam: Sara Chapman Bull', *Modern Review*, June 1911, in *CWSN*, op. cit., vol. 5, pp. 269–75.

110. Ole Bull, 17 May 1901 by Sister Nivedita in Pravrajika Prabuddhaprana, *Saint Sara: the Life of Sara Chapman Bull—the American Mother of Swami Vivekananda*, op. cit., pp. 499–500.

111. 'In Memoriam: Sara Chapman Bull', *Modern Review*, op. cit.

112. Nivedita to Yum, 13 April 1911, *Letters*, vol. 2, p. 1197.

113. Foxe, Barbara. *Long Journey Home, A Biography of Margaret Noble (Nivedita)*, op. cit., p. 218.

114. Nivedita to Yum, 31 August 1911, *Letters*, vol. 2, p. 1228.

115. Foxe, Barbara. *Long Journey Home, A Biography of Margaret Noble (Nivedita)*, op. cit., p. 219.

116. Nivedita to Ratcliffe, 5 June 1911, *Letters*, vol. 2, p. 1203; eventually the memoir of J.C. Bose was written by Patrick Geddes.

117. Nivedita to Yum, 19 May 1911, *Letters*, vol. 2, p. 1201.

118. Nivedita to Dr Cheyne, 23 May 1911, *Letters*, vol. 2, p. 1202.

119. Nivedita to Ratcliffe, 28 July 1911, Ibid., p. 1217.

120. Nivedita to Yum, 16 August 1911 Ibid., p. 1223.

121. Nivedita to Ratcliffe, 6 July 1911, Ibid., p. 1210.

122. Nivedita to Ratcliffe, 3 August 1911, Ibid., p. 1218.

123. Nivedita to Alice Longfellow, 5 September 1911, Ibid., pp. 1230–34.

124. Ibid., pp. 1230–33.

125. Alice M. Longfellow on Sister Nivedita in *Boston Evening Transcript*, 29 June 1911 in Appendix—1911, *Letters*, vol. 2, pp. 1247–48.

126. Nivedita to Mrs Wilson, 3 October 1911, *Letters*, vol. 2, p. 1246.

127. Nivedita to Yum, 17 March 1904, *Letters*, vol. 2, op. cit., p. 636.

128. 'Death', *An Indian Study of Love and Death, CWSN*, 2012, vol. 2, p. 281.

129. Abala Bose to Mrs Wilson, 18 October 1911, *Letters*, vol. 2, pp. 1252–53.

130. Christine to Josephine MacLeod, 16 October 1911, Ibid., p. 1251.

131. Josephine to unnamed, 3 November 1911, *Letters*, vol. 2, p. 1254.

132. Josephine to unnamed, 1911 (undated) in *Letters*, vol. 2, p. 1254.

133. Abala Bose to Mrs Wilson, 18 October 1911, Ibid., p. 1252.

134. Alice Longfellow to Josephine MacLeod, 19 November 1911, Ibid., p. 1254.

135. J.C.Bose to Mrs Wilson, 2 November 1911, Ibid., p. 1253.

136. 'The Voice of Life', Sir Jagadish Chandra Bose's inaugural address dedicating the Bose Institute to the nation on 30 November 1917.

137. The fragrant shefali blossoms also called *harsingher*.

138. Dr Bose to Mrs Wilson in 1916 quoted in Pravrajika Atmaprana, *Sister Nivedita*, op. cit., p. 242.

139. 'Margaret Noble: A Tribute to a Remarkable Career', *Daily News*, 26 October 1911.

140. S.K. Ratcliffe, 'Sister Nivedita: A Close Friend' in *Great Women of Modern India: Sister Nivedita*, Grover and Arora (edited), Deep and Deep Publications, New Delhi, 1993, vol. 2.

141. Ibid.

142. Abanindranath Tagore to Havell, 2 November 1911 in *Letters*, vol. 2, p. 1287.

143. Pravrajika Atmaprana, *Sister Nivedita*, op. cit, p. 290.

144. Ibid., p. 249.

145. *CWSN*, vol. 1, op. cit., p. xi.

146. Ibid., p. xi.

147. Quoted in Pravrajika Atmaprana, Sister Nivedita, op. cit., p. 230.

148. 'Bhogini Nibedita' in *Parichaye*, *Rabindra Rachanabali*, Government of West Bengal Centenary Edition, Calcutta 1961, vol. 13, pp. 192–99.

149. Nivedita to Yum, 14 July 1910, *Letters*, vol. 2, p. 1114.

150. Nivedita to Yum, 25 August 1910, Ibid., p. 1137.

151. Ibid.

152. Ibid.

153. Nivedita to Ratcliffe, 25 August 1910, Ibid., p. 1140.

154. Tagore's Introduction to Sister Nivedita's *The Web of Indian Life*, November 1917, op. cit., pp. ix–xii.

155. 'Bhogini Nibedita' 1318 (1911 in English calendar) in *Parichaye*, *Rabindra Rachanabali*, Government of West Bengal Centenary Edition, Calcutta, 1961, vol. 13, pp. 192–99.

156. My free translation and paraphrasing of major sections of the article.

157. Alice M. Longfellow on Sister Nivedita in *Boston Evening Transcsript* in *Letters*, vol. 2, p. 1248.

Index

283